STRATHCLYDE
30125
D0364532

ANDERSONIAN LIBRARY
WITHDRAWN
FROM
LIBRARY
STOCK

THE EYE IS DELIGHTED

Some Romantic Travellers in Scotland

Also by Maurice Lindsay:

Poetry

The Exiled Heart
Hurlygush
At the Wood's Edge
Ode for St. Andrew's Night and Other Poems
The Enemies of Love
Snow Warning
One Later Day
This Business of Living
Comings and Goings

Prose

The Lowlands of Scotland: Glasgow and the North
The Lowlands of Scotland: Edinburgh and the South
The Scottish Renaissance
Robert Burns: the Man: his Work: the Legend
The Burns Encyclopedia
Clyde Waters
By Yon Bonnie Banks
The Discovery of Scotland: Travellers in Scotland from the 13th to the 18th centuries
Environment: A Basic Human Right

Anthologies

Poetry Scotland 1-4 (4 with Hugh MacDiarmid)
No Scottish Twilight (with Fred Urquhart)
Modern Scottish Poetry: An Anthology of the Scottish Renaissance
John Davidson: with a preface by T. S. Eliot and an introduction by Hugh MacDiarmid
A Book of Scottish Verse
Scottish Poetry 1-5 (with George Bruce and Edwin Morgan)

Maurice Lindsay

THE EYE IS DELIGHTED

Some Romantic Travellers in Scotland

FREDERICK MULLER

First published in Great Britain 1971
by Frederick Muller Ltd., Fleet Street, London, E.C.4

Typesetting by Print Origination, Liverpool, England
Litho Printed by Redwood Press Ltd.

SBN 584 10082 5

Contents

Illustrations

The illustrations facing pages 264 and 265 are reproduced by gracious permission of H.M. the Queen, those from Mendelssohn's sketchbook by kind permission of the Bodleian Library. All others are reproduced by kind permission of the Mitchell Library, Glasgow.

Travellers' Tales

The paddle-steamer pulls its own bent image
over loch water, through a rippling screen
that makes itself, tall mountains, trees and islands
    twisted and squat, and seem to lean
out of the shapes of what we think they mean.

Tourists, anonymous behind dark glasses,
admire the scene, yet feel that something's wrong,
they're not sure what; the wind's in the wrong quarter,
    the season's late, the sun's too strong,
the ship's too slow, or perhaps the loch's too long!

According to our childhood expectations
landscape should wear the look of history,
and island waters lap soft wordless legends.
    No place, wherever it may be,
preserves impersonal objectivity.

Which is why journeys usually disappoint us:
until we're there, we always hope to find
escape from discontent, somehow forgetting
    the self we never leave behind
makes all we see half attitude of mind.

MAURICE LINDSAY

Acknowledgements

I should like to thank Mr. Eric Major, formerly of Messrs Frederick Muller, and Mr. A.R. Mills: Mr. Major for first suggesting that his firm might be interested in publishing this book and Mr. Mills for his patience in dealing with one whose pressures and responsibilities outside authorship resulted in delays which must at times have been exasperating.

I should also like to thank Mr. C.M. Black and members of the staff of the Mitchell Library, Glasgow, for assistance of various kinds, particularly in connection with the illustrations. I am especially indebted to Miss Margaret Crum, of the Bodleian Library, Oxford, for her help with the Mendelssohn drawings. While writing the chapter on Mendelssohn and Klingemann, I noticed that Mendelssohn frequently referred to his sketching activities. I therefore wrote to the principal libraries in Berlin and Leipzig in an effort to trace them, but without success. The British Museum, however, mentioned "a recent Mendelssohn bequest to the Bodleian". It turned out to be the gift (not bequest) of a series of sketch books about nine inches by six, and a further series of day books about three inches by two, the former containing the more elaborate sketches made by Mendelssohn during his Scottish tour, the latter roughly-noted musical ideas, engagements, expenses details and additional drawings. These, I discovered from Miss Crum, had been given by Mendelssohn's grandson, P.V.M. Benecke, a don at Magdalen College, to his friend Miss Denecke, who eventually gave them to the Bodleian Library during her lifetime, bequeathing her other Mendelssohn relics to her sister. Apart from an article by me in the December 1969 *Scottish Field,* describing the discovery of these drawings, they have not been published before.

Finally, I should like to thank my secretary, Margaret Miller, for her efficient patience in deciphering my handwriting, and my friend Morven Cameron for kindly reading my proofs. If any errors remain, the fault is, of course, mine.

M.L.

Prelude to the Journeys

. . . the eye is delighted with the most diversified landscape

Sir John Sinclair's *Statistical Account of Scotland,* 1796

There was a time when travelling through Scotland was difficult, dangerous and in some parts more or less impossible. Many of the earliest travellers were either foreign diplomats accredited to the Scottish Court, or soldiers, usually English, forming part of an invading army.

The first traveller, in the modern sense of the term, who came to Scotland to satisfy his curiosity and broaden his education was the wealthy young Elizabethan Fynes Moryson (1566-1618), who in 1617 published an account of his journey to Edinburgh, and across the Forth, to Falkland, in Fife. He was a lively-minded scholar, full of that restless energy which was so marked a characteristic of the Elizabethan age. He shared Sir Francis Bacon's views on the benefits of travelling; and since what Moryson had to say has become generally accepted without any need of contemporary re-definition, his words bear repeating:

"They seem to me most unhappy, and no better than prisoners, who from the cradle to old age, still behold the same walks, faces, orchards, pastures, and objects of the eye, and still hear the same voices and sounds beat in their ears . . . . Running water is sweet, but standing pools stink . . . .We are citizens of the whole world . . . .I think variety to be the most pleasing thing in the world, and the best life to be, neither comtemplative alone, nor active together, but mixed of both".

In the eighteenth century, Burns's first biographer, Robert Heron, pointed out the quickening effect of "those numberless, unconnected particulars, which, in every country, meet the traveller's eye. Among such a diversity of objects, some are unavoidably interesting. And whenever the mind is interested, its attention is engaged. It is thus roused from that languor into which, in long confinement within a narrow sphere, it is apt to sink".

Early in the nineteenth century Sir Walter Scott said much the same thing more simply: "What is this life, if it be not mixed with some delight? And what delight is more pleasing than to see the fashions and manners of unknown places?"

Until the development of the railways brought travel speedily and cheaply within the reach of everyone, a journey was an adventure undertaken at such a pace that it could be–indeed had to be–savoured to the full. There was thus ample time to set down personal impressions, either in letters to friends at home, or in journals for the stimulation of recollected satisfaction, or for eventual publication.

Elsewhere, [1] I have collected accounts of those travellers who opened up Scotland from the thirteenth to eighteenth centuries. My eighteenth-century travellers, Thomas Pennant and the French geologist Faujus St. Fond, were both firmly rooted in the classical, the Augustan traditions of that age. But it was in the latter part of the century that those undercurrents of romanticism, latent perhaps in any classical age, broke surface and so effectively overflowed their subjectivist banks that it has not since been possible for their waters to be drained back into their former channels.

This book presents some accounts of travellers, affected in varying degree by the new romantic sensibility, who came to Scotland in search of delight of one kind or another. Through their eyes, the Scotland we encounter seems much nearer our own than the Scotland of even such a rumbustious classicist as Dr. Samuel Johnson.

My span of romantic travellers begins with the poet Thomas Gray, takes in the Reverend William Gilpin, who invented a systematic way of looking at landscape, the Wordsworths, William and Dorothy, who invested Gilpin's system of looking with a deeper spiritual significance, and, among others, two sensitive Europeans, Hans Christian Andersen, the poetical teller of fairy tales, and the composer Felix Mendelssohn, whom Andersen counted among his many famous friends. It ends with Queen Victoria. Her death, in the early days of the era of the motor-car, marked not only the beginning of many movements leading to social

[1] *The Discovery of Scotland.*

changes, but a speeding-up of the pace of life itself. As travel has become simpler and cheaper, and therefore more widespread, there has been neither the time nor the necessity for the writing of journals. Nowadays, everyone can go and see for himself.

What, then, is the justification for bringing together these older travellers' writings, this "private literature", from earlier ages?

The modern traveller goes readily enough; he looks, but does not always stay long enough really to see for himself. The accounts of earlier travellers through Scotland make fascinating reading today not only because they draw the attention of the car-bound hurrying modern traveller to facts or features which might otherwise have passed unnoticed, but also because they provide us with a kind of time-depth appreciation. The pleasures we enjoy today are much enhanced by an understanding of the nature of the delight they gave to earlier, sensitive writers with seeing eyes.

Apart from giving what, in modern jargon, might be called this practical satisfaction-benefit, what all the travellers represented here have to say makes rewarding reading in its own right. Some of them were great writers, others were personalities of absorbing interest, and even the least of them was not without considerable descriptive talent. They may thus both enhance our physical enjoyment of Scotland, whether we be natives or travellers, and pleasure our minds with the interest and aptness of their literary moods and manners.

1

Thomas Gray: Pivot of an Age

Few children leave school without having had to learn Gray's *Elegy*. Few poems leave their traces on even the most poetical of memories as powerfully as this one does. Few poets are as shadowy figures as Gray in the imaginations of those who learn his lines.

I once attended a Burns Supper at which the chairman, after a bibulous evening, rose uncertainly to his feet to bring the proceedings to a formal close. "In the words o'the immortal Rabbie," he announced:

The plooman hameward plods his weary wey
An' leas the warld tae derkness an' tae me.

One or two of his fellow celebrants may perhaps have experienced twinges of doubt about the exact source of the quotation. No one offered any correction. And yet Gray, a scholarly retiring bachelor, was a kind of pivot on which the Augustan aspect of the eighteenth century first clearly inclined towards the Romantic age: not because of the diction he employed in his handful of completed poems—he once declared: "The language of poetry is never the language of the age, except among the French," a doctrine as startling as it is, and always was, untrue—but because of his attitudes. His interest in Scandinavian and Celtic mythology preceded 'Ossian' Macpherson's by a generation, and was reflected in Gray's two "Norse" odes, couched in a style and metrical form oddly foreshadowing Coleridge and Scott. Then there was his passion for travel, and his belief, though not by him ever so defined, in the arrangement of scenery to produce the "best" effect, a belief he pursued towards the end of his life when he travelled the Lake district with a Claude Lorrain spyglass, a device with a varnish-tinted lens which was designed to make landscape look like the canvases of the French painter after whom it was named.

Thomas Gray was born in 1716. His mother, Dorothy Antrobus, kept a milliner's shop with her sister, Mary. The shop was rented from Philip Gray, a money-scrivener whom Dorothy married in 1706. Thomas was their fifth and only surviving child. Their marriage was not a happy one, for Philip Gray was selfish and brutal: so much so that Dorothy took unsuccessful steps to initiate a divorce in 1735. It was her mother who paid the fees for Thomas Gray to go to Eton in 1727, where his uncle, William Antrobus, was an assistant master. At Eton, Gray's friends included Horace Walpole and Richard West, whose early death was later to cause Gray much sorrow.

In 1734, Gray matriculated at Peterhouse, Cambridge, though, after the manner of the times, he did not trouble to graduate. Horace Walpole was his travelling companion on his first long Continental tour, which began in 1739, and took in Florence, Rome, Naples and Venice. He returned alone in 1741, having quarrelled with Walpole, a quarrel they later made up.

In 1742, he produced, among other pieces, his "Ode on a Distant Prospect of Eton College," which prospect Dr. Johnson bluntly declared suggested "nothing to Gray which every beholder does not equally think and feel". Returning to Peterhouse, Gray took the degree of LL.B. in 1744. Poems were written slowly and infrequently, usually in response to particular circumstances. In 1750, he sent Walpole "a thing to which he had at last put an end". The "thing", on which he seems to have been working for five years, was his *Elegy Written in a Country Churchyard.* It seems strange that a poem which moves so effortlessly should have caused its author so much protracted anvil-work. Dr. Johnston tells us that Gray "did not write his pieces first rudely and then correct them, but laboured every line as it arose in the train of composition".

Many of Gray's later years were spent studiously at Pembroke College, where he removed himself, when, to quote Johnson again, Gray's fellow-commoners at Peterhouse "diverted themselves with disturbing him by frequent and troublesome noises, and as he said, by pranks yet more offensive and contemptuous".

In 1753, the year his mother died, Walpole persuaded Gray to allow the publication of six of his poems, one of them being the *Elegy*. In 1757, his two Pindaric Odes, *The Progress of Poetry* and *The Bard* also appeared. Astonishing as it may seem, on the strength of these eight poems and a few occasional verses published in magazines, a *genre* in which Gray was a deft practitioner, he was offered the Poet Laureateship in succession to Colley Cibber, an honour which, though he declined it, may have consoled him a little for the poor reception being awarded to his two odes.

For the next three years, during which he moved to London, living near the then-new British Museum, he became interested in Norse and Welsh poetry as a result of a curiosity kindled by his intensive reading in history. He "cockered and spirited" up sufficiently to ask Lord Bute for the Chair of Modern History at Cambridge. Lord Bute sent him a polite refusal.

By this time Gray's never very robust health had begun to deteriorate, so he began to travel again. In 1761, he made a tour of Suffolk and Norfolk, and in 1762 a visit to York, his home-time being now divided between London and Cambridge. There was a trip to Winchester, Southampton, Salisbury and Stonehenge in 1764, and another visit to York in the early summer of 1765. Then in August of that year, he set out upon a journey to Scotland, a journey which lasted just over two months.

He had been spending some weeks at the estate of Old Park, near Durham, the home of the poet's friend since College days, Dr. Thomas Wharton. From there, on 18th August, 1765, Gray set out for Scotland in company with the ninth Earl of Strathmore, his brother, the Honourable Thomas Lyon, and a Major Lyon, who was a cousin of Lord Strathmore.

The first night was spent at Hetton. On the 19th, the poet and the earl dined with Thomas Percy at Alnwick, and spent the night at Tweedmouth. Next day, they dined at Haddington and arrived at Edinburgh late in the evening. There they seem to have spent two nights[1] . The meals they paid for cost

[1] In a notebook in the British Museum, the Reverend John Mitford, one of Gray's early editors, gives extracts "from the Journal of Mr. Gray in the Possession of Mr. R. Wellesley", which only allow that one night was spent in Edinburgh.

"three shillings for dinner, sixpence in a Coffee House and four shillings for Supper". On the 22nd, if Gray's own dates are correct, they crossed the Forth and lodged at Perth. On the 23rd, they crossed the Tay and arrived at Glamis Castle in time for dinner.

Of "the way as far as Edinburgh", Gray thought "that there was not a great deal worth remarking". During his stay of a day and a half in Edinburgh, he had "leisure to visit the Castle, Holy-Rood-House, Heriot's Hospital, Arthur's Seat, etc". He recorded that he was "not sorry to have seen that most picturesque (at a distance) nastiest (when near) of all capital Cities". But if the place displeased, he must surely have enjoyed the company of Dr. William Robertson, the historian, who was at that time Principal of Edinburgh University, William Wright, Professor of Ecclesiastical History at Glasgow University, and Alexander "Jupiter" Carlyle, whose *Autobiography* is one of the literary delights of the period. All were the guests of Dr. John Gregory, the Aberdonian physician and inventor of the laxative known as Gregory Powder, who was to become Professor of Medicine at Edinburgh a year later.

Robertson later related to Gray's friend the Reverend Norton Nicholls, that "when he saw Mr. Gray in Scotland, he gave him the idea of a person who meant *to pass for a very fine gentleman*", a comment passed on by Nicholls to their common friend, William Johnson Temple, in a letter that has survived. But the most vivid comment–and incidentally, a possible explanation for the poor impression Gray made on Robertson–comes, as we might expect, from the pen of Alexander Carlyle: "We had a sight of the celebrated poet Gray at Dr. Gregory's, who, passing through the Highlands with my friend Major Lyon for his conductor, six or seven of us assembled to meet him, and were disappointed. But this eminent poet had not justice done him, for he was much worn out with his journey, and, by returning soon after supper, proved that he had been taken at a time when he was not fit to be shown off".

The crossing from Queensferry "in a four-oar'd yawl without a sail" can hardly have afforded Gray much relief, for he told his friend that he had been "toss'd about rather more than I should wish to hazard again".

Perth seemed to the poet "a large *Scotch* Town with much wood about it on the banks of the Tay, a very noble river", over which, next morning, he was ferried without incident on the last lap of the journey from Hetton to Glamis, a distance of about two hundred miles.

Gray later gave Wharton a very full description of Glamis and its surroundings, and one which relates sufficiently closely to what may be seen by twentieth century eyes that his eighteenth century view merits quoting at some length.

"The Castle stands in Strathmore (i.e. the Great Valley) which winds about from Stonehaven on the East Coast of Kincardineshire obliquely as far as Stirling near 100 miles in length, and from 7 to 10 miles in breadth, cultivated everywhere to the foot of the Hills on either hand with oats or bere-barley, except where the soil is mere peat-earth (black as a coal) or barren sand cover'd only with broom and heath, or a short grass fit for sheep. Here and there appear just above ground the huts of the inhabitants, which they call Towns, built of and cover'd with turf, and among them at great distances the Gentlemen's houses with inclosures and a few trees round them.

"Amidst these our Castle distinguishes itself, the middle part of it rising proudly out of what seems a great and thick wood of tall trees with a cluster of hanging towers on the top. You descend to it gradually from the South thro' a double and triple avenue of Scotch Firs 60 or 70 feet high, under three Gateways. This approach is a full mile long, and when you have passed the second Gate, the Firs change to Limes, and another, oblique avenue goes off on either hand toward the Offices.

"These, as well as all the enclosures that surround the house, are border'd with 3 or 4 ranks of sycamores, ashes and white poplars of the noblest height and from 70 to 100 years old. Other allies there are that go off at right angles with the long one, small groves and wall'd gardens of Earl Patrick's [Patrick Lyon, c. 1642-95, first Earl of Strathmore] planting, full of broad-leaved elms, oaks, birch, black-cherry-trees, Laburnums, etc: all of great stature and size, which have not till this week begun to shew the least sign of morning frosts. The third Gate delivers you into a Court with a broad pavement, and grass-flats adorn'd with statues of the four

Stuart Kings [only two of these leaden statues, James I and VI and Charles I, now remain] border'd with old silver-firs and yew-trees, alternatively, and opening with an iron palisade on either side to two square old-fashion'd parterres surrounded by stone-fruit-walls.

"The house from the height of it, the greatness of its mass, the many towers atop, and the spread of its wings, has really a very singular and striking appearance, like nothing I ever saw . . .The wings are about fifty feet high, the body (which is the old castle with walls 10 feet thick) is near 100.

"From the leads, I see to the South of me (just at the end of the avenue), the little Town of Glames, the houses built of stone and slated, with a neat Kirk and small square Tower (a rarity in this region). Just beyond it rises a beautiful round hill, and another ridge of a longer form adjacent to it, both cover'd with woods of tall fir. Beyond them peep over the black hills of *Sid-law,* over which winds the road to Dundee.

"To the North, within about 7 miles of me begins to rise the Grampions, hill above hill, on whose tops 3 weeks ago I could plainly see some traces of the snow that fell in May last.

"To the East winds away the Strath, such as I have before described it, among the hills, which sink lower and lower as they approach the sea. To the West the same valley (not plain, but broken unequal ground) runs on for about 20 miles in view. There I see the crags above Dunkeld, there Beni-gloe [Ben-y-Gloe, 'the hazy mountain'], and Beni-More [Ben More, 'the gentle hill'], rise above the clouds, and there is that She-khallian [Schiehallion, 'the maiden's pap'] that spires into a cone above them all, and lies at least 45 miles (in a direct line) from this place".

Glamis, through the imaginary connection of its thanage with Shakespeare's *Macbeth,* has attracted the interest of Scotsmen as widely different in temperament as the Chevalier St. George, who stayed there in 1716, and Sir Walter Scott, who spent a night in the Castle about the year 1800. Although certainly tradition, and perhaps also its foundations, take it back to the eleventh or even the tenth century, its present form of a French château in the style of Chantilly, its surface richly adorned with sculptures, corbellings, battlements, pinnacles, pepper-box turrets and the like, is the result of massive reconstructions and additions during the sixteenth, seventeenth and eighteenth centuries.

John, the ninth Earl, who was Gray's host, married Mary Eleanor Bowes, heiress of over a million pounds, of whom George VI's Queen Elizabeth is a descendant. He was a man of considerable energy and ability, and Gray obviously admired him.

"Lord S., who is the greatest Farmer in this neighbourhood, is out from break of day to dark night among his husbandmen and labourers; he has near two thousand acres of land in his own hands, and is at present employ'd in building a low wall of 4 miles long; and in widening the bed of the little river *Deane,* which runs to S and SE of the house, from about 20 to 50 feet wide, both to prevent inundations, and to drain the Lake of Forfar. This work will be 2 years more in completing, and must be 3 miles in length. All the Highlanders that can be got are employ'd in it; many of them know no English, and I hear them singing Erse-songs all day long.

"The price of labour is 8 pence a-day; but to such as will join together and engage to perform a certain portion in a limited time, 2 shillings. I must say, that all our labours seem to prosper, and my Lord has casually found in digging such quantities of shell-marle as not only fertilize his own grounds, but are disposed of at a good price to all his neighbours. In his nurseries are thousands of oaks, beech, larches, horse-chestnuts, spruce, fir etc: thick as they can stand, and whose only fault is that they are grown tall and vigorous before he has determined where to plant them out".

Gray's eye for the arrangement of natural properties led him to analyse the environment and imagine what might be done for it by way of landscaping.

"The most advantageous spot we have for beauty lies West of the House, where (when the stone-walls of the meadows are taken away) the grounds (naturally unequal) will have a very park-like appearance. They are already full of trees, which need only thinning here and there to break the regularity of their lines, and thro' them winds the *Burn of Glames,* a clear and rapid trout-stream which joins the River Deane hard by. Pursuing the course of the brook upwards, you come to a narrow sequester'd valley sheltered from all winds through which it runs murmuring among great stones.

On one hand, the ground gently rises into a hill; on the other are the rocky banks of the rivulet almost perpendicular, yet cover'd with sycamore, ash, and fir, that (tho' it seems to have no place or soil to grow in) yet has risen to a good height, and forms a thick shade. You may continue along this hill and passing by one end of the village and its church for half a mile it leads to an opening of two hills cover'd with fir-woods, that I mentioned above, thro' which the stream makes its way, and forms a cascade of 10 or 12 feet over broken rocks. A very little art is necessary to make all this a beautiful scene".

Soon after Gray reached Glamis, a letter arrived from Dr. James Beattie, Professor of Moral Philosophy and Logic in the Marischal College, Aberdeen. Beattie earned the warm support of many Scottish churchmen because of his valiant, but unsuccessful, attempt to refute the "sceptical" philosophy of David Hume. He later won admiration in other quarters when it became known that the poem, *The Minstrel*, which had appeared anonymously in London in 1771, was by him. He had already published a volume of verse in 1761, and so was probably known to Gray principally as a poet.

Dr. Carlyle and Dr. Wright had let him know that Gray was in Scotland. He therefore began his letter with as elegant an example of polished self-abasement as is to be found in eighteenth century literature.

"If I thought it necessary to offer an apology for venturing to address you in this abrupt manner, I should be very much at a loss how to begin. I might plead my admiration of your genius, and my attachment to your character; but who is he, that could not, with truth, urge the same excuse for intruding on your retirement? I might plead my earnest desire to be personally acquainted with the man whom I have so long and so passionately admired in his writings; but thousands, of greater consequence than I, are ambitious of the same honour. I, indeed, must either flatter myself that no apology is necessary, or otherwise, I must despair of obtaining what has long been the object of my most ardent wishes; I must forfeit all hopes of seeing you, and conversing with you.

"It was yesterday I received the agreeable news of your being in Scotland, and of your intending to visit some parts of it. Will you permit us to hope, that we shall have an opportunity, at Aberdeen, of thanking you in person for the honour you have done to Britain and to the poetic art, by your inestimable compositions, and of offering you all that we have that deserves your acceptance, namely, hearts full of esteem, respect and affection? If you cannot come so far northward, let me at least be acquainted with the place of your residence, and permitted to wait on you. Forgive, sir, this request; forgive me if I urge it with earnestness, for indeed it concerns me dearly; and do me the justice to believe that I am with the most sincere attachment, and most respectful esteem, &c. &c. &c. . . ."

Gray had to delay replying to Beattie, being on "a little journey" to Arbroath when it arrived. Gracefully he parried Beattie's fulsome eloquence.

"A Man of merit that honours me with his esteem and has the frankness to tell me so, doubtless can need no excuses; his apology is made, and we are already acquainted, however distant from each other".

However, he had already made other plans.

"I fear, I can not (as I would wish) do myself the pleasure of waiting on you at Aberdeen, being under an engagement to go tomorrow to Taymouth, and if the weather will allow it, to the Blair of Athol: this will take up four or five days, and at my return the approach of winter will scarce permit me to think of any farther expeditions northwards. My stay here will however be a fortnight or three weeks longer, and if in that time my business or invitation should call you this way, Lord Strathmore gives me commission to say, he shall be extremely glad to see you at Glames".

Business or invitation did call Beattie that way, and he seems to have spent two days at Glamis with Gray. They talked about poetry, and although no record of what was said has survived, Gray seems afterwards to have felt that his remarks might have upset his fellow-poet. On Beattie's return to Aberdeen, he wrote again, this time offering Gray the Degree of Doctor of Laws from Marischal College, an honour Gray declined, explaining:

"I have been, Sir, for several years, a Member of the University of Cambridge, and formerly (when I had some thoughts of the profession), took a Bachelor of Laws degree there. Since that time, tho' long qualified by my standing, I have always neglected to finish my course, and claim my Doctor's degree. Judge therefore, whether it will not look like a slight and some sort of contempt if I receive the same degree from a Sister-University. I certainly would avoid giving any offence to a set of Men among whom I have pass'd so many easy, and (I may say) happy hours of my life: yet shall ever retain in my memory the obligations you have laid me under, and be proud of my connection with the University of Aberdeen".

Gray then refers back to their conversation about Beattie's poetry.

"It is a pleasure to me to find, that you are not offended with the liberties I took when you were at Glames. You took me too literally, if you thought I meant in the least to discourage you in your pursuit of Poetry. All I intended to say was, that if either Vanity (that is, a general and undistinguishing desire of applause) or Interest or Ambition has any place in the breast of a poet, he stands a great chance in these our days of being severely disappointed. And yet after all these passions are suppress'd, there may remain in the mind of one, *ingenti perculsus amore,* (and such a one I take you to be), incitments of a better sort strong enough to make him write verse all his life, both for his own pleasure, and that of posterity".

Beattie, according to Mason, had "expressed himself with less admiration of Dryden than Mr. Gray thought his due. He told him in reply, that if there was any excellence in his own numbers, he had learned it wholly from that great Poet; and pressed him with great earnestness to study him, as his choice of words and versification was singularly happy and harmonious". This point about the poet whom Scott later called "Glorious John", was hammered home in the postscript to Gray's letter:

"Remember Dryden, and be blind to all his faults".

On 11th September, Gray and his host set out on that trip which had been his excuse to Beattie for not visiting Aberdeen. They drove westwards to Meigle, "where is the tomb of *Queen Wanders, that was driven to dethe by staned-horses for nae gude that she did".* Gray, somewhat puzzled, adds: "So the Women there told me, I'm sure".

The largest of the remarkable sculptured stones at Meigle,

now housed in a museum made out of the old school, is indeed said to commemorate the death of Guinevere, the unfaithful Queen of King Arthur, whose name in Scotland took the form of Guanora, Vanora, or Wander. She was reputed to have been imprisoned on Barry Hill, in Alyth Parish, three miles from Meigle. The Latin-writing historian John Bellenden, as translated into Scots by Hector Boece, says that all women abhor these stones, "and specially the sepulture of Guanora, as the title written thar upon showis– All weemin that stampis an this sepulture shall be ay barrant, but [without] ony fruit of their wamb, siclike as Guanora was".

Gray and the Earl drove through Coupar Angus, "on the River Ila [Isla], then over a wide and dismal heath fit for an assembly of Witches, till we came to a string of four small lakes in a valley, whose deep-blew waters and green margin, with a Gentleman's house or two seated on them in little groves, contrasted with the black desert, in which they were inchased. The ground now grew unequal, the hills more rocky seem'd to close in upon us, till the road came to the brow of a steep descent, and (the sun then setting), between two woods of oak we saw far below us the River Tay come sweeping along the bottom of a precipice at least 150 feet deep, clear as glass, full to the brim, and very rapid in its course. It seem'd to issue out of woods thick and tall, that rose on either hand, and were overhung by broken rocky crags of vast height. Above them to the West, the tops of higher mountains appear'd, on which the evening clouds reposed.

Down by the side of the river under the thickest shade is seated the Town of Dunkeld. In the midst of it stands a ruined Cathedral, the towers and shell of the building still entire".

It took from 1318 to 1501 to build this Cathedral which, sixty years later, was much more quickly reduced to a roofless ruin by the violence of the Reformation. Argyll and Ruthven, those Protestant noblemen who ordered the Lairds of Airntully and Kinvaid to "pass incontinent to the Kirk of Dunkeld, and tak doun the haill images thereof, and bring furth to the kirkyard and burn them openly; and siclyke cast doun the altars, and purge the kirk of all kinds of monuments of idolatry", cannot wholly be blamed for the desecration in this instance, for they added: "Find not but that ye tak good heed that neither the desks, windocks, nor doors be onyweys hurt or broken, either glassin work or iron work". However, this advice was ignored. The choir was re-housed in 1600 to serve as a parish church, and in our own day the National Trust for Scotland has restored the delightful domestic precincts of the Cathedral.

Gray admired the Duke of Atholl's mansion beyond the town. At that time, as "his grounds were interrupted by the streets and roads", he had "flung arches of communication across them, that add to the scenery of the place, which of itself is built of good white stone, and handsomely slated, so that no one would take it for a Scotch Town till they come into it".

Gray apparently alludes to the prevalence of thatching in the smaller houses of that period. The Duke's house has now become a hotel, and the arches have long since disappeared. Although Gray approved of the appearance of Dunkeld, there were other aspects of it which he found less endearing, for he told Wharton: "Here we passed the night: if I told you how you would bless youself".

The vast Breadalbane territory was the travellers' intended destination. So: "Next day we set forward to Taymouth, 27 miles further West, the road winding thro' beautiful woods with the Tay almost always in full view to the right, being here from 3 to 400 feet over: the Strath-Tay, from a mile to 3 miles or more wide cover'd with corn and spotted with groups of people then in the midst of their harvest. On either hand, a vast chain of rocky mountains, that changed their face and open'd something new every hundred yards, as the way turn'd, or the clouds pass'd. In short, altogether it was one of the most pleasing days I have pass'd these many years, and at every step I wished for you.

"At the close of the day we came to *Balloch* ['the foot of the loch'] so the place was call'd: but now for decency Taymouth, improperly enough, for here it is, that the river issues out of Loch-Tay (a glorious lake 15 miles long and 1½ broad) surrounded with prodigious mountains". Gray noted Ben Lawers on the north western edge of the loch; Schiehallion "that monstrous creature of God," to the east;

and directly west, Benmore, which "rises to a most aweful height, and looks down on the tomb of Fingal". Fingal, the legendary Ossianic hero, is reputed to be buried near the village of Killin, at the southern extremity of Loch Tay, in what was once the site of the ancient churchyard.

At the time of Gray's visit, the Breadalbane lands were among the most expansive in all Scotland, a fact which led Gray to record:

"Lord Braidalbin's *policy* (so they call here all such ground as is laid out for pleasure) takes in about 2,000 acres, of which his house, offices, and a deer-park about 3 miles round, occupy the plain or bottom, which is little above a mile in breadth. Thro' it winds the Tay, which by means of a bridge I found here to be 156 feet over. His plantations and woods rise with the ground on either side the Vale to the very summit of the enormous crags that overhang it. Along them on the mountain's side runs a terrain a mile and a half long, that overlooks the course of the river. From several seats and temples perch'd on particular rocky eminences you command the Lake for many miles in length, which turns like some huge river, and loses itself among the mountains that surround it".

The grounds particularly impressed Gray.

"Trees . . .grow here to great size and beauty. I saw four old chestnuts in the road as you enter the park, of vast bulk and height. One beech-tree I measured, that was 16 feet, 7 inches in the girth and (I guess) near 80 feet in height. The Gardiner presented us with peaches, nectarines, and plums from the stonewalls of the kitchen-garden (for there are no brick nor hot-walls.) The peaches were good, the rest well-tasted, but scarce ripe. We also had golden pippins from an espalier (not ripe), and a melon very well-flavour'd and fit to eat".

The house which Gray visited was not the present magnificent Taymouth Castle, but its predecessor, the Castle of Balloch, which dated from 1580.

"Of the house", Gray reported, "I have little to say. It is a very good Nobleman's house, handsomely furnished and well-kept, very comfortable to inhabit but not worth going far to see".

Of the Earl's taste, he had not much more to say. "It is one of these noble situations that man cannot spoil. It is, however, certain that he has built an inn and a tower just where his principal walks should have been, and in a most wonderful spot of ground, that perhaps belongs to him. In this inn, however, we lay, and next day, returning down the river 4 miles, we pass'd it over a fine bridge built at the expence of the Government, and continued on our way to Logie-Rait, just below which is a most charming scene. The Tummel, which is here the longer river of the two, falls into the Tay. We ferried over the Tummel in order to get into Marshall Wade's road (which leads from Dunkeld to Inverness) and continued our way along it toward the North".

George Wade, to whom Gray refers, became Commander-in-Chief in Scotland in 1726, and began the construction of what were described as "the important military roads which brought the inmost fastness in the north and west of Scotland within touch of the rest of Great Britain". These labours he directed included the construction of forty stone bridges: all of which gave rise to the historic bull:

Had you seen these roads before they were made
You would lift up your hands and bless General Wade.

Forty years after Wade began his work, Gray already thought the great engineering feat not wholly perfect.

"The road is excellent, but dangerous enough in conscience. The river, after running directly under us at the bottom of a precipice 200 feet deep, sometimes masqued indeed by wood, that finds means to grow where I could not stand: but very often quite naked and without any defence. In such places we walked for miles, together, partly for fear, and partly to admire the beauty of the country, which the beauty of the weather set off to the greatest advantage."

When Gray was making his Highland tour, there were still many people living who remembered the Jacobite Rising of 1745. It was therefore perhaps not surprising that his interest in Killiecrankie was aroused for what we today would consider the wrong reason. Wrote Gray:

"We approach'd the Pass of Killikrankie, where in the year '45 the Hessians with their Prince at their head stop'd short, and refused to march a foot farther". The reference is to the incident in which six thousand Hessians, under the command of Prince Frederick of Hesse-Cassel, who had landed at Leith, advanced from Perth with the Earl of Crawford to the relief of Sir Andrew Agnew, who was blockaded in the castle of Blair Atholl by Lord George Murray. In Sir Walter Scott's words: "Lord Crawford, however, in vain attempted to bring up the Hessians, for so great was their terror of being attacked in the Pass of Killiecrankie by the swords of the wild mountaineers, that they absolutely refused to march beyond it".

Apart from the beauty of this Pass, through which the Garry flows, and part of which is now owned by the National Trust for Scotland, the incident most strongly associated with it occurred on 27th July, 1689, after the battle fought on higher ground near Urrard House, a mile or so to the north. On that occasion, a force of Jacobite supporters of James VII and II under Graham of Claverhouse, "Bonnie Dundee", routed William III's army under General Mackay.

Although the action lasted only a few minutes, Dundee himself was killed; and so the Jacobite cause, through lack of leadership at a crucial moment, failed to hold the advantage its victory had gained for it. One of Mackay's men, Donald MacBean, is said to have made the Soldier's Leap in the Pass below, fleeing for his life before the Highlanders.

Close by the house of Faskally, Gray noticed "a hill cover'd with ash, with grotesque masses of rock, staring from among their trunks, like the sullen countenances of Fingal and all his family, frowning on the little mortals of modern days".

Here, unfortunately, Gray's letter to Wharton had to be abruptly ended, because, as he explained, "my paper is deficient". He thus did not record his views on "the black river Garry, the Blair of Athole, Mount Beni-ghloe, my return (by another road) to Dunkeld, the Sta-Bann and Rumbling Bridge". The district of Strathbran, in which is clustered Little Dunkeld, was, in the words of a contemporary topographical dictionary, "much frequented by parties visiting the romantic scenery in its vicinity. Among its principal attractions are, the *Rumbling Bridge,* thrown over a deep chasm, in which the Bran, rushing with impetuous violence among the rocks, forms a romantic cascade: and *Ossian's Seat,* or the *Hermitage,* situated on the North Bank of the Bran in the woods of the Duke of Atholl".

Gray summed up his impressions hastily. "In short", he wrote, "since I saw the Alps, I have seen nothing sublime till now".

On 7th October, unwilling to risk another crossing of the Forth, as he later told a friend "being a foe to drowning", Gray set out again for the south, passing through Stirling on his way to the Capital; not without apprehension, for, he confessed to Wharton, "I dread Edinburgh and the itch and expect to find very little in my way worth the perils I am to endure". A fortnight later, he was reunited with Wharton at Old Park.

From London, he pronounced on his Scottish tour to several of his friends.

James Brown, the Master of Pembroke, was told that the Highlands "would be Italy, if they had but a climate, and even that was not wanting for the few days I pass'd among them. There it is that the beauties of Scotland lie hid. Of the Lowlands which every true Scotsman celebrates as a Paradise, I shall only say, they are better than Northumberland . . .and the nearer they come to the mountains, the better they grow".

Gray seems to have believed that Brown would make a journey to Scotland by himself at some stage, for the poet provided his friend with a series of jottings, possibly originally enclosed with the letter already quoted, giving route notes for such a journey. Also included are some amusing general observations, reflecting on the poor quality of Scottish inn-keeping. When staying at an inn, Gray advises:

"See your sheets air'd yourself. Eat mutton or hard eggs. If they are broil'd, boil'd or roasted, say that from a child you have eat no butter, and beg they would not rub any over your meat. There is honey, or orange-marmalade, or currant-jelly, which may be eaten with toasted bread, or the thin oat-cakes, for breakfast. Dream not of milk. Ask your Landlord to set down, and help off with your wine. Never scold at anybody, especially at Gentlemen or Ladies".

Brown did, in fact, visit Scotland in 1767, but in the company of Gray's host, Lord Strathmore.

To William Mason, Gray's eventual literary executor, the poet wrote: "I am return'd from Scotland charm'd with my expedition. It is of the Highlands I speak. The Lowlands are worth seeing once, but the Mountains are exstatic, and ought to be visited in pilgrimage once a year. None but those monstrous creatures of God know how to join so much beauty with so much horror. A fig for your Poets, Painters Gardiners and Clergymen"–a hit at Mason, who was all four!–"who have not been among them. Their imagination can be made up of nothing, but bowling-greens, flowering shrubs, horse-ponds, Fleet-ditches, shell-grottoes, and Chinese rails. Then I had so beautiful an Autumn. Italy could hardly produce a nobler scene, or a finer season. And this so sweetly contrasted with that perfection of nastiness, and total want of accommodation, that Scotland only can supply. Oh! You would have bless'd yourself. I shall certainly go again. What a pity 'tis I can't draw, nor describe, nor ride on horseback!" Gray's proposed return visit, however, was not to materialise.

His old friend Walpole was told simply: "I am coming back from the Highlands very much better for my journey, and (what I little expected) very much pleased with what I have seen". These two men had once together visited the famous monastery the Grande Chartreuse (also visited by Wordsworth). Walpole had found the precipices, mountains, torrents, wolves and rumblings of the French Alps reminiscent of the painter Salvator Rosa, the late eighteenth century's ideal conventional interpreter of the wildness, the vastness and the energy of scenes like these. Gray, however, saw the apparatus of the sublimity of horror rather differently. Of this same Continental scene, he wrote:

"Not a precipice, not a torrent, not a cliff, but is pregnant with religion and poetry. There are certain scenes that would awe an atheist into belief, without the help of other argument. . .You have death perpetually before your eyes, only so far removed, as to compose the mind without frightening it".

This imaginative interpretation of mountain scenery, which perhaps came more easily to the young Gray touring the Continent than to the middle-aged Gray who travelled to Scotland, sounds out the mood Wordsworth was to deepen and develop. Before the Lake poet could do so, however, the theory of the picturesque was to be spelled out in detail by William Gilpin, and Mrs. Murray was to exemplify conventional Salvator Rosaling at its most enthusiastic extreme. On the sensitive mind of Gray, therefore, the pivot between the eighteenth and the nineteenth-century attitudes towards scenery delicately balances, sometimes tilting backwards, sometimes forwards.

The rest of his life passed uneventfully. Gray divided his time between London and Cambridge, and the houses of two or three of his closest friends.

On 24th July, 1771, while at dinner in the College Hall, he was overcome by a nausea which caused him to retire to his bed. His illness was diagnosed as "gout of the stomach"; he had been affected by gout in his feet for some years. At that time it was believed that when gout left the joints, it could attack the stomach. Sir Humphrey Rolleston, however, considered, on the evidence of the letter of Gray's friends, that the poet probably suffered from chronic kidney disease, terminating in uraemia (as, in all probability, also did Mozart, who met a similar end). Gray died in his room at Pembroke Hall at eleven o'clock on the evening of 30th July.

Samuel Johnson included Gray in his *Lives of the Poets*. The famous *Elegy* has kept its place in anthologies through the English-speaking world. His letters are relished by students of his period for their many vivid turns of expression.

Rarely, however, has a poet enjoyed such celebrity in his own lifetime, or such posthumous fame, on the strength of so small a body of achievement. The remarkable and continuing impact of his work lends added interest to the record of his enthusiastic enjoyment of Scotland.

2

William Gilpin:
In Search of the Picturesque

In the year 1776 a traveller came to Scotland who was not only a gifted artist and writer but also the formulator of an aesthetic that did much to shape the taste of his contemporaries in England: the theory of the picturesque.

William Gilpin was born in Cumberland in 1724, the son of Captain John Bernard Gilpin, an officer of the 12th Regiment of Foot and later Captain of an "Independent Company of Invalids" which was serving with the garrison at Carlisle when that town capitulated to Prince Charles Edward Stuart in 1745. Captain Gilpin also inherited considerable artistic ability from his father, William Gilpin, the Recorder of Carlisle, who had died the year young William was born. As a boy, Captain Gilpin had studied art with Matthias Read. When the Carlisle defeat put an end to his military ambitions he pursued art enthusiastically in middle and later life, seeing that his sons, William and Sawrey, were well-grounded in its technicalities.

William was educated at St. Bees, and at Queen's College, Oxford, where he graduated in 1740, returning home in 1746 to be ordained curate of Irthington. Two years later he was back in Oxford to take his Master of Arts degree. For several years he practised as a priest in London, devoting also a great deal of time to improving his drawing technique and to studying the art of his contemporaries, many of whom he came to know. Then, in 1752, he became headmaster of Cheam School, which responsibility curtailed his artistic activities for a time, although he managed to keep in touch with the world of art through his brother Sawrey, who had become a professional. By the 1760s, however, Cheam School was flourishing, and Gilpin was increasingly able to devote time to drawing. He was influenced by the work of

Alexander Cozzens, whom he may have met during his London days. From the middle 1760s the influence of Salvator Rosa became more and more apparent in Gilpin's imaginary scenic compositions; idealised landscapes, one might call them. During this decade, he began to make a series of short tours, writing accounts of what he saw, and sometimes making sketches to aid his memory. From 1768 onwards he created what was to become a new kind of travel literature, writing accounts of his tours, which grew more extensive, and illustrating them himself. He set out from Cheam during the summer holidays for periods ranging from a week to a month, covering Kent in 1768, Essex, Suffolk and Norfolk in 1769, South Wales in 1770, Cumberland and Westmorland in 1772, North Wales in 1773, the South Coast of England in 1774, the West of England in 1775 and finally the Highlands of Scotland in 1776. He recorded his impressions of these tours in little notebooks, many of which have survived, together with rough sketches of the scenes he visited. From these materials he later prepared for publication the full accounts. In the case of his Scottish book, *Observations on several parts of Great Britain, particularly the Highlands of Scotland, relative chiefly to Picturesque Beauty, made in the year 1776,* the first edition did not appear until 1789, by which time his book on Lakeland had made him famous.

In dedicating his Scottish account to the Earl of Harcourt, he remarks: "Picturesque ideas lie not in the common road of genius and learning. They require perhaps a distinct faculty to comprehend them—at least they require more attention to the scenes of nature, and the rules of art, than men of letters in general, unless stimulated by a peculiar inclination, bestow upon them".

In other words, Gilpin differed from all previous discoverers of Scotland in that he looked with the objective eye of a painter. Such were the taste and manners of his age that he sought to fit what he saw into a system of rules. Nature, if it could not be accommodated within the conventions of a picture, or did not answer in proportion and balance to what seemed to him to be aesthetically satisfactory, was at fault. But he swept away the emotional nonsense about horror and terror, pleasing or displeasing, which had obsessed most of his predecessors from Longinus to Burke and his eighteenth-century successors when they tried to devise theories to account for the sense of artistic sublimity, whether in art or nature. As Samuel Monk[1] commented of Gilpin: "While never denying the existence of a sublimity other than picturesque sublimity, he simply ignored it, and concentrated his attention on line and form and perspective". This, of course, led Gilpin to overlook the immediate emotional relationship between Man and Nature, a subject soon to become the concern of Wordsworth, then a boy growing up among the rainy silences of Cumberland. But, as Monk puts it, Gilpin was content "to throw the weight of his influence on the side of the eye and to leave to a greater man the vindication of the imagination".

Gilpin crossed the Esk at Longtown, and followed the course of that river into Scotland. His first inspection of that characteristic piece of Border architecture, the Peel tower, led him to set down a description of its former functions:

"They are commonly built in the form of a square tower. The walls are thick: the apertures for light small. They are divided generally into three or four stories, each containing only one apartment. The lowest was the receptacle for cattle, which were driven into it in time of alarm. The family occupied the upper stories. As these towers were chiefly meant as places of security against the banditti of the country, the garrison had seldom more than the siege of an hour or two to sustain. They could bear therefore crowding together, and were not anxious about their magazines. If they were attacked by one of the neighbouring garrisons, they could make no defence". He had looked up "among Haynes's state papers the Exploits done upon the Scotts in the year 1544", and found that between 2nd July and 14th November ninety-seven raids had been carried out by the English side, "which no doubt were repaid in kind by the Scotts; though probably not in so full a measure". On 7th August, for instance, Sir Ralph Eves, with fourteen hundred men, burnt Jedburgh, Ancrum and some smaller villages, slew eighty Scots and stole four hundred and twenty "head and nolt" and four hundred sheep, "with much inside goods": while on 27th August, Sir Brian Layton, among other exploits, "went

[1] Samuel H. Monk: *The Sublime* (1935)

Thomas Gray, 1716–1771

Above, Glamis Castle . . . 'very singular and striking' thought Gray; *below*, Dunkeld, where Gray spent the night—'if I told you how you would bless yourself'

to a tower of Lord Buccleugh's called the Moss-house, and smoked it very sore, and took thirty prisoners, and brought away eighty nags, two hundred nolt and four hundred sheep".

The gentle and civilized Gilpin comments: "I need not multiply extracts from this horrid catalogue, in which the pillage, ruin, and slaughter of thousands of individuals . . . are related with as much indifference as the bringing in of a harvest. We consider war as a necessary evil; and pride ourselves now on making it like gentlemen. Humanity certainly requires us to alleviate its miseries as far as we can".

Even in this once war-torn frontier countryside, Gilpin found himself "amused with the sweet vallies of the Esk". Passing through Langholm, he crossed by Mosspaul to the valley of the Teviot. Here: "Tho' the lofty skreens run down pricipately to the river, and contract the vallies, you see plainly they are the parts of a large-featured country; and in a state of landscape very different from those irriguous little vallies which we had left. . . .The downy sides of all these vallies are covered with sheep, which often appear to hang upon immense green walls. Several of the mountainous slopes. . . are finely tinted with mosses of different hues, which give them a very rich surface".

Hawick, then still a rural little town, seemed to Gilpin to have "a romantic situation among rocks, sounding rivers, cataracts and bridges". His drawing of the old bridge at Hawick, long since demolished, is among his very best. The bridge made him reflect that "When we meet with objects of this kind (the result of nature and chance), what contempt do they throw upon the laboured works of art?"

The picturesque eye, he explains, "has that kind of fastidiousness about it that is seldom pleased with any artificial attempts to please. It must find its own beauties; and often fixes, as here, upon some accidental, rough object, which the common eye would pass unnoticed".

Crossing the hills to Selkirk, he thought the scenery "unadorned", though "by no means devoid of beauty". He went on to explain his principle of adornment:

"As in history-painting, figures without drapery, and other appendages, make but an indifferent group; so in scenery, naked mountains form poor composition. They require the drapery of a little wood to break the simplicity of their shapes, to produce contrasts, to connect one part with another; and to give that richness in landscape, which is one of its greatest ornaments".

But at Ferney he was able to enjoy "a good scene of mountain-perspective. It is not often that these elevated bodies coincide with the rules of beauty and composition–less often indeed than any other mode of landscape".

From just beyond the village of Middleton, Gilpin obtained his first view of Arthur's Seat and decided that it was "of peculiar appearance; romantic, but not picturesque". At Dalkeith House, he enjoyed "a landscape by Vernet, in Salvator's style. It was a rocky scene through which a torrent rushes: the foaming violence of the water is well expressed". He decided that he had not often "met with a picture in the fashionable manner" which he liked better, even although this one was "not entirely free from the flutter of a French artist".

He reached Edinburgh high in his expectations, having heard that the Scottish capital was "one of the most picturesque towns in Britain". People, he explained, "often consider *romantic* and *picturesque,* as synonymous". This was not so. Take Arthur's Seat, for instance.

"Arthur's Seat, which is still the principal object, appears still as odd, mishapen, and uncouth as before. It gave us the idea of a cap of maintenance in heraldry; and a view with such a strong feature in it can no more be picturesque than a face with a bulbous nose can be beautiful. The town and castle, indeed, on the left, make some amends, and are happily introduced". What he described as "the old castle-like building, called Craigmillar" also had "a good effect".

Gilpin walked round Edinburgh and surveyed it from different angles, and so greatly added to his store of unusual pleasures.

"As you approach from the south, it appears like a grand city of noble extent. As you move to the right, its size gradually diminishes. But when you view it from the Musselborough road, which is in a direction due east, the street is gone; and the houses are all crowded together, as if they had retreated under the walls of the castle. And yet the appearance of the town and castle, thus united by perspective into one vast object, is extremely grand".

Having studied the city from its approaches, Gilpin now proceeded to inspect the castle at close range, it being, in his opinion, "the only object of picturesque curiosity in Edinburgh. They who go to see it are commonly satisfied with being carried *into* it, where they find a number of patched, incoherent buildings without any beauty. Since anything in it deserves the least attention; except the views from the batteries, which are very amusing; particularly those over the Forth. But he who would see Edinburgh Castle in perfection must go to the bottom of the rock it stands on and walk round it. In this view, the whole appears a very stupendous fabric. The rock, which is in itself an amazing pile, is in many parts nobly broken; and tho', in its whole immensity, it is too large an object for a picture, unless at a proper distance; yet many of its craggy corners, with their watch-towers and other appendages, are very picturesque".

Holyrood House was simply "a grand palace, occupying a large square". A few years before Gilpin saw the Chapel, "a modern heavy roof was thrown over light, airy Gothic walls: the consequence of which was, it crushed them. On the night of the second of December 1768, a crash was heard by the inhabitants of the neighbouring district; and in the morning, the roof, walls, and monuments were all blended in one confused mass of irretrievable ruin".

As he set out from Edinburgh on the road to Stirling, Gilpin took another look at Arthur's Seat, shuddered, and growled, "Arthur's seat presents an unpleasing view from every station".

Hopetoun House, originally built for the first Earl of Hopetoun by Sir William Bruce between 1699 and 1703, and then enlarged and embellished during the next fifty years by William Adam and his sons John and Robert, aroused Gilpin's admiration. First, there was the setting, the House appearing "behind a sloping hill, which hides one of its wings". Whether or not Robert Adam would have approved of Gilpin's way of looking at the classical symmetry of the facade of his masterpiece, set in its formal layout of lawns, is very doubtful.

"The horizontal lines of the house", said Gilpin, "and the diverging lines of the hill accord agreeably. A regular building always appears best when thus connected with some irregular object. A new source of beauty arises from the contrast: and indeed without it a regular building has seldom a good effect".

Moving up the southern bank of the Forth, he noted "hills and promentories, and winding bays, which had a fine effect in nature: and tho' deficient in point of objects to characterize the scene, they were still accommodated to the pencil". The coastline of the Forth prompted him to declare that: "A country may please the eye in all its naked and unadorned rudeness: but when a portion of it is selected for a view, its features must be uncommonly striking, if it can support itself without the adornment of some artificial object, which both characterizes the scene; and adds dignity to it".

Blackness Castle, under the terms of the Act of Union of 1707 one of the four fortresses to be maintained at full military strength, had before that been a prison for Covenanters, and earlier still, a royal Castle. It was seen by Gilpin against the sunset.

"All the detail and surface was lost in obscurity: while the landscape around was overspread with that grey, and dubious, tint, which brought the whole into exactest harmony".

The royal palace of Linlithgow, which had caught fire while General Hawley's troops used it as a barracks in 1745 and had lost its roof in the conflagration, might have been expected to arouse Gilpin's enthusiasm, but he was "prevented by the weather from taking such a view of it as we wished".

At Falkirk, where he inspected the Forth and Clyde Canal, then under construction–it was opened in 1790–he broke out in cheerfully moralising strain:

"Busy man is ever at work grubbing the soil on which he exists; sometimes casting up heaps, and sometimes throwing them down". Unlike Southey, when he saw that other artificial sea-link across Scotland, the Caledonian Canal, in a similar stage of construction, Gilpin, whose interest in men and their affairs was so much less intense than his concern for landscape, had nothing to tell us about the details of the work in progress he must have observed.

At Carron, a curious relic known locally as Arthur's O'on (oven) was still standing, "a rotunda, open at the top, like the

Pantheon at Rome, though of very inferior workmanship, and dimensions. From the ground to the summit of the dome it measured twenty-two feet—the diameter in the inside was nineteen and a half".

This monument was thought by some to have marked the tomb of King Arthur, slain by Medrunt the Pict, uncle of St. Mungo, in 537, though more probably it was some kind of chapel where a Roman legion kept its colours. In any case, it was vandalistically destroyed by a pig-headed laird, Sir Michael Bruce, later in the century, in spite of the protests of local antiquaries.

However, the main sight at Carron was the Ironworks founded in 1760 by Dr. Roebuck of Sheffield. Grates, pots and pans, iron castings, and, a little after Gilpin's time, Carronades, have been produced in quantity, near the site of the Carron river, where, according to James Macpherson's Ossian, the young Fingal defeated Caracalla, son of Severus, in the year 211.

Gilpin saw over the Carron Ironworks, and reported that: "The great forge" exhibited "a set of the most infernal ideas. In one place, where coal is converted into coke by discharging it of sulphur, and the fire spread of course over a large surface, the volumes of smoke, the opening flames, and the suffocating heat of the glimmering air" were "wonderfully affecting. How vast the fire is, we may conceive, when we are told it consumes a hundred tons of coal a day", an amusing reminder that ideas on combustibility have changed since the eighteenth century. He also admired "the massy bellows, which rouses the furnaces. They are put in motion by water; and receiving the air in large cylinders, force it out again through small orifices, roaring with astonishing noise. The fire of the furnace thus roused, becomes a *glowing spot,* which the eye can no more look at, than at the sun. Under such intense heat, the rugged stone instantly dissolves in streams of liquid iron".

For once, Gilpin noticed human beings. "Among the horrid ideas of this place, it is not the least, that you see everywhere, black, sooty figures wheeling about, in iron wheel-barrows, molten metal, glowing hot".

Carron Ironworks were to have a visit from another and greater writer a decade later, Robert Burns. He arrived on a

Sunday, and so, not surprisingly, was refused admission: a rebuff which gave him some "horrid ideas".

We cam na here to view your works,
In hopes to be mair wise,
But only, lest we gang to Hell,
It may be nae surprise:
But when we tirl'd at your door
Your porter dought na hear us,
Sae may, shou'd we to Hell's yetts come [gates]
Your billy Satan sair us! [serve]

From Carron, Gilpin moved on to Stirling, and immediately applied his code of visual rules to the Castle and its surroundings:

"There is nothing very beautiful in the scenery around it; but an object of such consequence will give dignity to any scene. . . Viewed upon the spot, the *outside* of it is very inferior to the castle of Edinburgh. . . But if it be inferior on the outside, it is infinitely grander within. Edinburgh castle is only a collection of barracks, magazines, and officers' houses; whereas in Stirling castle you find very noble remains of royal magnificence. . . a palace, a chapel and parliament house". Though the palace of James V had by then become a barracks and was inside "totally without form", outside, it was "very richly and curiously adorned with grotesque figures". Like James VI's, Chapel Royal, it has been restored to an approximation of its original grandeur by the Ministry of Works.

By the entrance to the Castle, Gilpin admired "the palaces of the earls of Argyle and Mar", which stand like "two royal supporters". Argyll's Ludging is now a youth hostel; Mar's Wark, as it was in Gilpin's time, a richly impressive Renaissance ruin.

From the Castle ramparts, he looked at the prospect "which has always been esteemed the most celebrated view in Scotland. It is not indeed picturesque; but it is exceedingly grand, and amusing. You overlook a flat valley of vast extent, stretching almost as far as Edinburgh, through which the windings of the Forth are very intricate and curious. . . Through the whole of this vast channel the river winds as through a vast gut".

He mused upon Bannockburn, "the most glorious action in

the whole annals of Scotland; as it entirely freed it from the English yoke", yet listened with enjoyment to the tale of an old gunner whom he met at the Castle, and who, in 1745, had helped to direct such "a terrible discharge of cannon, and small arms" on the Jacobite army laying siege to the place that "seven hundred were left dead upon the spot while the rest fled with trepidation".

From Stirling, he crossed the Forth and travelled by the foot of the Ochils through "a tract of country affording little amusement", to Kinross, where Sir William Bruce's Kinnaird House very properly impressed him. It had been a fine day, and in the garden by the shores of Loch Leven, he observed and described an evening scene in a manner which seems almost to look forward to the Impressionists, and is certainly a far cry from the representational solidity with which many future generations of English artists came to view landscape.

"A soothing stillness ran through the scene. It was one of those mild, soft evenings, when not a breath disturbs the air. Almost sun set, a light grey mist arising from the lake, began to spread over the landscape. Creeping first along the surface of the water, it rose by degrees up to the hills: blending both together in that pleasing ambiguity through which we can but just distinguish the limits of each".

He admired Loch Leven Castle, "which appeared floating on the lake", and was the scene of the imprisonment of Mary, Queen of Scots. She had been forced to sign a deed of abdication in favour of her infant son, James the Sixth, by Lord Lindsay of the Byres, and was in the custody of Lady Douglas and her son, the young owner of the castle, Sir William Douglas. But with the aid of his eighteen-year-old son Willie, and friends who had carefully plotted across the water, Mary was able to escape. This romantic story, worked by Scott into his novel *The Abbot,* moved Gilpin to flights of rhetoric nowhere equalled in any of his other writings:

"But neither the walls of Loch-leven castle, nor the lake which surrounded it, were barriers against love. Mary had those bewitching charms, which always raised her friends. She wore a cestus; and might be said to number among her constant attendants, the God of Love himself. His ready wit restored her liberty. Time, and place were obedient to his will. His contrivance laid the plan. His address secured the keys: and his activity provided the bark: to which he led her; with his own hand carrying the torch, to guide her footsteps through the darkness of the night.–Confusion ran through the castle. Hasty lights were seen passing and repassing at every window; and traversing the island in all directions. The laughing God, the mean while, riding at the poop, with one hand, held the helm; and with the other waved his torch in triumph round his head. The boat soon made the shore, and landed the lovely queen in a port of security; where Loyalty, and Friendship waited to receive her". Alas for Gilpin's brave fancy! One night at Niddrie Castle was all Mary was to know of security before she watched her last army suffer defeat at Langside, and, in defiance of the advice of Archbishop Hamilton, rode down the hill towards English Elizabeth, eighteen years imprisonment and death on the block at Fotheringay.

Gilpin next passed on to Perth, the approach to which he thought would have been "extremely picturesque, were it not for an awkwardness which totally incapacitates it for the pencil. The Tay runs in a direct line between parallel banks". If Nature erred, Man had done his best to compensate for the error in linking the offending banks by a bridge which Gilpin much admired. He was able to look through "the window of Gowry-house, from whence James the Sixth called for help; when he feared assassination from the earl of Gowry", an experience no longer available to modern tourists, the city fathers having pulled the historic old house down.

At Scone, where the kings of Scotland were crowned, he observed that "the celebrated stone-chair, the palladium of the Scottish empire, which formerly had its station here, is now one of the appendages of royalty in Westminster Abbey".

As Gilpin approached Dunkeld, he was delighted by the variety of the scenery around him. Feeling that he had begun to *"descend* into the Highlands", the changing scene made him reflective:

"There is something very amusing even in a hasty succession of beautiful scenes. The imagination is kept in a pleasing perturbation; while these floating, unconnected ideas become a kind of waking dream".

He admired the "picturesque bridge" over the Bran; the

Abbey (which is, in fact, a Cathedral); the seat of the Duke of Athole, "a villa, rather than a ducal mansion"; the "large circular valley" in which the town lies, and "the mountains that inviron the whole". He noticed that the hill of Birnam was then "totally divested of a wood", and lest any of his Shakesperean readers might think the prophecy in *Macbeth* had come true, added that "of Dunsinane no vestiges remain; except a deep double ditch".

From Dunkeld, he rode up to Blair Atholl. The waters of the Tummel set him thinking of the importance of catching "the tints of nature with your pallet in your hand", to assist his readers in the doing of which he included a numbered sketch with accompanying colour-chart. "The banks of the Tummel", he declared, "are chiefly pastoral, but when it is joined by the Garry, or rather received into it, we had an ample specimen of the sublime".

He visited the pass of Killiecrankie and thought "the very formidable defile" displayed "in one part or another of its ample course, every species of rough and picturesque scenery". Blair Castle, garrisoned both by Montrose and by Claverhouse and used as a resting place by Prince Charles Stuart on his way south in 1745, suffered badly the following year when the Jacobites were trying to dislodge some of Cumberland's men and some German mercenaries. When Gilpin saw it, the turrets and parapets had been removed, turning it into a plain Georgian mansion which he thought "mean", though the rooms were "noble and furnished in grand taste". In the Victorian era, David Bryce was commissioned to put the Gothic trappings back on again, and there they remain to this day.

On the way to Glen Lyon, Gilpin found that "many of the scenes were very noble. The mountains retiring in different distances from the eye, marshalled themselves in the most beautiful forms, and expanded their vast concave bosoms to receive the most enchanting lights".

Glen Lyon is the longest glen in Scotland, and in Gilpin's day it was even longer, the Lubreoch Dam, at the head of the glen, having absorbed Loch Lyon. But then as now, entering the glen is a memorable and dramatic experience.

"The steep sides of Glen-lion received us and afforded us several views, which were magnificent in their kind, into the deep recesses of the dell; where the river is sometimes seen, but oftener only heard; and where it's sequestered haunts are seldom interrupted by human curiosity".

Glen Lyon, with its vistas of trees seen from above, inspired Gilpin to one of his more poetic flights of description.

"The eye is often carried many fathoms below, into these depths of solitude; and it is often arrested in mid-way by the spreading tops of trees, from whence getting passage perhaps again through some opening among them, it is baffled a second time by the darkness of the recess".

But his eighteenth-century sense of practicality never lagged far behind his fancy, for he added: "Amusing as these views were, they would have been more so, if the edge of the precipice on which we travelled had been better grounded. Our attention, in some degree, was engaged by our danger".

He sailed on Loch Tay, and on the lower end thought that he had seldom met with a grander piece of lake-scenery. Taymouth Castle, the seat of Lord Breadalbane, was not the present magnificent building by the Elliots, William Atkinson and Gillespie Graham, with its ceiling which took seven years to paint and its interior by Crace Bernasconi, but its predecessor, demolished in 1799, a house standing "on a lawn, between two mountains, which open to the lake" so beautifully placed that Gilpin reflected: "Perhaps no country in the world abounds more with grand situations, especially in the highland part of it, than Scotland".

From Kenmure, Gilpin rode to Killin, finding the scenery at the head of Loch Tay disappointing, since it exhibited "no bold shore, broken promentories, nor other forms of beauty", and its surroundings were "rather tame hills than picturesque mountains". However, as he approached Killin, "the country began to amend and pleased us in spite of a drizzling rain through which we viewed it. Many of the hills were clothed with wood; and some of them finely disposed . . . But as the evening grew worse, and set in wet, we could not examine the landscape as it deserved".

Although Gilpin's visit to Scotland coincided with the cult of James Macpherson's Ossianic poems, there is perhaps a touch of unsympathetic irony behind Gilpin's observation that, "The town of Killin is celebrated for being the receptacle of the bones of Fingal. We were shewn the place, where tradition says, they were buried: but the traveller must view his tomb with the eye of faith".

At Killin, Gilpin heard, and recorded, a story similar to that upon which Burn's poem "Address to Bealzebub" was based. Some Highlanders on the Breadalbane estate had banded together to emigrate.

"Several expeditions of this kind to America, from different parts of Scotland (which were supposed to have been attended with success) began to make a noise in the country; and a discontented spirit got abroad, even in those parts, where no oppression could be complained of; particularly in the domains of the earl of Breadalbane; the happiness of whose tenants seems to have been among the principal sources of the happiness of their lord. The *word was given,* as it was phrased, in the beginning of March 1775, and a rendezvous was appointed at Killin, on the first of the ensuing May. Here convened about thirty families, making in all above three hundred people. The first night they spent at Killin, in barns, and other outhouses, which they had previously engaged. Early the next morning the whole company was called together by the sound of bag-pipes, and the order of their march was settled. Men, women, and children, had all their proper stations assigned. They were all dressed in their best attire; and the men were armed in the Highland fashion. They who were able, hired carts for their baggage: the rest distributed it in proper proportions, among the several members of their little families. . . Then taking a long adieu of their friends and relations, who gathered round them, the music began to play, and in the midst of a thousand good wishes, the whole train moved on. . . Many of them were possessed of two or three hundred pounds. . . which at least showed that they had not starved upon their farms. They were a jovial crew; and set out, not like people flying from the face of poverty; but like men who were about to carry their health, their strength, and little property, to a better market".

They spent a day marching to the head of Loch Lomond, and sailed down it, moving on to Dumbarton, where they "contained themselves, till their transport vessel was ready at Greenock".

Breadalbane did not attempt to hinder the emigres. There are some grounds for thinking that McKenzie of Applecross did not do so either, in spite of Burns's allegations to the contrary. Knox's *Tour of the Highlands* attributes a different attitude to him than Burns chose to adopt. In any case, the whole attitude to emigration underwent change within a generation, and by the time of the evil days of the Clearances, it was the landlords who wanted rid of their tenants to make way for more profitable sheep, and the Highlanders who, in many cases, only left their native airt when the factors set fire to the thatched roofs of their poor homesteads.

By Tyndrum and Dalmally Gilpin came to Loch Awe, "one of the grandest lakes in Scotland". He admired "the vast mountain of Cruachan", and "the castle of Kilchurn, which is a grand object under the impending gloom of the mountains.

A "very long and dreary ride" brought him to Inveraray, where the castle "fully ensured the grandeur of the approach. It seems equally adapted to all the purposes of greatness, beauty and accommodation". Robert Mylne and Roger Morris, with some assistance first from William Adam and then from John, had just finished rebuilding this seat of the Dukes of Argyll when Gilpin saw it, and found "two disgusting parts about it. . . the square appendages which are tacked to each side of the middle tower, for the purpose of furnishing the interior apartments of the castle with light". One of these "interior apartments", the dining-room, is probably Mylne's finest interior.

Gilpin thought that Loch Fyne had "almost all the beauties of an inland lake; and some which an inland lake cannot have, particularly that of a very crowded navigation". It was then "one of the favourite haunts of herring, and when the shoals were present, according to the natives the loch consisted of 'one part water and two parts fish'." Such are the ways of herring that those shoals which enabled Loch Fyne to build up a reputation for producing the finest kippers, no longer frequent its waters. When they did, the groups of little fishing vessels made "a beautiful moving picture, which is frequently varied by vessels of a larger size shooting athwart, threading the several little knots of anchoring barks and making their *tacks* in every direction".

The crews of these Highland boats were "a cheerful, happy race. Among the implements of each boat, the bagpipe is rarely forgotten; the shrill melody of which you hear constantly resounding from every part; except when all hands are at work".

Gilpin left Inveraray with regret, because of "those scenes, in which the grand and beautiful are as harmoniously combined as we almost in any place remembered to have seen them. We approached it through magnificent woods; and we left it through a succession of lake-scenery still more magnificent".

Of the hill above Inveraray, Duniquaich, Gilpin observed: "Nothing exceeds the dignity of a mountain so much as its rising from the water's edge. In measuring it, as it appears connected with the ground, the eye knows not where to begin, but continues creeping up in quest of a base, till half the mountain is lost. But a water-line prevents this ambiguity".

He rode round the head of Loch Fyne, through Cairndow, which he thought "a few miserable houses", though the valley of the Kinglass was "one of the wildest and most sublime vallies" he had seen. He felt immured between two ranges of mountains, "magnificent; and yet well proportioned; bare of wood indeed, but rich from a varied and broken surface. . . Through the valley ran a stream, trembling violently over the rocky fragments, that opposed its course: and to compleat the grandeur of the whole, the sky happened to harmonize with the mountains, shapeing the clouds into. . . those swelling forms which present so strongly the idea of puft cheeks", an idea which early cartographers frequently embodied seraphically when decorating the corners of their maps.

Glencroe widened "rather to the beautiful, than to the sublime", the latter depending upon "the softness of the herbage" on the mountain side. Loch Long also seemed to Gilpin to combine the qualities of a freshwater lake with a sea-loch. "Upon its shores and rocks lie seaweed, shells, and other marks of a tide; which alone shew it to be salt-water; for its banks have all the verdure and vegetation of an inland-lake".

Crossing the narrow stretch of land which separates Loch

Long from Loch Lomond, Gilpin reached Tarbert. He looked up to the narrow part of the lake, where "a mountain on the left, near the eye, runs boldly into the water; beyond which the lake retires, bay after bay, in perspective, among distant mountains into its deep recesses".

Of all the Scottish lochs, Loch Lomond not only offers a greater contrast than any other, but constantly changes its aspects under the movements of sun and cloud. When Gilpin rowed out to the middle of the loch, "the scene had shifted. It was more of a vista. The mountains shelved beautifully into the water, on both sides. . . On the right, Ben-Lomond, the second hill in Scotland, raised its respectable head". To the south, the surface of the loch was "broken by a number of islands, which are scattered about it, and prevent all *unity of composition.* Its banks also, in that direction, are tame scenes of pasturage and cultivation".

However, he explored some of the islands in the loch–his refusal to use this correct descriptive word makes one wonder how English readers would respond to a Scots travel-writer referring to Windermere, Derwentwater and the others as being in the Loch District!–and was particularly interested in Inch Caillach. He claimed that the idea behind such island burials as once occurred here owed its origin to a time when "the country abounded with wolves", and "the animals would often attack church-yards; against which the people guarded by insular graves". He regarded the smaller islands in Loch Lomond's total of thirty-six as "only a garnish to the rest", and was suitably sceptical about the time-worn legends of floating and disappearing islands connected with Loch Lomond since mediaeval times. There appears to be some substance, however, in the story he was told about the effect of the great earthquake which seriously damaged Lisbon in 1755, when Loch Lomond "arose suddenly many feet in large swells, and overflowed a considerable distance".

Between Loch Lomond and Dumbarton, he found the countryside "level, cultivated, and adorned with gentlemen's seats", to say nothing of the "pillar erected to the memory of Dr. Smollet"–Tobias Smollet, the novelist–at Bonhill. Dumbarton Castle, that "whole grand object", was "interesting", in that "such a rock as this, is as uncommon at land, as it is at sea". From the battlements, he looked up and down the Clyde, but was unable to see Glasgow because the weather was hazy. Dumbarton itself he judged to be "an inconsiderable place" which delayed him "only for refreshment" before continuing on to Glasgow.

That city, as we know from many sources, which Gilpin confirms, was then "a beautiful town, consisting of elegant houses". But he had his criticisms. If these houses "were a little more connected, the high street, which is ample in its dimensions, would in all respects be noble". He called the Cathedral a "vast pile" with "nothing very pleasing in its structure; and it accords ill with the modern splendour of the city", an understandable urbane eighteenth century view of Gothic architecture.

Leaving Glasgow behind, he set out for Hamilton, taking a look at Bothwell Castle, whose ruins impressed him more highly than the then still intact and lived-in Hamilton House which, to him, had "the appearance of one of the most disagreeable places we had seen in Scotland–heavy, awkward, gloomy". It was to provoke an even stronger comment from Dorothy Wordsworth, and in 1822 give place to the huge Hamilton Palace, still heavier and uglier, before the ground beneath it, mined to produce the wealth with which it was built, took revenge by producing a subsidence so severe that it had to be taken down in 1927. In Gilpin's day, like so many Scottish mansions, it held "a great profusion of pictures. In general, one should not say much for the taste with which these collections have been made", though a few were "very good".

However, a building in the grounds, Chatelherault Lodge, built by William Adam and named after the Duke of Hamilton's French title, impressed Gilpin as being "a sumptuous pile" containing "the odd assemblaye of a banquetting-house and a dog-kennel". Almost two centuries later, its fate is in question, there being all too many local councillors who think our stone-and-mortar heritage worth neither the trouble nor the expense of saving. What were in these days the sequestered paths around the Clyde made him reflect: "I do not remember ever meeting with a scene of the kind which pleased me more than the wild river-scenes about Chatelherault".

Moving southwards, he passed over "vast wastes of barren

tracts" on the way to Drumlanrig. In these "dreary regions, in which no one travelled", he "met the Clyde wandering about in very low constitution". Around Leadhills, where lead and, nearby, gold, had been mined in the days of the Stuart kings, and which had since become mere mountainy villages, he thought the "shades were unaccompanied with any picturesque ideas. Often, when mountains, forests, and other grand objects, float before the eye, their sweeping forms, clad in the shade of evening, have a wonderful effect upon the imagination. But here the objects were neither grand, nor amusing. All were one general blot".

So uncharacteristic was Gilpin's taste for his age that when he came upon the architecture of the late seventeenth-century Queensberry seat of Drumlanrig, part of which may be by Sir William Bruce and the rest by William Lukup, he admitted the approaches to be "magnificent" but deplored the attempts of the owners of the Castle at landscaping their gardens, finding it amazing how much "contrivance" had been "used to deform all this beauty". The banks of the Nith, nearby, formed "a delicious scene", with the grazing cattle "milk-white, except their noses, ears, and the orbits of their eyes".

From Drumlanrig, down the valley of the Nith to Dumfries, was "rather pleasant than picturesque", though just outside Dumfries, there was the "elegant Gothic" ruins of the Collegiate Church of Lincluden, which, had Gilpin taken time to look, he would have found to contain much heraldic ornament and the noble tomb of Robert II's daughter, Margaret, who became the wife of the Earl Douglas, and who brought to Scotland those French craftsmen who wrought much of the decorated work in this beautiful ruin; and where, not long after Gilpin passed by, Burns delighted to wander "Lincluden's leafy shades amang".

Dumfries, then still a bustling, important town and Burns's "Maggy by the banks o'Nith, A dame wi' pride eneuch," merely seemed to stand "pleasantly on the Nith". The water, and the view from the twelfth century bridge, seemed "amusing".

The bleak shores of the Solway gave him more satisfaction than the red sandstone prosperity of Dumfries. "There is something pleasing in those long stretches of sand, distant country, and water, which flat shores exhibit. The parts are often large, well-tinted, and well-contrasted. Often, too, their various surfaces appear ambiguous, and are melted by light mists into one mass", an accurate observation of the ingredients of the charm of the Solway seascape; although "to make pictures" of it, "the foreground must be adorned with objects–masts of ships, figures, cattle or other proper appendages to break the lines of distance".

Passing through Annan, Gilpin reached Gretna Green, "the great resort of such unfortunate nymphs as happen to differ with their parents, and guardians, on the subject of marriage". He found it "a not disagreeable scene". He might have been less favourably impressed today.

But Gretna's associative powers were, even then, considerable. Gilpin writes: "Places furnish their peculiar topics of conversation". At Dover, the landing and embarking of foreigners was "the vulgar topic". At Portsmouth, "ships, cannon, gun powder", and "blowing the French to the d——" kept conversation humming. But at Gretna, Gilpin found that "the only topics are the stratagems of lovers; the tricks of servants; and the deceits put upon parents, and guardians": adding that "of all the seminaries of Europe, this is the seat, where that species of literature called novel-writing may be the most successfully studied".

As he crossed back over the Border, after a trip of just under three weeks, Gilpin set down his considered verdict on Scotland.

"Even in countries like this in which we now travelled, where the soil and climate are thought to deny the luxuriant growth of wood, there is abundant amusement. . . The coarsest face of nature is a comely face, and though her features, in these barren countries, have no great share of sweetness, and beauty, yet there is always something wildly graceful and expressive in her countenance". Mindful, perhaps of those wet Highland days that had limited the range of his seeing, but not damped his enthusiasm, he added a weather warning. Remember, he said, that "a grand light, or shade, thrown upon an object, gives it a consequence, without which it may escape notice".

Gilpin's *Scottish Observations* did much to attract attention to Scottish scenery, and to suggest a more ordered way of looking at it than anyone else had hitherto systematized.

He looked at landscape, and saw it for what it was. No one else had quite looked in that way before. In the years that followed, many others also did so as a result of the vivid and, on the whole, sensitive impressions of what he saw that Gilpin set down in his oddly punctuated yet effective prose.

In 1777, the year after he had made his Scottish tour, Gilpin accepted the offer of the living of vicar of Boldre, in Hampshire, passing on the rectorship of Cheam to his son. He had turned Cheam into a preparatory school which became a model of its kind, and to which the sons of many families of distinction had been sent.

At Vicar's Hill, his Boldre home, he busied himself not only with his religious duties, but also with generously playing the role of drawing master to numerous talented amateur artists, many of them well-connected young women. He used the profit from his books, and from the sale of some of his drawings, to found a school at Boldre. He landscaped his garden at Vicar's Hill with an imagination and physical energy which suggested yet another talent that circumstance gave him no opportunity fully to develop.

In his closing years, his drawings were much sought after, and among those interested in his work were the Royal Family. He died peacefully in his manse, of dropsy, in April 1804.

One of his lady pupils, Caroline Bowles, a niece of General Sir Henry Bernard (who was to command the British forces at the victory of Vimereria in 1808, and who had drawing lessons from both Gilpin and his brother Sawrey) was to achieve fame by becoming the second wife of the poet Robert Southey in 1839. Three years before her marriage, she had published a narrative poem, *The Birth-Day,* in which she recalled her visits as a young girl to Gilpin in his study at Vicar's Hill, where she remembered finding him busy with:

> *. . . grave tome, or lighter work of taste*
> *(His no ascetic, harsh, soul-narrowing creed),*
> *Or that unrivalled pencil, with few strokes,*
> *And sober tinting slight, that wrought effects*
> *Most magical–the poetry of art!*
> *Lovely simplicity! (true wisdom's grace)*
> *That condescending to a simple child,*

Spread out before me hoards of graphic treasures;
Smiling encouragement, as I expressed
Delight or censure (for in full good faith
I played the critic), and vouchsafing mild
T'explain or vindicate; in seeming sport
Instructing ever; and on graver themes
Winning my heart to listen, as he taught
Things that pertain to life.

3

Sarah Murray:
Lady into Guidebook

Gilpin had travelled in order to satisfy his own artistic curiosity, and had published the accounts of his tours because of his desire to spread an interest in his theories of the picturesque. The Honourable Mrs. Murray of Kensington, however, travelled in order to see Scotland herself with the definite object of producing the first guide-book of any consequence. Not a great deal is known about her life. She was born in 1744, and married, first, the Honourable William Murray, younger brother of the Earl of Dunmore. He, however, died in 1768. For her second husband, she married George Aust, but retained her previous name for her literary purposes. Her book *A Companion and Useful Guide to the Beauties of Scotland, to the Lakes of Westmorland, Cumberland and Lancashire; and to the curiosities of the District of Craven in the West Riding of Yorkshire, to which is added, a more particular Description of Scotland, especially that part of it, called the Highlands*, came out in two volumes in 1799. A second edition, published in 1803, extended the scope of the work to take in the Hebrides, and the last edition of 1810 included a survey of new and recent roads. Mrs. Murray died at Noel House, Kensington, in 1811.

She prefaced her work with an address "To the Managers of the Literary Reviews;" announcing to them:

"I am an Author, neither for fame (my subject being too common a one to gain it), nor for bread. I do not publish from the persuasion of friends, or to please myself. I write because I think my Guide will be really useful to people who may follow my steps." Indeed, she begins her book with a table of routes and mileages, before getting on to the descriptive matter dealing with what lies at the end of these journeys. Nor was she under any illusions as to her literary limitations, for she says:

"I have no wings to soar Parnassus' height; no talents to treat the wild path of imagination; but having a little of *ce gros bon sens qui court les rues*, I am able to relate, in my own fashion, what my eyes have seen." And her own fashion, as your eyes shall shortly see, was by no means so devoid of talent as she professed to suppose.

She travelled in a specially equipped chaise, rather like a modern caravan, and set out to enjoy herself; a purpose she succeeded in fulfilling, even if, in the words of Samuel H. Monk, in the process her "simple love of nature" led her into situations which were "the *reducto ad absurdum* of the cult of nature in the eighteenth century."

She entered Scotland, like Gilpin before her, through Longtown and along the Border Esk to Langholm, "a drive that must give pleasure and satisfaction to any one who had a taste for natural beauty." At Langholm, she found the inn "too bad to sleep in", then discovered that the Duke of Buccleuch had taken all the available horses, except for "two miserable beasts", which were accordingly brought out and harnessed to her chaise. As the inn at Langholm offered "nothing inviting" her to stay there, she decided to move on to Hawick, pulled by her two "miserable beasts". The ascent up to Mosspaul proved adventurous:

"I hastened into the carriage, it still raining prodigiously hard. As soon as I was seated, I perceived a fine honest-faced old Scot, twisting a cord from one fore-spring to the other.—'Friend, what are you doing?'—'Making a seat, my Lady, the one horse being hardly able to stand for rheumatism and broken knees; and the other will not suffer me to ride him being woefully galled on the back.'—'Well, but surely such poor creatures will never carry us to Hawick?'—'Never you heed, my Lady, have patience, and they will carry you cannily: I will be bound for it, they'll gang the last mile better than the first.'

"Necessity has no law, and I was therefore obliged to be silent. Presently I observed the good old man at the head of the horses, twirling his fingers at their snaffles, with pieces of slender packthred. 'What is all that for, friend? What are you doing now?'–'Only making reins, my Lady.'–'We cannot, surely, go with safety, with reins of that twine, up such hills as are before us?'–'Never you heed, my Lady, I'll answer for your safety: after a wee bit, we shall gang weel and cannily.' When this very slender tackle was completed, the honest man mounted his seat, and we soon crossed the bridge over the Ewes, which at Langholm joins the Esk, and came to a prodigiously steep hill; here my heart failed me, not being able to walk, by reason of the hard rain and almost a hurricane of wind. The old Scot, however, quitted his perch, and took hold of the head of the should-be riding beast; I ordered my man to lead the off horse; and what with whipping, hooting and coaxing, the poor lame creatures at length got the chaise up that first hill, where they stopped to recover a little the dreadful pull."

After all this exertion, it must have been trying to discover that at Mosspaul, at the head of the glen, "no horses are kept, nor can you get anything there for those in your chaise, except a little meal and water." So she drove on through Teviotdale, towards Hawick, with enthusiasm undamped.

"All I could see through torrents of rain, was delightful, particularly below the junction of the branches of the Teviot . . . with the main stream; which came rolling down amongst rocks and woods, in a very charming style. Anyone, less delighted than I am with wild nature, would perhaps be somewhat alarmed at such a road, and such scenery, in a violent rainy day. The road, too, rough and steep, and not wider than a carriage; with huge clifted rocks on the right, sometimes covered with wood, at others, bare and frowning through the shade of other overhanging precipices; and water gushing in spouts from innumerable apertures. On the left, the river deep below, foaming and rolling down its close bed of rocks and precipices."

No wonder she was glad to get to Hawick after such an arduous day, even although the main inn turned out to be "a very middling place . . . old and shabby", with "but one sitting room . . . and only one *tolerable* bed chamber with two beds in it." Because the Duke and Duchess of Buccleuch "stopped short at Hawick that day", no doubt delayed by bad weather, Mrs. Murray had to put up at a "very dirty and uncomfortable inn"; in view of which it was perhaps surprising that she found Hawick's "surrounding beauties" so "enchanting".

Mrs. Murray was no idle lie-abed. "If you mean to travel for pleasure . . . make a resolution (and keep to it steadily). *Never* be out after dark. If you will adhere to my plan, and be early in a morning in your chaise, you may see each day's portion of beauty and have daylight to lodge you safe in your intended quarters."

Presumably she was early in her chaise next morning on the road to Selkirk. "Nothing can be more deplorable than its appearance", she wrote of that town; "nothing but dirt and misery to be seen." She stopped off to enjoy "a very slender breakfast", and then re-entered her chaise.

In her book she recorded the story told to her later by friends who, on arriving at Selkirk one evening and inquiring for their beds, were "startled with the noise of two falling out of their dirty boxes in the wall of the room where they were sitting; and were told, these were the nests in which they were to sleep." However, she herself did not delay her journey at Selkirk, but rode on to Tweeddale.

Here, by Fernilee, where Alison Rutherford wrote "The Flowers of the Forest," and in what was later to become Andrew Lang country, she was wholly enchanted, as well she might have been.

"The fancy, in Arcadia, cannot paint a more soft, more sweet, or more lovely scene . . . It is pastoral beauty completely perfect. Not an object can hurt the eye, or ruffle the mind. The soul, for four miles, must be lost to every other sensation but that of soft delight, heightened by an elevation of sentiment, which nothing but such enchanting scenes as those on the Tweed can produce."

However, Edinburgh was her immediate destination, so on she travelled. Her first glimpse of the city, from the road beyond Middleton, impressed her favourably.

Once arrived, she made a point of inspecting the "tottering bow window", since restored, of the house in the High Street "where Knox thundered his address to the people." She was not to know that the connection between this house and John Knox is, at best, problematic. Her inspection of the Old Town, "sloping on each side of the High Street" between the Castle and Holyrood House, was thoroughly practical. The houses were high, yet there was "but one staircase leading to all the flats in the house; and it may easily be imagined in what condition this common, cork-screw, stone staircase, must always be", an experience which the occupants of modern high rise housing are finding repeating itself, even with the "corkscrew" straightened out somewhat, and the addition of an elevator.

Then there were the famous Edinburgh winds.

"The violent gusts of wind, continually to be felt in the streets of Edinburgh, are, I imagine, owing to its situation; and must be the cause of health to its inhabitants (they are very healthy); for had not the atmosphere of that city some powerful refiner, such as a constant high wind, it would, by its nauseous scents, poison the race of beings in it."

By 1799, James Craig's New Town, begun in 1768, was still in course of construction. Mrs. Murray thought the South Bridge "very wide, with handsome shops on each side, except over the arch", and commented on the North Bridge being thrown over "the dry trench to the New Town", the Nor Loch, of course, having been drained before building began. She found Robert Adam's University "at a stand for want of money." In "one of the old churches", she heard "the good and venerable Dr. Blair, whose sermons have been edifying the world for some years past." This was that same Hugh Blair who occupied the Chair of Rhetoric at Edinburgh University, who persuaded Burns–"an astonishing proof of what industry and application can do" was the poet's verdict on him–not to include some of his bawdier pieces in his Edinburgh edition, who was a wholehearted believer in the genuineness of Macpherson's *Ossian* and whose sermonising was less charitably described by Gosse in later years as "Blair's bucket of warm water". When Mrs. Murray heard him preach he was eighty-one years old and within a year of his death.

The original Princes Street, to be the victim of Victorian and later hotch-potching, was then "a noble street, or rather row of houses, looking over the dry trench up the backs of the houses in the old town." She noted another interesting resemblance that is too often overlooked in our own day: "Much of the New Town is built with free-stone, hewn, something like that of Bath." The New Town of Edinburgh is, indeed, as significant a part of our European Georgian heritage as Bath.

That the rawness associated with any major development was still present in the New Town is attested by her comment: "There cannot be much passing and repassing in the new town in summer, for in almost every street the grass grows."

It, at least, was free of that nightly effluvium euphemistically dubbed in the Old Town "the flooers of Edinburgh". Mrs. Murray relates: "I was one fine evening walking up the *inviting* Canongate, nicely dressed, in white muslin: an arch boy eyed me, and laid his scheme: for when I arrived opposite a pool, in the golden gutter, in he dashed a large stone, and, like a monkey, ran off chuckling at his mischief." When one reflects upon what made the gutter golden, it is easy to understand Mrs. Murray's annoyance. Yet more vividly, she complains that the Canongate "still bears strong marks of its old customs," it being necessary to cry out "haud your haund" to have any hope of escaping the cascading slops from a twelfth story window. "Even in the middle of the street, where decent folks generally walk for fear of accidents, they are not exempt from splashes, unless they are in high good luck."

But though smells were bad in the Canongate, at the foot of it, in the Palace of Holyrood House, there was a flutter of borrowed royalty, for the "French of fashion", headed by Compte d'Artois, who had escaped the Revolution, were in occupation.

Mrs. Murray was a great one for heights, and climbed the Calton Hill, not yet encumbered with its Greek columns in commemoration of Waterloo, but harbouring dangers making her advise her readers to "be sure to have a gentleman or man servant with you" if they followed her example, as she hoped they would. For she found that "There scarcely can be a finer view than that from Calton Hill . . . I have never seen the view of Naples to its bay, but I am told, those who have seen both, are in no doubt to which of the two to give the preference." Such a pity that it was the "common, daily, and nightly lounge of vagabonds and loose tribe of the town", who insulted unaccompanied "women of any discription."

Not content with the Calton Hill, Mrs. Murray climbed Arthur's Seat and Salisbury Crags. She next set out on an excursion to Roslin, missing out Dalkeith House because: "I did not go to Scotland to see houses, nor dressed places. The simple beauty of nature, is my hobby-horse; and where can a hobby-horse of that breed find greater scope than in Scotland?" Nevertheless, that over-dressed place Roslin Chapel, the choir, Lady Chapel and beginning of the transepts of what was to have been a fifteenth-century Collegiate Church, with its elaborately carved Prentice Pillar, left her "struck with astonishment at the beautiful structure and workmanship of the ceiling, and pillars."

On her departure from Edinburgh, she noted, along the road to Queensferry, that almost every house had "a garden well stocked with vegetables", and that every available corner of land was used to grow potatoes.

There must have been a crane of some sort operating at the Queensferry passage over the Forth, for she reports: "The contrivance they have for hoisting carriages in and out of the ferry-boats, is very clever: my chaise was drawn out pretty far upon a stone pier, and in a very few minutes it was laid safe upon deck; and in as short a time relanded, as soon as the ferry-boat touched the shore on the opposite side."

She saw the estuary of the Forth in its late-September splendour.

"The morning was gloriously fine when I set out from Edinburgh, but it began to cloud and darken for some time before I reached the Ferry: the clouds, however, suffocated their burden, and Eolus kept close his bags, until I was within ten yards of the end of my passage. It began to rain as I landed, and I had not been in the inn on the north side of the water, three minutes, before it poured; the wind blew a hurricane; and the sea tossed high."

When the storm had subsided, she made her way to Kinross, jotting down only a conventional reference to Loch Leven and its island castle, and losing no time in pressing on to Rumbling Bridge, the Salvator Rosa-like qualities of which thrilled her even more resoundingly than they had previously pleased the Reverend Gilpin. She enjoyed "the loud thumping of the Devil's Mill", so-called, she explains, because "it pays no more respect to the Sunday than it does to the other days of the week", and to get a better view of the cascading, constricted water of the River Devon, she got herself onto "a huge rock in the middle of the water, looking down into the chasm under the bridge, where the towering rocks on each side, covered with beautiful wood, form a magnificent and awful shade over the murmuring water, issuing from its dark and confined passage." The bridge was the older one, put up by a local mason, William Gray, in 1733, and lies below the later bridge, built in 1816, which is a hundred and twenty feet from the water. It is easy to appreciate that Mrs. Murray's rocky standpoint was "a very difficult one to gain, and . . . still more difficult to be continued. It is in the middle of the river, on a huge slippery rock, amidst other innumerable fragments, over and against which the impatient water loudly dashes; having huge towering rocks, full of clifted chasms, over-run with wood on each side; and in front, the small arch of the bridge just visible, through the thick shade of wood and rock, at least one hundred feet above the eye. In such a situation, it is almost impossible to preserve one's head from swimming." She "attempted to sketch the scenery; but in the attempt" was several times obliged to shut her eyes, and take hold of the rock on which she sat, lest she should "drop from it into the whirling, foaming stream."

That other fall, the Cauldron Linn, however, seemed to her something of an anti-climax after the Devil's Mill; "more a scene of solemnity, surprise and astonishment, than that of beauty."

In what she punningly called "the woeful town of Dollar, high among gloomy hills and dark fir-woods"—clearly the proximity of the Ochil Hills had disturbed her sense of perspective!—she inspected the ruins of Castle Campbell, on the hillside in Dollar Glen, and thought that "the rooms within (by what remains of them), must have been dismal dungeons; but in the times when that castle was inhabited men were more like wild beasts than human beings." And, of course, in the times when Mrs. Murray saw Dollar it was still a village, Playfair's Academy not being built until 1816, the first stage in the development of the rural academic little town we know today.

Passing along the foot of the Ochils, she admired the

distant view of Stirling. But before she reached that town she noticed "on the side of a steep craggy mountain, a herd of moving creatures; and when I came near enough to see them distinctly, I discovered they were human beings, gathering in corn; they appeared like a flock of sheep hanging on the craig's side." It seemed to her "wonderful that corn should grow there, and still more wonderful how a plough should ever get at such steep and broken precipices."

She noticed the obvious similarity of situations between the Castles of Stirling and Edinburgh. Such was her enthusiasm to savour the grander aspects of everything she saw that, having admired the view from the ramparts, and the meanders of the River Forth through the valley below, she drove round the road at the foot of the Castle rock, apparently rather differently aligned than it is now. The sight was pleasantly frightening.

"To look up, huge loose fragments hang over the head, suspended in a loose soil: appearing in such a state, as if the jolting of a carriage were sufficient to shake them from their very slender hold: and that they would come tumbling down, crushing to atoms, and whirling to the middle of the river, everything in the way! . . . But the pieces of rock must undoubtedly adhere much more firmly to the great mass than they seem to do, for I heard of no mischief ever being done by them." It seems odd to find her prophesying fearfully that in time, part of the distant castle "may slip down and take a watery bed in the Forth".

From Stirling, she drove west, through the "pleasant fruitful valley" to Doune, where the ruined former royal Castle, one of the best-preserved mediaeval castles in Scotland and then still in the hands of the earls of Moray, attracted less of her attention than its interest and importance might seem to merit. But she was anxious to reach Callander, in order to discover for herself "the wonders of the Trossachs". In 1799, Scott's *Lady of the Lake* had not yet been conceived–it did not appear until 1810–and so her enthusiasm reflects a climate of interest shared a few years later by the Wordsworths, which Sir Walter's poem, with its masterly descriptive passages and swift-moving romantic story, subsequently popularised.

Her account may not have the poetic intensity of Scott's

descriptions, but it does have an enthusiastic vividness which makes us aware of the difficulties and dangers involved in Highland explorations of this sort before the post-Scott steadily developing tourist boom began to smooth the traveller's way.

The first morning of her exploration was gloomy: "the waters roared, and the mountains looked black, particularly Ben Lidi [Ledi]", and "heavy rain made me despair of seeing . . . the surrounding scenes of Loch Catherine [Katrine], which, I had been informed, were more romantic than any other in Scotland." She took shelter in her chaise, and the weather cleared up by noon. So she "mounted a very steep rough road, cut out of the mountains; and then went winding in labyrinths of crags, intermixed with patches of verdure; bogs, rushes, and some wood, with pouring torrents from every quarter; the carriage often hanging over a precipice, and the wheels every moment up and down, over large pieces of rocks and stones, in chasms, torn by rushing waters down the sides of crags."

Since 1859, Loch Katrine has had the prosaic role of supplying water to Glasgow along a sunken aquaduct thirty-four miles long. The modern traveller thus sees a different view than that which thrilled Mrs. Murray, for the level of the loch was raised seventeen feet, and the Silver Strand, opposite Ellen's Isle, submerged. Still, few even today would disagree with Mrs. Murray's spontaneous outburst: "When I caught sight of Loch Catherine, I was astonished, I was delighted!—a faint ray of sun was just then penetrating through the mist, still resting on the tops of the surrounding mountains and crags: tinging the wood on their sides, and gleaming on the beautiful islands in the lake."

She got a boatman to row her out upon the loch so that she could make sketches. Back on shore, she recorded: "It soon after began to rain, and all the scenes I had passed in the morning were obscured by mist and the approach of night, for it was scarcely driving light when I reached Callander." So primitive were the standards of inn-keeping, often combined with farming in the country districts, that she found, on entering the inn, her rooms "stripped of their carpets, to cover new-made or new-making hay ricks, in order to screen them from the rain."

Next day she hired a little boy as guide, and, by "the road that leads from Callander, over the hills, to Comrie", reached Brackland Brig, and "the cascades at it of the water of Kelty." She was disappointed to find "nothing that indicated the romantic horror" which she had been led to expect, but was consoled to find the falls "grand and beautiful; dashing in different directions, heights, and breadths."

She had a passion for waterfalls in passes, and next day "admired the Pass of Lennie, through the Grampions, and the fine cascades of the Teith, running from Loch Lubnaig." To the east of the loch, at "a house called Ardhullary", properly *Ardchullarie*, she noted that James "Abyssinian" Bruce arranged his papers and finished his account of his *Travels to the Source of the Nile*, which he published in 1790. Mrs. Murray thought that he could have had "no interruption in the desert of Hullary, where nothing is to be seen but high mountains on every side; a winding lake, with dashing rivers issuing from it, and entering into it; and the lofty Ben Lidi, occupying an immense space." Today, this kind of isolated solitude less than forty miles from Glasgow, or indeed almost anywhere in Scotland, is as remote an experience as the century in whose terminal year Mrs. Murray's words were first read.

She covered the seven miles to Lochearnhead, where she found "the whole scene delightful", and Strathearn, "from Drummond Castle, only the keep of which then remained, the main building having been razed by the Jacobite Dukes of Perth to ensure it could not become a royalist garrison, to Lochearnhead, which "for rich picturesque and sublime scenery" to be at least equal "if not surpassing any other scene in Scotland." Perhaps she was prejudiced, for this was the countryside from which the brother of her first husband took his title.

Comrie, which in the eighteenth century experienced mild earth tremors due to its situation on the "fault", she thought "finely situated and beautifully romantic," noting that the inhabitants had become so accustomed to the shocks that they "were actually going to build a town on the convulsed spot, which will probably, one day or other, open and form a lake; as the noise under ground is like the gushing of water making fresh passage through the rocks," a prophecy as alarming as her prospect of the slipping Stirling Castle, but fortunately also unrealised. The worst shocks were felt in 1839, though no lives have ever been lost.

"Sweetly situated" Crieff pleased her, as did the remains of Drummond Castle, standing "on a pretty eminence" to the south east, the grounds of which had been laid out by the second earl of Perth in the seventeenth century. She stayed at Ochtertyre–not to be confused with Ochertyre in Kincardine parish, just outside Stirling, where, as Mrs. Murray was jaunting about Scotland in her chaise, John Ramsay of Ochertyre sat compiling his "lucubrations" which later made up *Scotland and Scotsmen* and sending off gossipy letters to his cousin in Edinburgh, Mrs. Dundas–but the Ochertyre in Monzievaird parish owned by the Murray family. From there, she covered the road to Amulree, explored Glen Almond, and discovered the story behind Allan Ramsay's song *Bessy Bell and Mary Gray* at that "sweet Eden . . . Leadnock", spelled today without the "a".

She inspected the reputed last resting-place of the two ladies, and "plainly saw the marks of two graves, by the rising sod: the third, that of the lover," said to be at their feet, she could not find. After walking from Logie Almond to Lednock through "woods that were once made and kept open for the convenience of the families of Leadnock and Logie", and finding the paths "now entirely obliterated and choked by thick wood, briars, springs, and every obstacle that rude nature has combined to destroy them", she arrived, scratched and torn by thorns and soaked to the knees in mud, to be regaled at Lednock House with "some nice mutton pies and potatoes . . . a very acceptable refreshment after my lonely, blundering walk."

"There is a view of the town of Perth, coming from the south", the intrepid lady declared, having repaired the ravages of her bout with rude nature, "where the Romans halted to admire, and cried out in one voice–*Ecce Tiberem!*'. I think they paid a very bad compliment to the Tay, as there can be no comparison between it and the sluggish Tiber." She admired the prospect of the junction of the Earn with the Tay and, climbing the hill of Moncrieff, "the charming prospect that delighted the marching Romans . . . the broad sweeping Tay, coming from the north, and winding round the base of Kinnoul Crags, flowing majestically to the east, and towards the rich Carse of Gowrie and Dundee . . . In front . . . the town of Perth, its noble bridge, the South Inch, the spires, and other edifices in the town; the waving corn, in part of the fertile district of Strathmore, with the grand chain of Grampion Mountains, in the back-ground."

She drove towards Perth on a Monday, and was surprised to see "a multitude not far from the road's side, with a wooden stand raised in the midst of the throng; some of the congregation were standing, others sitting, forming altogether an amazing concourse of men, women, and children. It was a field-preaching day. It is impossible for *all* to *hear* the sermon: but, good souls, if they are only within the holy *sough* (or sound), that perfectly satisfies them."

Mrs. Murray gives some interesting social details of life as she found it in Perth in 1796. Butter was "about ten-pence a pound, twenty-two ounces." Coal came up the Tay from Newcastle because it was "procured full as cheap" as "Scotch coals . . . from Fife and Stirlingshire." A labourer at Perth got "fifteen pence a day", with an extra penny plus his "meat and drink" at harvest time. Masons' wages were twenty pence a day. Potatoes were cheap, though apparently more expensive than at Crieff, where she had heard of three hundred and sixty pounds of potatoes being sold for four shillings.

She visited "the old Castle of Gowrie", where an abortive attempt was made in 1600 to confine James VI, and found it occupied by "military men". (It is now, to Perth's shame, demolished.) She crossed the Tay, made her way to the junction of the rivers Isla and Tay, and from the walls of the ruined, once royal Castle of Kinclaven, which was said to have been founded by Malcolm Ceannmor and which the poet Blind Harry claims was won back by Wallace from the English, she enjoyed "some of the finest apricots I ever eat in my life."

Scone, the crowning-place of the Scottish kings; Stobhall, "in the very old style of building", built in 1578 and then owned by the Drummond family; Meikleour House, "more like a beautiful English place than any I saw in Scotland", the home of Lord Nairne, but much enlarged in 1869, in turn attracted her passing attention as she drove north to

William Gilpin, 1724–1804

Above, Dumbarton Rock. 'Such a rock as this,' wrote Gilpin, 'is as uncommon at land as it is at sea'; *below*, the Head of Loch Fyne. For Gilpin the Loch had almost all the beauties of an inland lake

Blairgowrie. At Craig Hall, the home of the Rattrays visited by Scott three years before, she descended the glen of the River Ericht, and reached "a scene of rock, wood, and water" which made her fancy herself "at the end of the world, at the gate of Paradise!"

Unshakeable in her pursuit of waterfalls, she set out from Craig Hall to Alyth. "Torrents of rain fell during our drive thither, so that the burn, which comes from the forest of Ailyth, and runs through the town, was rushing down its precipitate bed with the utmost violence." However, through the narrow, sloping streets, "slippery with wet", her chaise wended its determined way, to the banks of the Isla, where "a *gude* wife" guided her, first, "to the top of the great cataract, and then to the bottom of it, down a long, dangerous and slippery bank; and then from one huge stone to another" until she arrived at "the pool into which the river falls."

In 1799, the majority of Mrs. Murray's English readers would never have seen a waterfall, since only the rich could follow the descriptive trail her chapters blazed. She was therefore forced to try to make them feel these dark and watery experiences she enjoyed so much if she was to hold their interest. The "Reeky Linn", with one exception, seemed to her the finest falls in Scotland. So perhaps we ought to let her have her purple passage about it.

"Imagine yourself upon prodigious masses of slippery rock, severed from the mountain, damming up, in some degree, the vast body of water in front, precipitating itself from an immense height over jagged heaps of rock upon rock, in every possible form, with a violence that sends out its spray to a very great distance; and falling into a pool, of which no one knows the depth: and then to the right, goes dashing against tower beside tower of rocks, rising majestically to the sky, with sprigs of mountain ash, birch, and oak, thinly and carelessly scattered over them. To the left is a curved recess of rocks equally high with the opposite towers; in which, either by cliffs, or ravages made by the force of the dashing water, caves in numbers, deep and black, appear, to affright the timorous, or the guilty wight. To attempt to get at these caves is almost certain destruction; but what dares not he do, whom guilt has rendered desperate?" A former owner of Craig Linn, she explains, having killed a man, sought the dangerous safety of the caves, only to encounter the Deil, in the shape of a black dog, running up the sheer rocks opposite the caves; whereupon the poor wretch decided that punishment from human hands was the lesser of the two evils he faced.

Having changed her clothes and eaten a picnic in her chaise, she drove back, and was not surprisingly "happy to re-enter the hospitable walls of Meikleour house, after a long and fatiguing dripping day."

She left Meikleour with "the utmost regret." At Dunkeld, where she noted with pride that the Duke of Atholl was a Murray, she felt that "pens far abler" than hers had made further description superfluous. So she passed on to Blair Atholl, finding the road "one of the grandest, as well as the most beautiful of all the passes through the Grampion mountains", the Tummel being "far more violent than the Tay."

At Faskally, where in our own day the scene has been considerably altered by the manufacture of the North of Scotland Hydro Electric Board's artificially-dammed loch, she watched a salmon try to leap the Tummel. Today, it would have been able to proceed up a glass-lined fish-ladder, watched by curious visitors. When Mrs. Murray was there, however, "at the fall there was a great bag, made of net-work, fastened to a roundish hoop of iron, and hung like the pockets at the corners of billiard tables, from a long pole; this bag is usually either fastened horizontally upon some rock, or held by a fisherman just under the fall, to catch the fish, if they do not succeed in their leap."

As she approached Blair Atholl, she saw the tombstone of Bonnie Dundee, killed in the skirmish at Killiecrankie. Related by marriage to the owner of the house of Lude, "one of the prettiest places in Scotland", she got her chaise up the hill on which it stands "with great anxiety and dread of mischief to the poor horses." The Duke of Atholl had shooting lodges in Glen Tilt and Glen Bruar, and she visited both. In Glen Tilt she experienced for the first time Athole brose, a beverage "made of whisky, eggs and honey. To a lover of whisky it is a delicious treat, and much prized by the people of Atholl." She instanced a case where its efficacy was clearly proved.

"The daughter of an inhabitant of Atholl, having been placed at one of the first boarding schools in Edinburgh, was seized with a violent fever; her father was sent for, as she was thought in great danger; and upon his arrival, being told his child was at the point of death, and that everything the physician could do for her had been done, without effect; he earnestly exclaimed, 'but has she had any Athole brose?' 'No'. He then had a good dose of it instantly prepared, and making her swallow it, she soon recovered."

She inspected the Falls of Bruar, and, indomitably as ever, followed the tracks Burns had traced in 1787 when he visited Atholl House. Burns left one of his poetic thank-you pieces on his host's table when he departed, advising the Duke, through the "mouth" of Bruar Water, to:

"Let lofty firs, and ashes cool,
My lowly banks o'erspread,
And view, deep-bending in the pool,
Their shadows' watery-bed:
Let fragrant birds in woodbines drest,
My craggy cliffs adorn;
And, for the little songster's nest,
The close, embow'ring thorn."

The Duke took the poet's advice. Mrs. Murray applauded his plantings, and thought that "the beauty of the scene repays the fatigue of following it up to the summit of the high fall."

During her stay at Blair, she "lived upon red deer venison and moor-fowl" from "the prodigious tract of country" over which the Duke could hunt. But in due course northwards she went, to the inn at Dalwhinnie.

"A person accustomed only to the scenes in the vicinity of London, or the greatest ports of England," she reflected, "would be dismayed at the sight of this lonely habitation, the only one for miles around, where not a tree or a shrub is seen; only desolate crags, and a boggy heath of great extent on every side; nothing cheering, but the bubbling water running to the Spey river. Dalwhinnie pleased me", she nevertheless declared: "and, though the evening was chill, and a mist coming on, I took my way to the head of Loch Ericht."

The wilder the countryside, the more thrilled she became. As she moved north, she noted that "the crags around Rothemurchus [Rothiemurchus, the country of Clan Grant] are covered with wood, and the verdant meads are ornamented with fine trees." Rothiemurchus Forest is, in fact, one of the few stretches of natural Scots pine forest to survive. "The cap of winter upon the crown of luxuriant smiling summer below, was a contrast I had never before beheld."

In these days, and until comparatively recently, the nobler the natural scene, the more primitive were its creature comforts likely to be, as Mrs. Murray discovered.

"Aviemore inn was within sight when I came down to the side of the Spey; and my heart jumped at the idea of passing the night in a spot so grateful to my sensations, because nature there shines in its natural garb, and in high beauty: but no sooner had I put my foot within the walls of that horrible house, than my heart sunk; and I was glad to escape from its filth and smoke very early the next morning." Indeed, she escaped without breakfast, stopping eight miles up the road to get water from a cottage and make breakfast in her chaise: a strange contrast to the hospitable welcomes to people of every degree of wealth which the Aviemore Centre now offers all the year round!

But "artless, witless nature", as Landor so familiarly called it, soon restored her delight. She passed Lochindorb, in the middle of the desolate Dava Moor, with its ruined castle built by Edward I of England between 1303 and 1306 round a hunting lodge of the Lords of Badenoch, and from where the Wolf of Badenoch terrorised the Lowlands of Moray, burning Elgin Cathedral in 1390. "The beautiful bloom of the heath, its great variety and fragrance, its novelty, and the *tout ensemble* of the scene, amused me till I became in a degree enchanted." Most of us who have travelled in the Highlands have at one time or another experienced Mrs. Murray's kind of enchantment.

She struck east, making for Fort George, and when she came within sight of the Cromarty Firth: "The sun was shining with great lustre upon the lofty rocks on the north side of the entrance to the Firth, and I never saw rocks look finer or grander than they did."

She regretted that she had to pass the fifteenth-century Cawdor Castle, so strongly associated with Shakespeare's *Macbeth*, without stopping. But on she pressed, passing "a house well situated on an eminence, called Kilravock", where the lady of the house, the redoubtable Mrs. Rose of Kilravock, was then regularly receiving frequent and interesting letters on life and literature from her famous cousin in Edinburgh, Henry Mackenzie, author of that fashionable novel *The Man of Feeling*.

Mrs. Murray drove up to the "make-believe" fort of Fort George, which had been built in 1748 as part of the post-Jacobite pacification plans for the Highlands. By the end of the eighteenth century its role was over, though later it was to become the depot of the Seaforth Highlanders. Even so, Mrs. Murray discovered that a defensive posture was still being maintained.

"As the carriage drove to the outer gate, 'stop' was the word, with fierce sentinels on every side saying, 'who goes there?' My name being given, they slowly marched to the governor or fort major, for permission to enter. After waiting a considerable time, the outer gate was thrown open, and the postillion bid to come on. Thump, thump, went the horses' feet over a draw-bridge and through a covered way, with wood on the bottom, sounding like thunder; and when I was fairly in the fort, they closed the huge gates, grinding on their hinges, leaving me in the midst of red coats, cannon, musquets, and bayonets. I felt a little unusual on the occasion . . ." However, the Governor welcomed her courteously, explained the military mysteries to her, and apparently put her up for the night, before she set out next morning for Culloden and Inverness. The rising of the Forty-five was perhaps still too fresh in public memory to seem romantic to an English tourist and Mrs. Murray offers no comment whatever on that battlefield where the hopes of the Jacobite cause were so finally and cruelly butchered.

She found Inverness "a neat town, charmingly situated". She commented on a manifestation of one of the less civilized traditional Scottish habits:

"While I was at Inverness there was not a trace of its ancient castle; some person having lately removed the small remains of its ruins to build offices, or some such thing, for his own convenience: What an Hottentot!"

Spending four days with friends at Dochfour, she made a day trip to Beauly, the country of the Frasers of Lovat, whose Norman ancestry accounts for the French flavour of its name. Here the mountains of Rossshire seemed to her "a fine sublime heap, not to be described."

Her way back took her through the Great Glen. With her passion for waterfalls, she could not resist a visit to the Falls of Foyers, on the southern shores of Loch Ness. "I saw . . . the river issuing with violence from its confined space above, and dashing over broken rocks down to the pool; but a projecting slip of green bank, and other obstacles, screened from me the better half of the cataract. The rocks on each side the fall are clad with hanging trees, chiefly of birch, mountain ash, and young oak, peeping through the expanded spray. The river, after running from the pool, has several other projections to compass, before it reaches the foot of the promontory on which I placed myself; I was in ecstacy with all around me; but to get to this station was a bold adventure (for a woman) when the ground is wet, being obliged to creep from one slippery bank to another, and to step from rock to rock, supported only by stumps and branches of birch, and in continual danger of tumbling headlong over pieces of rock, and into bogs. But I was determined nothing should hinder me from seeing this grand object in all possible points of view." The volume of water, however, was reduced when, in 1896, the first hydro-electric scheme was constructed to supply power to the nearby aluminium factory.

Moving on, she thought, "the first view of Fort Augustus from Strath Errick, in a fine day . . . like a little paradise", in which respect it resembled "the happy valley described by Doctor Johnson in his Rasselas, or Prince of Abyssinia." At the Fort itself, she had the same difficulties of entry from "the creeping sentinels" as she had experienced at Fort George, although once her letters of introduction had been presented, she was again "received with every mark of kindness and hospitality", and there spent a night.

Next morning, driving down to Fort William, the waterfalls tumbling towards the lochs had her "the whole way in constant exclamation: here is another; oh, how fine! how beautiful! how dashing!–hopping and rushing sometimes down mountains perpendicular to the road, so that I was continually obliged to draw up the glasses of the carriage to prevent the spouts coming upon us."

She took time to investigate not only waterfalls, but the conditions under which the Highlanders lived just outside Fort William. "A person accustomed to the comforts and luxuries of life," she reflected, "cannot conceive how it is possible for human beings to exist, in a state so near that of the brute creation": and she went on to describe it accurately and without any of that malice sometimes attributed to English travellers by Highland writers on the defensive.

The Scots house, she explains: "consists of a butt, a benn, and a byar; that is, a kitchen, an inner room, and a place in which to put cattle. In the centre of the gavel end of the butt, is heaped up dirt and stones, in which is fixed small iron bars; leaving a hollow by way of grate, with a hob on each side: there is also a crank that moves any way, to which is hooked the meikle pot. There is no resemblance of a chimney, but the hole at the top; so that the whole side of the gavel is covered with soot from the fire to the vent. The dirt floor is full of holes, retaining whatever wet or dirt may be thrown upon it; consequently it is always a mire. In one corner is a box nailed to the partition, between the butt and the benn. This box opens with a door in front, in which is a heath, or other bed, with a great number of blankets. Into this box creep as many as it can hold; and thus they sleep, boxed in on every side, except the small door at the front. In the house I was in, close to the box bed, stood another box similar to the bed, containing provisions of milk, oatcakes, broth &c. and eating utensils. If the family be large, the benn too has a similar bed or beds; between which and the byar, there is only a very partial partition. A small farmer will say, he delights to sleep thus close to the byar, that he may lie and see, and hear, his beasts eat.

"Another pretty fashion among them (and it is universal), their dunghill is close to the door of the house, or hut . . . Next the dunghill stand their peat stacks . . . In most of the sequestered parts of the Highlands, the substitute for tallow candles, are the stumps of birch and fir trees . . . These stumps appear to have lain buried in the bogs for a vast time; and when prepared for candles, they really give a charming light, but of short duration . . . It is a pleasant sight to see an old woman of seventy or eighty, dressed in her snow-white cursche, sitting by a cozy fire, holding this clear tape for her daughter and grand children, while they are, some spinning, others singing and dancing, and a group of youngsters playing on the ground with each other, and their faithful sheep dog."

As is not uncommon, Ben Nevis was hidden in cloud when she passed it. Although she noticed next day that "his majesty" had "a strong inclination to uncover" and finally saw "every part that is possible to see from the road", she found its shape "beauty, mixed with the sublime and terrific". Not even her intrepid curiosity urged her up its glen.

However, she made a crossing of the Corryarrick Pass, a section of the military road built between Dalwhinnie and Fort Augustus by General Wade in 1731-4, marvelled at the view from the summit, over two thousand five hundred feet—"all is boundless space (except by the sky) of a rough ocean of mountains"—and at the tearing waters about Corryarrick itself.

From Dalwhinnie, she drove by Rannoch, finding her eye "amazed at the dark majestic scene of Schiehallion", to Kinloch, where she crossed the Tummel by that then Highland rarity "a very good bridge". From the north end of Loch Ericht, she decided that she must visit the southern end; so she was "placed upon a shelty, which was led through the burn of Gauir by an Highlandman, hip deep; but he cared far less for that than I did for the splashing of my petticoats. As soon as I left the side of the Loch, to mount the river Ericht's side, I could no longer take care of myself; therefore the good Highlandman again became my friendly leader. I stuck as fast to the pummel of the saddle as I could, and thus mounted and descended such places as were sufficient to scare a lowland female out of her wits."

She left the Rannoch district regretfully, thinking "it would be a very desireable place to live in, were it not for its great distance from any medical assistance."

By way of the Falls of Moness (wetly but dutifully explored), Taymouth, where the "extended centre" of the pre-Victorian castle struck her as being "in a very old style of building, with short round towers stuck on from the top of each corner", and Glen Lyon, she reached Fortingall where, on her arrival at the kirkyard to inspect the ruin of the famous old yew tree, said to be two thousand years old, and which Pennant found measured fifty six and a half feet in girth, "the sound of the carriage at the kirk-gate brought out the clergyman from his manse adjoining. No set of beings can surpass the inhabitants of the Highlands (of every description), in hospitality and attention to strangers; but at the same time they are extremely curious, and must know everything, of everybody who comes their way; who they are, what they are, whence they came, and whither going."

At Killin, beneath Ben Lawers, she recorded that here the bones of Fingal were supposed to rest, though she contented herself with the reflection that Lord Breadalbane, who owned the former MacNab seat Kinnell House, had had the ground about the supposed grave "examined without success, as to finding the bones." However, she visited the linn, wondering how the inhabitants of Killin "are not all deaf (like those who are employed in iron and copper works), from the loud and never-ceasing noise of the rushing waters."

In Glen Dochart, "all the surrounding objects" conspired "to make the small Loch Dochart, a view of the sublime and beautiful united." Through Strathfillan, she drove to the inn at Tyndrum, "a tolerable one for so desolate a place". But she was not to have a quiet night.

It happened that the Falkirk Tryst, that great cattle market transferred from Creiff to Falkirk in 1770, and as late as 1865 described by Augustus Hare as "a curious sight, an immense plain covered with cattle of every description, especially picturesque little Highland beasts attended by drovers in kilts and plumes", was just over. Says Mrs. Murray: "Many of the sellers of black cattle and sheep were on their return to the Western Highlands, and islands, and began to fill the inn. The rain and wind were excessive, and the night so dark, that it was impossible to see. In this dreadful weather, nothing but rap, rap, at the door. 'Who comes?' was the frequent question: 'Drovers, madam.' This continued till the house was in a perfect uproar: my servants could not get a place to put their heads in. My man took his sleep in the carriage; and the poor horses were almost crushed to death in the stables." Falkirk Trysts induced much celebratory merriment among the drovers, for whom it was the main event of their year, but they and it disappeared with the development of the railways.

From Tyndrum, she turned up towards Glencoe, to visit the place where in the winter of 1692 the shameful massacre of the MacDonalds was perpetrated by Campbell of Glen Lyon, on the orders of William III and his Government in London, after the Campbells had enjoyed for twelve days the hospitality of their victims. Crossing the Moor of Rannoch, she thought it "nothing but a dreary black boggy moor, the loose soil of which is quite black, broken by pools and small lakes, and very thinly covered, where the water does not remain, with the coarsest brown heath, rushes and bogs."

When she reached the object of her journey, "the spot where old MacDonald and the greatest part of his clan were massacred", she "could not help paying the tribute of a sigh for their melancholy fate. To be in friendship one hour, and butchered indiscriminately in the next, by those whom they had feasted and caressed, is a tale to shudder at."

But more awaited her shuddering when she arrived at her "sty" in the King's House inn. She was exhausted and hungry after her day's journey.

"I soon eat my bit of supper, half-choked with smoke, and in danger of getting cold by an open window, the damp from the rain pouring in, and my petticoats tucked to my knees for fear of the dirt, which was half an inch on the floor; but notwithstanding all these obstacles to peace and rest I had no sooner laid my head upon my pillow, than I fell fast asleep, and did not awake till morning."

Next day she drove to Dalmally, and along the fifteen miles between it and Inveraray through "the noise of a constant rushing violent cataract." The rain increased. Waterfalls splashed down the rocks beside the road, and "dashed" against the windows of her carriage, "sufficiently to alarm a timorous mind": but not her mind, since she was able to apprehend it as "a grand and awful scene that penetrated my soul".

She admired the ornamented bridge outside the Duke of Argyll's new castle, "constructed of dark bluish-looking stone", and its "Gothic tops". But then, she thought Inveraray "the noblest place in Scotland . . . I asked a lady if the streets were ever perfectly dry. She answered me, *never;* nor is there a bit of fresh meat to be got in the town during the whole winter."

Next day, in rain again, she set out for Loch Lomond, eating her lunch in her chaise near "a very pretty place called Ardkinglas, where is a new modern house just then finished." The "new modern house" built by the Campbells was burned down in 1840, and replaced by the Noble family with the present house which Sir Robert Lorimer put up for them in 1907. Lunch did not lift her depression. Going through "such black, bare, craggy, tremendous mountains, as must shake the nerves of every timorous person, particularly if it be a rainy day", she asked: "and when is there a day in the year free from rain, in Glen Croe? and on the hill called, 'Rest-and-be-Thankful?' no day; no, not one!"

After spending a night at Arrochar, she crossed the narrow neck of land to Tarbet, Loch Lomond, and found the drive down the lochside "superlatively beautiful." She thought the southern view from about two miles south of Tarbet "enchanting."

"The mountains, the woods on the banks, and the cultivation as the mountains recede from the lake, with the high blue hills in the horizon to the south, all contribute to render this view, in point of beauty, equal to any in nature, when seen in a clear day, with a favourable light."

Dumbarton had "nothing striking" about it, though the Castle rock seemed to her "a very great curiosity. The Castle, in the light of utility as a defensive fortification, is a mere nothing; though a farcical fuss in time of war is made to gain admittance. The sketch book of such an inoffensive draughtswoman as myself, was, with great solemnity, ordered to be left in custody whilst I walked to the top of the Castle . . . I obeyed orders, but laughed in my sleeve at the prohibition of my innocent portfolio."

And so she reached Glasgow.

"Glasgow is amazingly enlarged; I was there eleven years previous to this tour, and I could hardly believe it possible for a town to be so altered and enlarged as I found it to be in 1791. Its situation is very fine; but the town is like all other great manufacturing trading towns; with inhabitants very rich, saucy and wicked."

To forget " the din of Glasgow, its pride, its wealth, and worldly ways" she left it as soon as possible to walk by the side of the Clyde at Bothwell Castle, where there was "no drawback, except in a few spots; a little, and but very little of the slime of the Nature dressers, who shave too neatly for dame Nature's lovely honest face."

By the "tolerable town" of Hamilton, she looked at the outside of the Duke's Palace, "an old, and rather forlorn-looking mass of building, attended by walls to the worst end of the town", and drove on past the Falls of Clyde, to Lanark.

Lee Palace, the home of the Lockharts, and the Lee Penny, which Sir Simon Lockhart took from the wife of a Saracen prisoner when crusading with the good Sir James Douglas in the Holy Land, and which was believed to have healing properties, engaged her interest. It was soon to inspire Scott to write *The Talisman.*

From Lanark, she visited Carstairs and Douglas Castle, the ruined mediaeval home of a family which became so powerful that they threatened the throne of Scotland, until James II checked their influence by murdering their chief. On the way south to Moffat, she looked at early snow (it was 10th October) covering the top of Tinto Hill.

The "German" style Spa, within a mile of the town of Moffat, was "tolerably frequented". Here, goat's milk, as well as the waters, was supposed to encourage good health.

In the midst of torrential rain, and by swollen river-banks, she drove through Annandale, which eventually she quitted for what she called "the dreary road to Lockerby, Ecclefechan, Gretna, and Longtown", and so ended the major Scottish tour which was to provide her with material for the original and widely popular first edition of her *Companion and Useful Guide.*

So immediate and sustained was the success of her guide that she decided to return to Scotland and penetrate further in a more systematic manner than any previous traveller bent solely on recording information for the benefit of others. As she addressed her reviewers in the preface to her third edition, published in 1805, "Gentlemen, had you put an extinguisher upon my former feeble light, there would have been an end of my *Guideship*." In fact the *British Critic* for October 1799 stated: "The author's talents at description are successfully exerted . . .", while the *Monthly Review* for May, 1800 thought her an "agreeable traveller", though one who, they suspected "rather over-rates the difficulties and dangers which it was necessary to encounter, before a perfect view of the country could be obtained."

For her second edition of 1803, Mrs. Murray made a journey to some of the islands of Scotland. By February 1804, the *Monthly Review* had found less grudging admiration for the "fair author" who appeared "to be possessed of such enthusiasm that difficulties and dangers operate on her mind as inducements", so that "we frequently behold her exposing herself to situations from which the most hardy of the other sex would willingly retire." The edition of 1805 was substantially a reprint of the 1803 edition, with the addition of an account of some new roads in Scotland and an examination of a cave in Skye. The research for her Hebridean journeys appears to have been undertaken on several different occasions and the book in which she recounts these later experiences does not possess as strong a thread of narrative as that which held the first volume together. Although the great Dr. Johnson and the French geologist Faujas Saint-Fond both made their Hebridean tours twenty or so years before her, her quick eye and racey pen set down homelier impressions which are still of considerable interest to us.

On her way to the islands, she was shown the silver head of St. Fillan's crozier in the small inn of Suie, at the foot of Benmore, by a member of the Dewar family, whose distant ancestor was said to have been in the service of the saint. It is now preserved in the National Museum of Antiquities, in Edinburgh. Passing down Loch Awe, she spent a night at Dunstaffnage Castle, a Campbell home with a house built against one of the ruined walls. The first castle on the site is believed to have been founded by Ewin, a Pictish king who was a contemporary of Julius Caesar, and to have been occupied by the later Dalriaden Kings till 844, when Kenneth MacAlpin succeeded to the throne of Pictavia.

The main object of Mrs. Murray's curiosity was the island of Staffa. She made her way to Oban, arriving there on a July evening in the year 1800. On 23rd July, she "entered the Oban cutter, and set sail about noon with a tolerable breeze. Dunolly, Kerrera, Lismore and the hills of Morven attracted her passing attention. Duart Castle, which from about 1390 was the stronghold from which the MacLeans of Duart carried on a feud against the MacDonalds, induced her to recount how one of its MacLean owners, Lachlan MacLean, in 1523 had his barren wife conveyed to a tide-swept islet between Mull and Lismore where the rising tide would have secretly drowned her, had not a passing ship rescued her and returned her to her brother, the Duke of Argyll, at Inveraray, while MacLean carried out "a good mock funeral for his much loved, much lamented lady". She adds that the Duke, being "a mild and amiable man", took no revenge on MacLean, though the Duke's brother, less mild and amiable, years later, in an Edinburgh street, and when MacLean was eighty years old, stuck a knife in the owner of Duart. This not untypical Highland happening provided Scott's friend Johanna Baillie with the plot of her play *Family Legend* a few years after Mrs. Murray had heard the story.

She sailed past Duart Castle—restored in 1912 for Sir Fitzroy MacLean by Sir John Burnet, after it had been a ruin for more than a century—and Ardtornish, the ruined seat of the Lords of the Isles, which Scott described as "frowning steep, twixt cloud and ocean hung", on a headland at the entrance to Loch Aline. Here, a Lord of the Isles negotiated an alliance with Edward IV of England against the Scottish Crown, a deal which ultimately led to the forfeiture of the Lordship of the Isles. Passage in a cutter dependent on a steady breeze was a slow affair, and Mrs. Murray had time to enjoy that interplay of light and shadow which is so rewarding an experience on a Hebridean journey.

"We advanced slowly, as it every moment became calmer and calmer, so that at times the cutter hardly moved. The weather was hot and the mists were floating, sometimes along the sides of the majestic mountains, at others covering their summits, and again rolling through the vallies below, in a style I never had seen before; it was like Ossian's 'Shadowy breeze that poured its dark wave over the grass'. It was a perpetual change of light and shade, on majestic scenery that was beyond description glorious and enchanting."

This delay meant that she could not reach Aros, as she had intended; so she went ashore with her fellow passenger, Sir John Murray, in the bay by Ardtornish House, where she spent "one of the hottest and closest nights" she ever felt. At breakfast, following an alleged family custom, she drank whisky from a scallop shell "as Fingal and his heroes were wont to do." Thus fortified by whisky and romance, she inspected the old castle, of which now little more than the keep and fragments of its once formidable outer defences survive. When she boarded the cutter again for Aros, Sir John decided to wait behind "that he might have a conference with the Rev. Mr. McNicol, the minister of Lismore, on the subject of Ossian's poems." So calm was the water, that the seamen advised her to allow herself be rowed across the bay to Aros, by another great ruined seat of the Lords of the Isles about seven miles south east of Tobermory, where, two hours later, she arrived.

"The sea was a mirror, the mountains brilliantly clear, and not a sound to be heard but the dashing of the oars. I was for a time quite lost in admiration, and to complete the magic-like scene, I requested the seamen to sing Gaelic songs, which they did the greatest part of the voyage. It is astonishing how much their songs animated them, particularly a chorus, that made them pull away with such velocity, that it was like flying more than rowing on the surface of the water."

Her hosts at Aros, a Mr. and Mrs. Maxwell, saw her boat coming, and though they had never met her before, gave her such a welcome that she exclaimed:

"I am such a fortunate woman, that I was once told, if I were thrown from the peak of Cruachan, I should without doubt light safely on my feet at the bottom of it."

Knowing well the rapidity with the climate changes in these parts and how easily bad weather makes Staffa inaccessible, her host lent her horses and urged her to ride over to the point of embarkation without undue delay. The ride along Loch-na-Keal she called her "first cavalry expedition".

"In ascending I was obliged to lie on the horse's neck, and in descending almost on his tail, but for all that, though with trembling, I could not help gazing at the huge masses of rock piled like folio books one upon another, all the way up the mountain, hanging over my head." Her destination was Ulva House, which stands on an island in the Loch, and was visited in 1773 by Dr. Johnson, who was received by the sixteenth and last chief of the Macquarries.

On the next stage of her journey, having travelled at two miles an hour for eight hours, with only a short break "to eat my biscuit and drink my wine", she arrived at Torloisk. On the 26th of July, four rowers in a "very small boat" set out with her upon the Atlantic Ocean for Staffa.

"The sea was as smooth as glass, which enabled the boat to get quite close to the shore, tacking continually amongst innumerable small rocks separate from Staffa, lying on the west side of it."

The first sight and sound of Fingal's Cave is a remarkable experience for travellers much less susceptible than Mrs. Murray.

"When I faced the mouth of the cave, what I could see of the inside, and what I gazed at on the outside, made my blood thrill through every vein; but when I got within it, I forgot the world and everything it contains. The omnipotence of the Deity filled my soul. I was lost in wonder, gratitude, and praise. My nerves were so wound up, that the smallest sound distracted me. Never shall I forget the sublime heaven-like sensations with which Fingal's Cave inspired me."

The boatmen manoeuvred into the cave.

"The boat was not large, and the aperture it had at ebb tide to enter, is a trifle larger, so that we were obliged to worm in a little and little with a pole, continually pushing the boat from off one side to the other, until we got fairly into the cave, where the sea at all times widens considerably, particularly at high water. Whilst the boat was working through its narrow passage, I felt as if a huge monster had got the boat on his back, and was gently raising it, and again as gently letting it sink to its first level. As there was no surf, I could not conceive what occasioned that motion; but my alarm was soon quieted, by being told it was nothing but the swell of the sea."

She stepped "up the stumps of the pillars", and admired the prisms and pillars of this basaltic cave, their colours at a little distance "like rubies, pearls and other precious stones."

Leaving the cave, she landed outside and walked round the island, where there were only a few deer and sheep. She was then rowed back to Mull, reaching Torloisk about nine at night. It gave her some pleasure to record that in the year 1800—she paid a second visit in 1802—she was only the ninth "female stranger" to visit Staffa, the first that had gone alone, and additional satisfaction to discover that when Faujas St. Fond and his party had visited Staffa in 1784,[1] he was marooned by bad weather for several days; that Dr. Johnson "had not the happiness of visiting Staffa" as he passed by it in 1773 on his way to Iona; and that Thomas Pennant had only seen it "at a distance."

From Torloisk, she rode to the inn at Achnacraig, then the ferry-station for Kerrera and Oban, through which cattle were shipped for the South. From here she set out on 31st July to ride "from one end of Mull to the other", a distance of forty miles. She disagreed with the then popular estimate of the centre of Mull as being "a barren, dreary, dreadful district", but felt that "the want of inns" on the island was a considerable discouragement. "How is it possible," she asked, "for any one less enthusiastic than I am, to get a view of the numberless curious spots in Mull? Gentlemen's houses in that island are mostly situated widely from each other; consequently strangers in travelling through Mull will meet with many difficulties, and the island by that means must remain a spot of insignificance and disgust."

However, eventually she reached Bunessan, near the mouth of Loch Scridain, and on August 10th set out with a party for Iona. She landed at the bay where St. Columba is supposed to have first set foot when his Irish coracle brought him there in AD 563. Mrs. Murray collected some stones from the beach, and then rode round to the "town", which at that time consisted of huts "scattered among the ruins, chiefly around the nunnery, and along the causeway."

Her feminine nature urged her to doubt St. Columba's alleged dislike of women. Ignoring the rigours and realities which faced her sex in the sixth century, she felt sure that the nuns were only banished temporarily to the nearby rocky and inhospitable Island of Women "during the time the foreign colony of holy men were erecting the buildings, lest

[1] See *The Discovery of Scotland.*

their charms and allurements should, by rendering the men less industrious, impede the great work."

Iona suffered severely at the hands of the Norsemen after Columba's death in 597, and his daub-and-wattle monastery buildings were swept away. Somerled, a Celtic chief of Argyll, married into the Norwegian royal family and eventually secured Iona, to which his son introduced a colony of Benedictine Monks who built the present buildings, but drove out the remnants of Columba's Celtic monks.The Benedictines remained in possession of Iona until the Reformation. The MacLeans of Duart seized it thereafter, but in 1693 it came under the overlordship of the Duke of Argyll. In 1899, the eighth Duke presented the ruined Abbey to the Church of Scotland. It was re-roofed by 1910. To the plans of the architect Ian Lindsay, the work of restoring the conventual buildings began in the nineteen thirties, much of it achieved by voluntary labour under the inspiration of Lord MacLeod. In 1800, however, the Abbey was still a pathetic ruin, as the Nunnery still is. Mrs. Murray observed:

"It is a great pity that both the cathedral and nunnery are going fast to decay. Part of the ground around the cathedral, when I was at Iona, was planted with potatoes and other vegetables; the rest of it was over-run with the most luxuriant weeds and wild plants I ever beheld."

Fighting with "stubborn wild plants" up to her waist, she sought out the tombstones of the ancient Irish, Norse, French and Scots kings–among them Kenneth MacAlpine, first Celtic king of Scotland–brought to Iona for burial for more than four hundred years.

Although Mrs. Murray found no one on Iona who believed in second sight, the superstition was still cherished that "the last person buried keeps watch around the burying ground, until another body is interred, to whose spirit the office of guardian is immediately delivered up", a superstition that she attributed to Druidical origins.

Impoverished as was their way of life, four hundred people were still living on the island in 1800. No one, Mrs. Murray claims, had ever been executed for a capital crime "in the memory of any person living", and only one man had been sent to prison, in 1793: from which statistics she presumed that the morals of the islanders were good.

She discovered that grain on Iona rarely "lies on the ground longer than six weeks, for in that short time the people plough, sow, and gather their crops into their barns." This was because the soil is "a white light sand, on which the sun in a wet climate has an astonishing effect in point of quick vegetation." The absence of trees, and thus of fuel, necessitated boat journeys to the mainland of Rossshire to lift and stack peat, bringing it over in the Autumn once it had been dried. Many of the inhabitants, both men and women, trudged southwards on foot every year to find work at harvest-time.

After thoroughly exploring the island, Mrs. Murray had "a meal of fine fish and excellent potatoes", to which "hunger added the best of sauce", at the inn, and then sat by the shore while a minister who had travelled with them baptised a number of children.

"While we were seated on the rocks impending over the bay, numbers of women and children came after us, and by degrees some of the old ones crept from one piece of rock to another, until they were close to us. The men and boys kept at a respectful distance, not that they had less curiosity, but were more bashful than the women. The manners of the females appeared to me to be innocent, simple, and crouching, like spaniel dogs approaching their masters. If fear had not deterred them, I verily believe the poor things would have gladly fondled us. Very seldom indeed are their eyes accustomed to look upon strangers of either sex, and a few shillings distributed amongst them afforded a transient joy not easily described."

She noted that the "habiliments of the commonality" were "chiefly made of a thin coarse woollen cloth which they fabricate, and dye of indigo colour blue . . . The form of the women's dress is generally a petticoat, and a sort of bed-gown of that cloth, and a white mob cap, or an handkerchief wrapped closely round their heads and under their chins. The men wear waistcoats and trousers of the same sort of cloth, and beaver hats."

When the minister rejoined them, they sailed back to Bunessan, in Mull.

The changing state of the economy in Mull made her fear for the island's future.

"In former times a chieftain kept his family about him, and thought nothing of riches beyond his paternal inheritance. Hunting, shooting, and fishing, were the sole employments of the greater portion . . . Others cultivated land just sufficient to produce a crop of oats and barley, for the consumption of the clan of which they made a part . . . They had no luxuries, consequently few wants . . .

"But since the year 1745 great change has taken place in the Highlands, for now every gentleman makes the most of his land by industrious cultivation, and cattle and sheep are reared for exportation . . . He sends abroad his sons . . . to our fleets and armies. Many of these brave men are lost, but some return with spoils from the east and west; but alas! with them they have imported luxuries, and wants unknown to their forefathers, which have caused the downfall of some ancient clans, and many respectable families."

The suggestion that social life in the Highlands might perhaps have survived in its old state had it not been for the rising of 1745, is a romantic Rousseau-like notion which does not stand up to serious examination. Rising standards of living, and the steep increase in costs which occurred during the troubles with France, produced a situation in which too many people were trying to get an inadequate living out of the Highlands, using out-of date methods of production. The Clearances provided a cruel and inhuman solution, imposed by anglified lairds who had lost much of the traditional paternal feeling which had held the clan system together for so long. Lacking her own government since 1707, Scotland was in no position to devise any alternative solution, which might have encouraged a greater concentration on the means of production and the introduction of industry.

Mrs. Murray made several excursions along the shores of Lochbuie, and spent some days with the MacLeans of Moy, "and their numerous family of amiable children."

Lochbuie Castle, which had been inhabited until 1740, was in 1800 used as a storehouse. Its dungeon, which Lochbuie took her to see (she accepted without comment the Highland custom of calling a laird after his territory) made her blood "run cold to look at. The depth of it . . . probably is to the level of the sea, which washes the base of the castle where the dungeon lies. No steps ever led to the bottom of it. Culprits were let down by ropes, and over the aperture a huge flat stone was laid, which no single human strength could move."

On the day she was to leave to ride to Achnacraig, her host persuaded her to avoid the rain and stay another day; whereupon her servant "Dugall . . . expostulated . . . 'In truth, sir, it can't hurt her, for the rain will only drive on her back.' "

Sailing back to Oban, the sailors were much amused that Mrs. Murray should want to travel with a collection of stones. They were even more curious about a little mahogany box, which they suspected contained money. So she took its key from her pocket, undid the box, "and presented each of them with a small tumbler of wine out of it. Their surprise was extreme: the construction of the box, the bottle, the knife and fork, spoons, and other knick-knacks it contained, seemed matters of as much curiosity and astonishment to them, as Staffa and its prisms had been to me."

Back at Oban, she hired a small cart to carry her to Easdale, once famous for its slate quarries. She was driven by a Chelsea out-pensioner who had been wounded by the Spanish floating batteries during the Siege of Gibraltar in 1779. The purpose of this trip was to sail out to inspect the Corrievrechan whirlpool, which lies between the southern end of Jura and the little island of Scarba, and makes a "boiling" sound caused by the movement of the tide being constricted between two pieces of land.

She landed in a creek beside the whirlpool, and settled down to watch its agitation at high tide, while she began a meal. A ship from Dantzig came into the channel just as the agitation was beginning and in alarm, Mrs. Murray's boatmen rowed out to warn it of its danger, the belief then being that "no boat or vessel of any size whatever" could "with entire safety enter the gulf of Coire Vreaikain, either from the east or west (the gulf runs nearly in that direction) at flood tide." The northern seamen, however, resented the slur thus cast on their seamanship. When they had anchored their vessel on the safe side, they joined Mrs. Murray's party for dinner. The visual spectacle which accompanied their eating Mrs. Murray certainly thought worth waiting for.

"When the tide had been flowing about two hours, small billows rose and burst over the Coire; but at mid flood tide I saw, particularly if any wind met the tide, the sea began to rise a great way below the Coire, and then gradually swell to the vast billows rolling on, some white and foaming, others glassy and smooth, still getting higher and higher, till they came to the grand whirlpool, where they burst with an amazing noise, forming hundreds of small whirls in the surf around, and for a quarter of a mile in a direct line, in the current of the tide. Thus I beheld, for an hour, a succession of rising and breaking of billows, some low, others, if a gust of wind met the coming wave, to a vast height: and the noise in breaking was proportionately tremendous and loud."

After watching this spectacle for between three to four hours, they set out on the homeward journey, but got caught in the backlash of the whirlpool, whereby the sailors' oars were useless and they were carried, amidst a "clattering pell-mell in the Gaelic language", in the wrong direction. So the sailors jumped ashore, and by means of ropes, managed to pull the boat clear of the influence of the tide.

Mrs. Murray claimed not to have been frightened by this experience; but "poor Mr.———, wrapped in his tartan cloke, as soon as the confusion began, slipped off his seat to the bottom of the boat, and silently watched for the moment that (as he probably imagined), was to whirl him to a better world; and so great was his internal agitation, that his face was the colour of crimson, with drops of perspiration as big as peas, running down it."

Back on the mainland, she visited Dunolly Castle, which stands on a rock more than eighty feet high surrounded on three sides by the sea, and had been the seat of the chiefs of the Macdougals since the eleventh century; and Port Appin, in the country of the Stuarts of Appin, who lost their lands and their influence after 1745.

She crossed by ferry from Port Appin to the island of Lismore, "a very fertile island . . . the land extremely productive of grain and pulse." She was surprised to find that the parish of Lismore took in not only the whole district of Appin, but also Glen Creran and Glen Etive. To help the parish minister there was an assistant called the Minister of the Glens, who was paid thirty pounds a year: "and for this trifling gratuity, this much to be pitied gentleman" was "obliged to attend his sequestered flocks in their respective glens alternately, at the risk of breaking his neck if he rides over the rough passes."

On the way back to the Port Appin ferry, the minister pointed out to Mrs. Murray "a stone having the form of a chair. I was invited to seat myself in it, because having been the chair of a saint, it was said to have the virtue of preserving all who sit in it, from rheumatism. I had no ailment at the time, but there was no harm in securing my person from future pain by so easy a charm, so down I sat, and in the effort of rising from the deep, narrow cavity, I broke one of the glasses of my spectacles, to me a disaster worse than rheumatism in that secluded region, for I could nor replace it till I returned to Edinburgh.

During her tours of 1801 and 1802, Mrs. Murray engaged Angus Cameron of Rannoch to "serve and take care of me till I quitted the Highlands." Before she did this she explored much of the North of Scotland.

She thought the coastline from Appin to Ballachulish "indiscribably charming". She went to the head of Loch Leven, and was with difficulty persuaded from following the course of the River Leven up to its source by Angus Cameron, who told her that she could only do this if she was prepared "to put on a kilt (the little short petticoat of the Highlander's dress) to be prepared for wading water." Such a suggestion daunted even her intrepid spirit, so she contented herself with "walking up the banks of the river for about three miles from the head of Loch Leven, where I had the infinite pleasure of viewing what must enchant every eye that delights in landscape scenery." The development of an aluminium plant at Kinlochleven has unfortunately provided the modern eye with much to disenchant it.

While at Ballachulish, she decided to visit Loch Sunart, Loch Shiel, and the mines at Strontian, to collect "some of the newly discovered earth called Strontianite." She sailed on Loch Shiel with the family of MacDonald of Dalilia, and in due course collected "many prodigeously fine specimens" of Strontian ore.

Whether because of her own increasing age, or because her fame had slackened her enthusiasm to record everything she saw, the extra chapters added by Mrs. Murray to her third edition of 1810 are scrappily written, often not much more than notes to augment her earlier impressions. She spent a fortnight with the Grants of Rothiemurchus, during which she rode to Loch-an-Eilean, in the Rothiemurchus Forest, and "there entered a boat and rowed towards the ruin on the island." The castle has associations with the "Wolf of Badenoch", Alexander Stewart, Robert II's natural son. Ospreys nested here until about 1900.[1] "The scene was such that I began to fancy myself in a state of enchantment," wrote Mrs. Murray of this remarkably beautiful island. She also spent a month with the dowager widow of Macdonald of Boisdale in 1802 on the island of Ulva, "one of those unheeded islands, although abounding in rare productions." With one of the daughters of the house—of whom Mrs. Murray wrote: "Had I been a man, I most assuredly should have been robbed of my heart by the lovely Flora of Ulva"—there were expeditions to view the basaltic pillars, similar to though less impressive than those on Staffa, and to collect "crystals, zeolite, porphyry, spars", and other geological treasures. She saw corn being ground in querns, and she listened to the working-songs of the islanders. She was all but shipwrecked on Coll, and hospitably received by Colonel MacLean of Coll, from where she sailed to Eigg. There, she reflected on the difficulty of compelling proprietors to halt enforced emigration to America, of which she disapproved heartily.

Rum also received her, though she was "unable to reach the island of Canna."

Skye treated her to bad weather, though the sight of cascades "dashing in every direction" down the cliffs at Talisker revived some of her inborn enthusiasm for waterfalls.

From Loch Sligachan, she crossed to the island of Raasay. Her boat "had not rowed five minutes before it blew a hurricane, the rain descended in spouts, the sea was excessively rough with dreadful squalls, so that I was seriously apprehensive for our safety", an experience I, too, underwent though in a shallow motor-boat, in 1947. She spent ten days on Raasay waiting for the weather to abate sufficiently for her boat to push off again.

Back on the mainland, she made her way by Loch Duich to Fort Augustus, and presumably thereafter back to the sophistications of Kensington, from which she had so often

[1] They have returned to the district in recent years, nesting near Boat of Garten.

and so bravely adventured into those remote parts of Scotland where travelling conditions were always slow and often hazardous, and bespectacled English ladies with note-books and sketching-pads in their portmanteaux still a comparative rarity.

One suspects that Mrs. Sarah Murray or Aust cheated oblivion with an entry in the *Dictionary of Natural Biography* more because of the relationship of her first husband to a nobleman than by her literary achievement. She was the first systematic woman traveller in Scotland who toured as a professional writer, and yet her open and warmly enthusiastic nature still communicates from her pages. She does not deserve to be quite forgotten.

4

Thomas Thornton: *With Rod and Gun*

Sir Walter Scott opened up the Highlands to the general tourists with the curiosity aroused by his long poem *The Lady of the Lake,* published in 1810, and his widely-read series of historical novels, beginning with *Waverley* in 1814. The people whom Scott, and to a lesser extent James (Ossian) Macpherson half a century before him, inspired with sufficient enthusiasm to undertake the uncomfortable journey to Scotland were not talented, comparatively wealthy enthusiasts, like the painter William Gilpin and the journalist Mrs. Murray, but travellers in search of a change of scenery heightened in interest by the romantic glamour with which Scott's verse and prose had so strongly tinged it.

A decade earlier, Colonel Thomas Thornton, of Thornville Royal, in Yorkshire, found another reason for visiting Scotland. He came because it provided ample opportunity for the satisfaction of his gargantuan sporting tastes.

He was born in 1757, the son of a Colonel William Thornton who had been present at the battle of Falkirk, and who served under Cumberland at Culloden. His soldiering behind him, Colonel William became Member of Parliament for York, but died suddenly at the age of fifty, leaving his son a minor.

Thomas Thornton was schooled at Charterhouse, and thereafter at Glasgow College. He then retired to the family seat of Thornton Royal, where he formed a fox-hunting pack, kept race-horses, shot, fished, cultivated extraordinary feats of athletics, trained falcons and joined the West York Regiment of Militia, of which he subsequently became Colonel. Hawking and falconry, however, remained his outstanding passions. He undertook his sporting campaign in the Highlands of Scotland in 1784, although his book *A*

Sporting Tour Through the Northern Parts of England and Great Part of the Highlands of Scotland was not published in London until 1804. A second edition appeared in 1896. The first edition was reviewed, somewhat acidly, by the then Mr. Walter Scott, who complained that Thornton wrote as a sportsman rather than as a naturalist.

"The performance is termed a Sporting Tour, not because it conveys to the reader any information, new or old, upon the habits of the animals unfortunate enough to be distinguished as *game*, nor even upon the modes to be adopted in destroying them *secundem artem;* but because it contains a long, minute and prolix account of every grouse or black-cock which had the honour to fall by the gun of our literary sportsman—of every pike which gorged his bait—of every bird which was pounced by his hawks—of every blunder which was made by his servants—and of every bottle which was drunk by his friends."

Hard-drinking, quick-shooting, game-slaughtering English military buffers are, indeed, a bore if their company has to be too long endured. But the good Colonel was the forerunner of a whole army that has since trampled on Scottish moors, and dangled by Scottish rivers. He is therefore inevitably interesting as the precursor of a powerful and continuing fashion. Besides which, we shall not stay long enough in his bluff company to allow him inflict on us those *longueurs* with which he so evidently affected the author of *Waverley.*

The preparations which Thornton made for his trip involved the chartering of a sloop, *Falcon,* the purchase of a kind of portable kitchen, and the engagement as travelling companion of an artist, George Garrard (1760-1826), a pupil of the younger Gilpin, well-known both as an animal painter and as a landscape artist. After spending ten days visiting various places on the east coast of England, Thornton and his party—which included a sizeable mounted staff referred to as "the cavalry"—crossed the Tweed at Coldstream and descended on Kelso, where they were "detained a few minutes at the turnpike", which gave them "a very favourable opportunity of admiring a healthy, well-made, *sonsy* lassie," The inn proved "large, but incommodious", and one where, "notwithstanding the bad accommodation, they knew how to make a very handsome bill."

The Colonel "killed several small trout, but had no great sport, as the water was . . . here found too clear." He noted of the Tweed: "This river is a very dangerous one to the fisher, being full of shelves and rapid streams, so that, in the eagerness of playing a fish, should he lose his feet, he must be hurried immediately into a very deep and dangerous stream."

Next day Thornton and his friends rode to Lauder, and after a night at an inn "only tolerable", they set out very early on June 12th to reach Dalkeith so that they could breakfast with the King's Own Dragoons, who were stationed there. A few miles up the road, Thornton was "not a little surprised to find my progress stopped by a number of people, crowded together, to hear a person, who occasionally peeped out of a sentry-box. Enquiring what could be his intentions, I found it was a parson preaching to a half-drowned audience. As I was not, however, of the Kirk of Scotland, I drove on, somewhat astonished that the auditors could not be contented with hearing that gentleman's tenets delivered regularly once a week.

The view approaching Dalkeith was spoiled by rain.

"The landscape, however, notwithstanding this disadvantage, was wonderful; the different villas scattered around Edinburgh, and its castle perched on a rock, commanding the town; a view of the Firth of Forth, the Island of Bass, and the singular rock of Hamilton, bounded by the Pentland Hills to the left, and the coast of Fife, above which are faintly seen covered with snow, the Highland hills, compose a scene which must excite the admiration of every traveller."

It so excited the admiration of Garrard that although it was hardly sketching weather, he, "all eagerness, would not be diverted from the attempt, and having kept himself tolerably dry in the gig, he begged we could allow him to follow us, as it was now likely to be a fair day."

Arrived at Dalkeith, however, the servent sent on in advance by Thornton informed his master that "all the officers were marched to Edinburgh to quell some riots." These were at Canonmills. As a result of a bad harvest, and other causes, Edinburgh was suffering from a food shortage. The erroneous rumour got around that Mr. Haig, who managed a distillery in Canonmills, was using oats and potatoes for distilling at a time when many people were almost starving and food prices were high. On 4th June, a large mob had attempted to destroy the distillery, but were repulsed by Mr. Haig's employees. One man was killed. On 7th June, the mob returned, but this time were dispersed by the militia, who were stationed in readiness. It was presumably to aid this force that the dragoons moved in from Dalkeith.

Thornton and his entourage continued on to Edinburgh, though not without encountering fresh difficulties, making him remark: "a worser day's journey I seldom or never experienced: continual showers of rain involved the whole surrounding country in such a density of vapour as totally to preclude all perception of distant objects, whilst the extreme heaviness of the roads added a weight to every step we took."

But there was more to contend with than heavy rain and sodden roads.

"The carters, a set of men who, affecting English liberty, drive against the carriage of every peaceable traveller they meet, are, on the approach to this town, a perfect nuisance. Even the law is unable to cope with these gentry, who, as a body, defy all correction, and really ought to be noticed by the gentlemen of the neighbourhood at large. It is fortunate that the carts they drive are but small, and lightly laden, otherwise his Majesty would annually lose a greater number of his subjects."

Thornton set down at James Dun's Hotel, number 39 St. Andrew's Square. This, Edinburgh's first fashionable New Town "hottle", as the citizens dubbed it, was the scene of many society assemblies, and included among its distinguished guests Edmund Burke and Samuel Rogers, the banker poet. Thornton was "accosted" by his friends Sir Thomas Wallace and Burns's friend and patron the Earl of Glencairn, who together persuaded the Colonel to divide his time in Edinburgh between their houses.

While in Edinburgh, he left his party dining at the equally fashionable Fortune's Tavern, situated in the Old Stamp Office Close in what had formerly been the town house of the Earls of Eglinton, to attend a performance by the famous actress Mrs. Siddons.

"The impression on the crowd around us was really astonishing: long murmurs, deep sighs, and tearful handkerchiefs were plentifully displayed by the ladies, who seemed really striving to outdo each other in sensibility. This fashionable affection of feeling"–Henry Mackenzie's weepy novel *The Man of Feeling,* published in 1771, was still the rage of the towns–"for it could be little else, as the larger part of the audience, owing to the fullness of the house, could scarcely hear a syllable, was succeeded by faintings, and the whole was so perfectly *outré* that, much as I am an admirer of Mrs. Siddons's acknowledged merit, I confess I wished myself more than once back at the hotel."

However, the arrival of a friend, an officer struck on the head during the riots that morning though not seriously injured, enabled Thornton to sit out the performance to the end and then return to Fortune's where his party was still carousing.

Thornton's reactions to the appearance of Edinburgh are typical of those generally recorded by travellers of the period. Looking east along Princes Street, then "a long continued line of regular stone houses", Thornton wrote: "To the right, rising as it were from the depth of a vast *fosse,* called the North Loch, stands the old city, fantastically piled on the summit of an immense rock, nearly two miles in length, and abruptly terminated by the ancient castle, which impends, in sullen grandeur, like the stronghold of some giant of romance."

But more than romance occupied the good Colonel's attentions in Edinburgh, for he "ordered in two large chests of biscuits, several Cheshire and Gloucester cheeses, together with a number of Yorkshire hams, reindeer and other tongues, hung-beef etc., in order to be amply provided for a large party."

Leaving Edinburgh on 17 June, the entourage drew up at Kirk o' Shotts, "but found the inn so bad, and the whole house so inebriated" that they rode on to Holly Town (Holytown).

Next day they drove to Glasgow, noting how it was bounded by "the delightful hills of Campsey", and admiring "the villas, whimsically built according to the taste of their respective proprietors", making "the approach to that magnificent city truly noble."

His first day in Glasgow was spent inspecting with his

companions "the regularity of the streets and universal magnificence of the buildings." In the evening, they were invited to a ball.

"The ballroom was elegantly fitted up, and my companions agreed that handsomer women, or, in general, better dressed, were not to be met with: their style of dancing, however, quite astonished these *southrôns,* scarce able to keep sight of their fair partners."

The ladies retired at three in the morning, but the gentlemen stayed on "to pay the proper compliment of toasting their respective partners." Thornton was "detained", against his wishes, "till *six* in the morning, and then got away, leaving the majority by no means disposed to retire."

Another day was spent taking a walk round Glasgow Green: "a large, spacious piece of ground, not unlike a park, being walled in, except to the west, which is girded by the river Clyde. This piece of ground has a very excellent walk in it, and is the mall to the town. In the centre stands a very useful square building, inclosing a court, where the washerwomen reside, and dress and dry their linen.

"The soil of this green is very rich, and affords excellent pasturage for large herds of cows, and here the gentlemen resort to follow their favourite amusement, the game of golf, which is universal throughout Scotland, as well as Holland . . . It is a wholesome exercise for those who do not think such gentle sports too trivial for men, being performed with light sticks and small balls, and is by no means so violent an exertion as cricket, trapball or tennis."

After breakfast, he visited the College, "a piece of architecture in no respect extraordinary" (One must allow for the predilections of Georgian taste, together with the feelings for his *alma mater,* of one who may not have been a notable scholar, though Thornton claimed to have spent "many, many happy hours" within its walls). He then went to see the "High Church", as he dubbed the Cathedral, "that great, stupendous, and inelegant pile of building." This day was rounded off attending a private dinner at the newly opened Tontine Hotel, in Argyll Street. Thornton thought the famous coffee-room "very elegant indeed, but much too large for the company likely to resort to it"—he was wrong in this verdict, for it became the most fashionable resort of its kind in the city—but was full of praise for a meal which included "turtle and every other luxury in profusions."

A day or two was spent fishing for pike and perch in Bardowie Loch, a few miles north west of Glasgow—he caught ten pike and two perch at one session—then, on 27th June, the party set out for Luss. Even this short journey in these days was not without its hazards, for, Thornton recalls, they:

"Came to Kelvin, but found the bridge over the river had been broken down, and, though newly repaired, was scarcely passable: we had the prudence under these circumstances, to get out of the carriage, and by that means probably saved our lives, as the shaft-horse swerved, when half-across, in such a manner that it was impossible but that, with our additional weight, he would, otherwise, have gone over, and we must have been dashed to pieces in the torrent below, foaming at a tremendous distance with the agitations occasioned by the preceding heavy rains."

In due course they approached Dumbarton, which they had expected to reach before a gathering shower broke.

"But we were mistaken, for, at the distance of about half a mile, a sudden jerk broke one of the traces, owing to the neglect of the groom, who had not sufficiently attended to my constant orders to examine every part of the carriage, harness, etc., most minutely, and particularly so when entering the Highlands, where no assistance could be expected but from our own ingenuity.

We inquired for a cobbler, as the likeliest person to assist us, and having found one, in quarter of an hour the damage was repaired. It now rained pretty freely, but we went on at a good trot, and got to Dumbarton tolerably wet, but were nevertheless much pleased with the indistinct view of the castle, Clyde, etc., seen through the heavy vapours that surrounded them."

The Colonel thought Dumbarton "a small, indifferent town". But driving over the "ridge of moors that divides Loch Lomond from the Firth of Clyde", he thought the view of Loch Lomond behind him and the view of "the Firth of Clyde, crowded with shipping" ahead "worthy of the pencil of Claude."

Next day, he was taken to see over a calico-printing and

Above, Glencoe, where Sarah Murray 'could not help paying the tribute of a sigh' for the melancholy fate of the MacDonalds; *below*, Inverness, found by Mrs Murray to be 'a neat town, charmingly situated'

In Inveraray Mrs Murray asked a lady if the streets were ever perfectly dry. 'She answered me, *never* . . . '; *below*, Glasgow, where, Mrs Murray declared, the inhabitants were 'very rich, saucy and wicked'

bleaching works in the Vale of Leven, which at that time was developing into one of the main local centres of that industry. Although he was impressed by "the quantity of labour performed by the number of hands employed", a more unctuous judgment occurred to him as he watched the work in progress.

"This undertaking is conducted chiefly by women; but, as far as personal charms are in question, I confess I never was so much disappointed: out of fifty, there was scarcely one even tolerable, which is widely different from the case of the Scottish ladies, who, in general, excel their southern neighbours. On reflection, I am quite convinced that a certain degree of luxury is absolutely necessary to create and protect beauty, that the want of it hardens features, and that hot rooms, late hours and other fashionable excesses, destroy it."

He made an excursion to Inchmurrin, one of the islands in Loch Lomond, where he alleged that "a few wild boars" had been "turned in there" by Lord Graham, heir to the Duke of Montrose. Thornton reckoned that the Cameron House estate, which reaches along the shores of Loch Lomond, and was and still is, owned by the descendants of the sister of the novelist Tobias Smollet, was ideally situated, in that it had the benefits of cheap coal from Dumbarton, noble sailing, good coursing, sea-fish in the Clyde and fresh in the loch; indeed, was so well placed that no situation could be "more enviable, particularly to a sportsman; for, though some parts of the Highlands may be still superior for summer shooting, they are, in other respects, not so desirable." During his stay, the Colonel shot duck, a mallard and a cormorant, and his dog, Pero, was kept busy retrieving from the rushes at the loch-edge. On subsequent days trout by the dozen, cormorants, scuts, ducks, sea-gulls, sand-pipers and even a raven, fell to the Colonel's efficient tackle. His nonchalance about these performances is truly remarkable.

"After firing a few more shots at different birds," he tells us on one occasion, "we dined, and then rowed across towards an island to the south, and seeing the trout rising freely, I put my fly-rod together, and killed a dozen or two presently".

While visiting Rossdhu, the home of Sir James Colquhoun, the builder of Helensburgh, and his wife, Lady Helen, after whom that town was named, Thornton dined on one of his own perch. While returning to the inn at Luss, he encountered Jane, Duchess of Gordon, the wife of the fourth Duke. She had several times invited Burns to her drawing-room parties in Edinburgh, and Burns wrote an indignant letter to the editor of *The Star*, when that newspaper had published "some silly verses" on her. She was then on a walking tour of the Highlands, and Thornton was duly deferential.

Indeed, Thornton's attitude to people to some extent did depend upon their social status. When a boatman in his seventies accidentally jumped on, and broke, Thornton's rod, Thornton exclaimed: "Without being a warm man, it would have been excusable to have thrown him overboard, and have given him a good ducking." However, he contented himself by refusing to pay for the old man's services.

After a week spent in "trolling" the waters of Loch Lomond and shooting over its surface, Colonel Thornton and his party set out for Loch Tay, travelling by Glen Falloch and Killin, where Lord Breadalbane had an inn the like of which Thornton "never saw a better". He took the view that Killin offered an ideal site for a nobleman's seat, and could not understand what had made the Breadalbane family elect to build at Taymouth instead.

Thornton "found it delightful sailing down this enchanted water . . . The views up and down the lake . . . were very beautiful; and we had the additional pleasure to see the carriage and servants always in view, as it were, above us, constantly within call, had we either found any inconvenience in the vessel, from the wind being too boisterous, of which, however, we had little apprehension, or had there been a dead calm, which we at first feared; but as we advanced, a very refreshing breeze came from Ben More, and gently swelling our canvas, we glided on exactly at the rate which suited us for trolling."

After dining afloat, the party landed for the night by the inn at Kenmore, whereupon the boatman awaited his wages. The landlord thought three shillings for the day's rowing reasonable, since the man had been fed. However, anxious to be thought generous, the Colonel gave him all his change, which amounted to nine shillings and sixpence, and so suffered "no small mortification" when the man "was dissatisfied, and behaved very unhandsomely."

The moral for visiting Englishmen, Thornton thought, was for them "always to make a previous agreement with every countryman whose services they may want, but particularly with a Highlander: many of them have but one idea, which is that an Englishman is a walking mint, and they are never satisfied, should you give, as I have often done, four times as much as the man would have had from an inhabitant for executing the same business."

Taymouth, which Thornton had first seen when at College in Glasgow, had made such an impression on him then that "whenever I thought of anything extremely pleasant Taymouth constantly presented itself to me. It now appeared equally enchanting, the weather and every other circumstance conspiring to render it so."

Moving up to the River Tay, opposite Dunkeld, where Telford's bridge had not yet been built, Thornton provides us with a vivid reminder of the daily hazards of travelling in the eighteenth century:

"We soon came to the ferry, but were prevented from crossing for some time by a number of wild-looking horses, and their owners, little less wild than themselves, who were waiting there for a passage. The servants claimed the right they supposed we had of crossing first, and made a considerable hubbub; but as it appeared to me that, in crossing a public ferry, no other precedence could be claimed than the priority of application, or, as it is usually styled, 'first come first served', I desired them to desist, and highly amused myself with seeing the embarkation.

"The men pulled and hauled in their horses, accoutred, in general, not with bridles, but with *brands*"—two pieces of wood, through which a halter ran, generally made of twisted birch—"which, when the rider or conductor wishes to stop his steed, he pulls, and, consequently, pinches the animal by the nose. This effect happening, I presume, to several of the shelties at the same time, a great confusion ensued, attended with much kicking from men and horses, and more noise, for all were equally engaged. So ridiculous a situation, without any great danger, created infinite laughter from those on shore. We thought the oversetting of the boat at one time impossible to be avoided, but it was prevented, fortunately, by three of the horses, who had extricated themselves from their drivers, leaping, like goats, into the river, and dragging one, more obstinate than the rest, with them. The first horse swam to the opposite shore; the rest followed. The Highlander, thus emersed, might have run the risk of being drowned, had not a friend caught him by the kilt as he floated near the boat. He was hauled in, and the remainder of the cargo landed without further trouble."

Thornton then travelled up by the banks of the Garry to Blair Castle, the seat of the Duke of Atholl, but then in its reduced state following its siege and bombardment during the rising of 1745. In the later eighteenth century renovation, its turrets and parapets were removed, turning it into a plain Georgian house, in which state it remained until the Scottish baronial style became fashionable, and David Bryce put them back. Thornton inspected the "wonderfully thick" walls of the place–the oldest part, Comyn's Tower, dates from 1269–and walked through the "plantations".

Next day, he visited the Falls of Bruar. Garrard busied himself with his sketch-book, from "a stone overhanging a precipice, where, had his foot slipped, it would have been his last sketch", while the Colonel reflected that waterfalls were "subjects which no pencil can draw with the force they convey to the spectator, the chief astonishment being excited by the roaring sound of the water, which is inexpressible."

They spent the night at the inn at Dalnacardoch, and next day caught between them thirty trout. They also caught one char, which are not usually to be found in Highland waters. Back at the inn, the party sat down to a dinner the first course of which consisted of "Hodge podge, Pudding, Greens, Trout and Char, Roast Mutton" and the second "Brandered Chickens, Cold hams, Snipes, Cheshire cheese and biscuits", all this being washed down by claret, port, limes, Jamaica rum, and "incomparable porter from Calvert's".

July 10th was spent travelling through the hills to Dalwhinnie, and so on to Raits, in Strathspey, where Thornton learned that his cutter, which had made passage from Hull to Forres, had sprung a leak on the voyage, and had been in some danger. However, it was escorted into port by a Whitby smack, and the cargo, which included provisions and two small boats, was trundled by cart and by sledge to Raits.

The appearance of the house of Raits, which he had rented, together with its associated sporting rights, disappointed him. However, the fishing on Loch Insh, and on the Spey itself, to say nothing of the shooting, soon restored his spirits. On 18th July, Thornton's "returns" showed: "wild ducks, nine; snipes, three; plovers, two", and on July 20th, "one hundred and one trout". There was an embarrassing excursion to stalk and shoot a roe deer, which resulted in the killing by mistake of a "shaven goat", and which made Thornton nearly fall off a rock by a dangerous precipice, "overcome with a fit of laughter which this truly comic and well-executed scheme had occasioned."

On July 24th, the carts and sledges having arrived from Forres, the Colonel made a systematic inventory of his stores and provisions. This shows that in addition to enough food to last until the end of October, he had brought with him to the Highlands two Red Falcons, four Red Tercals, four setters, six pointers, one deerhound, two double-barrel shotguns, three single barrel, one rifle, eighty pounds of powder, eleven bags of shot and "flints sufficient". Rarely can so methodical a campaign of sporting slaughter have been organized by any previous traveller!

In the weeks that followed, Thornton threw himself into the business of "killing" things, to use his own favourite expression, great and small. To the sportsman, bent on similar pursuits, the details of his "bags" might be of interest. Most readers would probably find this antique catalogue of fishy stories and statistics as boring as did Scott.

There were, of course, high moments in Colonel Thornton's murderous progress. On one occasion he hooked a monster pike which looked "not less than twenty or thirty pounds" on Loch Aline. Believing the fish had "run himself tight round some root", Colonel Thornton and his friend Captain Walker "rowed up, therefore, to the spot," when the fish soon convinced me he was at liberty, by running me so far into the lake that I had not one inch of line more to give him. The servants, foreseeing the consequences of my situation, rowed, with great expedition, towards the fish, which now rose about seventy yards from us, an absolute wonder! I relied on my tackle, which I knew was in every respect excellent, as I had, in consequence of the large pike killed the day before, put on hooks and gimp, adjusted with great care; a precaution which would have been thought superfluous in London, as it certainly was for most lakes, though here, barely equal to my fish." Captain Walker played the fish for some time so that Thornton might eventually have the honour of landing it. Just as they thought it played out, "we were again constrained to follow the monster nearly across the lake, having the wind too much against us . . . I dreaded losing such an extraordinary fish, and the anxiety of our little crew was equal to mine.

"After about an hour and a quarter's play, however, we thought we might safely attempt to land him, which was done in the following manner. Newmarket, a lad so called from the place of his nativity, who had now come to assist, I ordered, with another servant, to strip and wade in as far as possible, which they readily did. In the meantime I took the landing-net, while Captain Walker, judiciously ascending the hill above, drew him gently towards us. He approached the shore very quietly, and we thought him quite safe, when, seeing himself surrounded by his enemies, he in an instant made a last desperate effort, shot into the deep again, and, in the exertion, threw one of the men on his back. His immense size was now very apparent; we proceeded with all due caution, and, being once more drawn towards land, I tried to get his head into the net, upon effecting which, the servants were orderd to seize his tail, and slide him on shore; I took all imaginable pains to accomplish this, but in vain, and began to think myself strangely awkward, when, at length, having got his snout in, I discovered that the hoop of the net, though adapted to very large pike, would admit no more than that part. He was, however, completely spent, and, in a few moments we landed him, a perfect monster! He was stabbed by my directions in the spinal marrow, with a large knife, which appeared to be the most humane way of killing him, and I then ordered all the signals with the *sky-scrapers* to be hoisted; and the whoop re-echoed through the whole range of the Grampians. On opening his jaws to endeavour to take the hooks from him, which were both fast in his gorge, so dreadful a forest of teeth, or tusks, I think I never beheld: if I had not had a double link of gimp, with two swivels, the depth between his stomach and his mouth would have made the former quite useless. His measurement, accurately taken, was *five feet four inches* from eye to fork."

When the fish was opened up, it was found to contain "another pike half digested" as well as a hook "wonderfully honey-combed; but free from rust, so that I cannot doubt its having been at least ten years in his belly."

The fish weighed forty eight pounds, and Thornton had his "head and backbone" preserved and the flesh "salted down".

For the rest, he shot ptarmigan in Glenennich, fished for pike in Loch-an-Eilean, "a most enchanting spot" where "every turn presents a fresh beauty", shot duck down the Spey, hawked snipe in the mountains around Raits, saw stags on the mountains above Aberarder but had to leave them alive having forgotten to bring his gun, saw goshawks (a bird which does not now breed in Scotland) nesting in the forest of Rothiemurchus, rescued his servant Lawson from drowning, walked and rode prodigious distances, and from the top of one mountain, near where he set up a camp, pronounced an encomium on Highland scenery:

"South Britons may talk of their beautiful, highly-finished landscapes, of which I have seen the most deserving to be viewed in England, and have been pleased with their elegance and neatness; but, from their small extent, they soon grow flat and lose their effect. Here the case differs; for the immense extent of these views, and the reflection of the sun, presenting various tints, each differing from another, though all beautiful, give this country every advantage, and a decided superiority over all the laboured works of a Brown or a White."

With a Colonel Macpherson, he dined on 18th September in celebration of the passing of the Act which gave back the forfeited estates to those from whom they had been taken after the rising of 1745. Macpherson had been a captain during that "horrid period", as Thornton calls it, and was taken prisoner along with Donald Macdonald of Kinlochmoidart and held at Carlisle. Macdonald was executed in September 1746, but Macpherson was freed for lack of evidence.

At dinner, "the table was covered with every luxury the vales of Badenoch, Spey and Lochaber could produce", the health of "George the Third, and long may he reign" was drunk with "as much unfeigned loyalty as ever it was in

London . . . the ladies gave . . . several very delightful Erse songs, nor were the bagpipes silent." But there was more to come.

"At ten o'clock, the company repaired to the terrace adjoining the house, to behold as fine a scene, of its kind, as perhaps ever was exhibited.

"Bonfires in towns are only simple assemblages of inflammable matter, and have nothing but the cause of rejoicing to recommend them; but here, the country people, vying with each other, had gathered together large piles of wood, peat and dry heather on the tops of the different hills and mountains, which, by means of signals, being all lighted at the same time, formed a most awful and magnificent spectacle, representing so many volcanos, which, owing to their immense height, and the night being totally dark and serene, were distinctly seen at a distance of ten miles. And, while our eyes were gratified with this solemn view, our ears were no less delighted with the different bagpipes playing round us; when, after giving three cheers to the king, and same to Mr. Pitt, etc., we returned into the ball-room."

He returned to the inn at Aviemore "highly delighted at having passed a day so very agreeable."

On September 25th, many pike, duck, trout and moorgame later, he dined with Grant of Rothiemurchus, whose "very commodious house", though "not in the best situation", had "a table . . . the most enviable in the world, as is his estate."

Lodging a night at the inn at Grantown, "very neat and clean, and so cheap a bill I scarcely ever met with", he made his way east towards Forres, visiting Castle Brodie, the home of Brodie of Brodie, one of the oldest untitled landed families in Scotland, tracing their ownership back to at least the middle of the eleventh century, and Darnaway Castle. Approaching Forres, he noted the roads "crowded with numbers of the country people, both men and women, who adopt the Lowland fashion, the men not retaining the least mark of the Highland dress, which is entirely exploded, except the bonnet, and even that has a different shape, not near so smart as the Highland; and in their persons they want that lively gait peculiar to a Highlander: nor are the women, in my opinion, better featured." However, the surface of the road on which these plainer people walked was, Thornton conceded, "improved".

At Forres, where his reception at the Falcon Inn won his praise, he noted the enclosed hedges round the fields, and recorded that the land, which was in "a high state of cultivation", let for "three pounds ten shillings to four pounds an acre".

On the road to Elgin, he mused upon the appearance of the three witches in *Macbeth*, advancing his view that they were not, as Shakespeare claimed, fates, but "the Valkyrie of the northern nations, Gunna, Rota and Skulda, the hand-maids of Odin, the active Mars," and styled "the Chusers of the Slain, it being their office in battle to mark those devoted to death", quoting Thomas Gray in support of his then fashionable theory:

"We the reins to slaughter give,
Ours to kill and ours to spare.
Spite of danger he shall live,
(Weave the crimson web of war)."

Elgin, which "in filthiness" exceeded all the towns in the North East, won his admiration for its "few good houses . . . chiefly built over piazzas; it has little trade excepting its great cattle fairs, but is rich in ecclesiastical antiquities. The people here, as in all the little towns on this coast from Inverness, are employed in making thread and linen, as well as woollen cloth, chiefly for their own use." The final destruction of the Cathedral, resulting from the sale of the lead from the roof in 1567 to support the soldiers of the Regent Moray, made Thornton inveigh against "the rude violence of the reformers that reduced it to desolation."

At Castle Gordon, the seat of the Earl of Huntly, built originally in 1501 though with later additions some of which were not quite finished when Thornton arrived with the Duchess of Gordon's brother, Herbert Maxwell, the travellers "found a very large party in the drawing-room. After ten we were entertained with music, and some pretty Erse songs, being the first time I ever heard them accompanied by instruments. We then adjourned to the ball-room, and, after dancing many good reels, strathspeys, and some country dances, retired to supper."

All of which prompted Thornton to reflect: "Nothing surely can be more delightful than this mode of living: it seemed to me a perfect paradise:" which doubtless it was for those privileged few whom the labours of others enabled to enjoy it.

Next day the party divided, some to shoot, others to fish. Thornton was interested to find that the Duke shared his enthusiasm for "the diversion of falconry, and has several fine hawks of the peregrine and gentle falcon species, which breed in the rocks of Glenmore." He was also fascinated by "a true Highland greyhound, which is now become very scarce. It was of a large size, strong, deep chested, and covered with very long and rough hair. This kind was in great vogue in former days, and used in vast numbers at the magnificent stag-chases, by the powerful chieftains."

Breakfast at the Castle was served at nine, and the guests were then marshalled into parties, so that the "day is thus completely enjoyed, not loitered away in total *ennui.*" One of the fellow-guests who certainly disapproved of *ennui* was the Scots judge Lord Monboddo, then is his eighties, yet possessing so much "good natural stamina" that he was "able to undergo the fatigue he sustained" at Castle Gordon "several days together".

Thornton next drove on to Grantown, where the Grant family provided him with plenty of those sports he so energetically pursued. Early in October he was to be found reducing the quantity of wild life around Loch Laggan, before making his way to Moy Hall, the seat of the chief of the Clan Mackintosh. Here, he shot through the heart a roebuck, "the most timid and innocent of all animals."

On 6th October, he entered Inverness, then "a town of considerable magnitude, said to contain about eleven thousand inhabitants. Some of the houses in it are tolerably built, but the streets are narrow and dirty." At that time, "groceries, haberdasheries, hardware, and other necessaries from London" were imported, while cording and sacking were exported, and "linen and woollen cloth" were made for local consumption. Thornton noted that: "The people of Inverness speak both Erse and English; the latter with remarkable purity", erroneously attributing this to the influence of English garrisons instead of to the softening effect of their native Gaelic on the pronunciation of English.

He stayed at a comfortable "modern" inn recently "errected at the expence of a society of gentlemen", rose early next morning, and rode down towards Loch Ness over a road "most execrable, being covered with an infinite number of loose stones, which are dangerous to the rider, and very bad for a carriage." A deluge of rain made the then remarkable (but since reduced) Falls of Foyers worth a diversionary visit. "Waterfalls should always be viewed," Thornton remarked, "from a position at least on a level with the stream or river . . . Seen from above, much of their grandeur is lost", an outlook with which Mrs. Murray would have heartily agreed.

At Fort Augustus, then still a military stronghold though now a religious house, Thornton found the Duke and Duchess of Gordon, with whom next day he had breakfast. Loch Oich, Loch Garry, the house of Glengarry and the site of Locheil House (burnt in 1745, but rebuilt since Thornton's time) engaged his jaunting attentions.

At Fort William, he received "very indistinct and contrary accounts" of his intended route thereafter. He himself is somewhat vague as to how he reached Dunstaffanage Castle, on the south side of Loch Etive. However, he arrived, duly admired, and set out for Dalmally, where he found a ball in progress at the inn. Fourteen couples were dancing "the Glen Orchy kick", whatever it may have been. Thornton did not dance, but observed "that every district of the Highlands has some peculiar cut; and they all shuffle in such a manner as to make the noise of their feet keep exact time." He was much amused by "the arrogance of the master: his mode of marshalling his troops, his directions, and other manoeuvres", which were "truly ridiculous." His own party then "set down to a plentiful, neatly-served supper, and having tasted nothing since breakfast, devoured all before us."

Next morning, he returned to look at Kilchurn Castle, on Loch Awe, "long and waving; its little isles tufted with trees and just appearing above the water." From there, he rode to Inveraray, on Loch Fyne, which inspired him to produce a purple passage perhaps the nearest he ever came in manner to the strains of Augustan verse.

"There never was a spot so judiciously assisted as this has

been, nor was nature ever more profuse; she seems here to have exerted all her powers. Hills vie with woods, whether the clothing or the clothed shall have the pre-eminence. The forms being so regularly and pleasantly broken, that the agreeable variety of shade, in general so much wished for, is found here at every angle; nor is the watery element willing to relinquish her magnificence to the terrestial goddess of the woods, the immensely noble Loch Fine supports the contest, supplying every species of sea-fish, and adds infinite grandeur to the scene, reflecting the different beauties of the surrounding mountains."

At Inveraray Castle, Thornton met other guests, including Lord Stonefield, and enthused over the building, its contents and its grounds. Inveraray itself, that delightful example of the Argyll family's interest in eighteenth century town planning, struck Thornton as being "hardly worth notice", though he allows it to have been "neatly built". With the Marquis of Lorne, the Duke's eldest son, Thornton killed three brace of razorbills.

Driving towards Glencroe, Thornton passed what he called Arkenless, "a temporary residence of Sir James Campbell." There was then under construction a new Ardkinglass, though this structure in its turn has since given place to yet another, by Sir Robert Lorimer.

As Thornton arrived at Tarbet, on Loch Lomond, it "blew a hurricane, which afforded me an opportunity of admiring the dreadful magnificence of the lake, the waves ran mountainous high, and from fresh-water waves breaking so much shorter than salt, they are infinitely more dangerous." He again called on Sir James Colquhoun at Luss—what endless patience the owners of these great houses must have had to put up with the visitations of curious travellers like Thornton!—before proceeding to stay with a Mr. and Mrs. Ruits, who had a house called Bel Retiro, just above the Luss.

Next day, he passed Dumbarton Rock, which looked "quite beautiful", crossed the Firth of Clyde by ferry, and arrived at Finlayston House, near Port Glasgow, where Burns's friend the Earl of Glencairn expected him to dinner.

After taking part in a shooting contest between Lord Eglinton and Lord Thanet on 14th October, Thornton drove to Bothwell Castle, which he thought "exactly in the style, as well as corresponding in magnitude, to the Welch castles."

His host that night was the Duke of Hamilton, who received Thornton in the massive pile that was Hamilton House. The talk was of sport, and next day the Colonel saw the Duke's horses, and Chatelherault, "a very whimsical building in the form of a banqueting house" which survived the parent mansion, taken down in 1927.

After a further three days' shooting, Thornton set out for Edinburgh, travelling by Lanark but visiting the Falls of Clyde on the way. At Edinburgh, he returned to Dun's Hotel. A friend took him to a meeting of the Highland Society, and he had to listen to a pibroch on the bagpipes in "a room much too small for any instrument". However, although he preferred the Northumbrian and Irish pipes, the good Colonel clearly liked folk-music. As for the rest:

"The present style of music is a constant critical attention to labour, art, and trick; the anxiety and *terror* that the performer seems to labour under, destroys that exquisite satisfaction that I admire in more simple compositions.

Another inconveniency arises, which is that the present masters are so totally absorbed, that there is no end of their concertos, which alone make them disgusting to nine-tenths of their audience."

So much for Yorkshire musical appreciation in the hey-day of Haydn and Mozart!

From Edinburgh, Thornton travelled to Kelso, regretting that the time did not permit him to pay his respects to the Duke of Buccleuch at Dalkeith. At Kelso, the races were in progress, and there was "a charming scene of confusions: cooks, writers, servants, and ladies running against each other." He does not tell us where he stayed, but he visited Sir John Vanbrugh's Fleur Castle, built for the First Duke of Roxburgh in 1718, and in the evening attended a ball given by the Caledonian Hunt.

Next day, he drove through Hawick, and heavy rain, to Langholm, staying the night of 23rd October in "the muckle toun", a night of sharp frost that froze the streets. The following morning he passed through Gretna, and crossed back over the border to England. After making a diversion to the Lake District, he arrived home early in November, full of gratitude for the pleasures Scotland, "that romantic country", had afforded him, and inspired by its "highly-varied charms" to write up his notes into a book.

Even at the height of late Victorian times when the Highlands of Scotland became a game-preserve for the rich, few Englishmen can have caught, shot, or otherwise executed so huge a quantity of wild life as did Colonel Thomas Thornton. Certainly, few of the sportsmen who followed his gun-sighting footsteps recorded their pleasure with such honest and infectious enthusiasm.

5

The Wordsworths:
Poet and Journalist

Dorothy and William Wordsworth were two of the five children born to the young attorney John Wordsworth, man of business and "law-agent" to Sir James Lowther, the chief land-owner and political influence of a large area of the County of Cumberland, and Ann Cookson, whose father kept a draper's business in Penrith. These two were married in 1766, and settled in a large house in the High Street of Cockermouth, owned by Sir James. There their children were born: Richard, the eldest, who became a shrewd and cautious lawyer, and later advised his famous brother and sister in their affairs; William, the poet, on April 7th, 1770; Dorothy, his sister and companion, on 25th December, 1771; John, the "silent poet", who became a sea captain, and perished when his ship, *The Earl of Abergavenny* went down with all hands; and lastly, Christopher, who became a scholar, earning distinction in the academic world.

The Wordsworths were a happy family, in spite of financial worries. Although Sir James Lowther was one of the largest and richest landowners in the North of England, he neglected to pay his man of business much of his salary. The Wordsworths were able to exist on the strength of the great man's word, together with the income from the small estate of Sockbridge, between Penrith and Pooley Bridge, which John Wordsworth had heired from his father.

In 1778, four years after the birth of her youngest son, Ann Wordsworth died, possibly of pneumonia contracted as a result of sleeping in a damp bed. The father was inconsolable, and probably never really recovered from this loss. He himself died on December 30th, 1783, after having lost his way on Cold Fell while returning on horseback from a business trip to Millom, and been forced to spend a wintry night on the shelterless hillside.

On their mother's death, the family had been split up when William went to Ann Tyson's school at Hawkshead. After John Wordsworth's death, the Cockermouth home was dispersed. Dorothy was brought up by a cousin on her mother's side, a Miss Threkeld (afterwards Mrs. Rawson), who lived at Halifax. For eight years, the brother and sister did not meet. In due course Wordsworth proceeded to St. John's College, Cambridge. During his first vacation, a reunion with his sister took place when the future poet visited his two guardian uncles at Penrith and Whitehaven. At Penrith, he also met again the friend of his childhood who was one day to become his wife, Mary Hutchinson.

During the following summers, Wordsworth undertook walking tours in Switzerland and Northern Italy. In 1791 he settled in France, absorbed the idealism behind the uprising of the French Revolution, and there met and became the lover of Annette Vallon of Blois, by whom he had a daughter, Caroline. It seems fairly clear that Annette Vallon was deeply in love with Wordsworth. Her intellectual attainments, however, were in no way the equal of the poet's, and her hopes for their marriage were dashed, not only by the complications and separations caused by France's wars, but by Wordsworth's gradual realisation that what had happened had been the expression of a passion generated only by physical attraction.

Already he had made up his mind to dedicate his life to the service of poetry, an ambition which a legacy of nine hundred pounds bequeathed to him by his young friend Raisley Calvert made a little easier to realise. Already he had decided that the mind most in sympathy with his own was that of his sister, Dorothy, whose own dearest wish was to keep house for the brother she so profoundly admired.

The modern reader, confronted with the passionate references made by these two to each other in their early days, can hardly be blamed if he wonders what Freud might have made of such a strange relationship. Yet clearly, it was a "marriage" of two powerful and passionate minds, a unique relationship with no physical implications whatever, and, indeed, expanded from a domestic duet to a trio when in 1802 Wordsworth married Mary Hutchinson.

In the autumn of 1795, the brother and sister made their first home at Racedown, Dorsetshire, where one of their guests was Samuel Taylor Coleridge. A friendship sprung up between the three of them, as a result of which the Wordsworths moved to Alfoxden, near Nether Stowey, in Somersetshire, to be nearer Coleridge. Here, the *Lyrical Ballads* were in part written, and put together to be published in 1778 by Joseph Cottle of Bristol.

That same year Coleridge, unhappily married, neurotic to such a degree that he was frequently physically ill, and already giving signs of that dissipating restlessness which was a by-product of the variegated nature of his great talents, accompanied the Wordsworths to Germany, but soon left them. He went to Göttingen to study the German language and German metaphysics. The Wordsworths spent the winter at Goslar, reputedly the coldest winter of the century, huddled over German stoves.

Early in the spring they returned to England, to spend the summer with their friends the Hutchinsons. In the autumn, Wordsworth and Coleridge embarked on a walking tour through the Lake District, as a result of which Wordsworth decided to settle at Grasmere.

On the shortest day of the year 1799, Dorothy and William arrived at the Town End of Grasmere which, for the next eight years, was to be their home. (The name Dove Cottage was given to it after Wordsworth's time). They had walked from Wensleydale, over the high range of mountains that divide Yorkshire from the Lake District, driven on by icy winds. Here at Grasmere they indulged in that "plain living and high thinking" which satisfied the deepest needs of them both, William suffering nervous pains in the side when composing and relying on the faithful Dorothy to carry out the work of copying out his finished poems. Dorothy herself kept up the detailed journal she had begun when they first set up house together, only reducing it to note form and ultimately giving it up when Wordsworth brought home his bride and there was thus another woman in the home to whom she could confide her thoughts.

William and Mary Hutchinson were married on 6th October, 1802. It was after the safe arrival of their first child, John, on 18th June, 1803, that the brother and sister, accompanied by Coleridge, decided to make their Scottish tour. Mary's sister, Johanna came to keep her company during the six weeks William and Dorothy expected to be away.

There were perhaps three compelling reasons why the Wordsworths should want to visit Scotland. Throughout their childhood, the southern uplands of Scotland must have been visible to them in their walks around Cumberland. The Scottish poet Robert Burns's *Poems Chiefly in the Scottish Dialect*, had been read avidly by William soon after the book appeared in 1786, and indeed were probably a more potent influence on the formation of his own style than any other poet's work, even that of the much admired Crabbe-influenced parson John Langhorne, author of *The Country Justice.* Wordsworth had made a journey to Glasgow by himself in September, 1801, to attend the second marriage of his legal friend Basil Montagu, and had his interest in the Highlands stimulated as a result.

Before they could set out, fifty pounds had to be borrowed from Daniel Stuart, the editor of the *Morning Post*, where some of Wordsworth's poems had first appeared. They bought a horse and a simple Irish carriage in which to make their journey. Coleridge, who accompanied them on part of the tour, described their transport to their common friend Robert Southey:

"We have bought a stout Horse, aged but stout and spirited, and an open vehicle called a Jaunting Car. There is room in it for three on each side, on hanging seats, a Dicky Box for the driver, and a space or hollow in the middle for luggage, or two or three Bairns . . . Your feet are not above a foot, scarcely so much–from the ground, so that you can get off and on while the Horse is moving without the least danger. There are all sorts of Conveniences in it".

This purchase seems to have made William feel it necessary to justify the plan to his lawyer brother, Robert, to whom he wrote:

"Do not imagine we are going to launch out in expense, we expect it will do our health good, and shall travel with one horse only. We do not expect to go into a more expensive house for some time than the one we now occupy and therefore can afford to take this recreation".

Coleridge felt gloomy about the prospect before them. "I never yet commenced a journey with such inauspicious heaviness of heart before," he told Southey, though he hoped that "the exercise and excitement" would be "of so much service as to outweigh the chances of injury from wet and cold".

They set off from Keswick in their Irish Jaunting Car on August 15th "at twenty minutes after eleven o'clock", travelling on the first day to Caldbeck Falls, passing next day the seat of the Bishops of Carlisle, "Rose Castle upon the Caldew, an ancient building of red stone with sloping gardens, an ivied gateway, velvet lawns, old garden walls, trim flower-borders with stately and luxuriant flowers". Dorothy tells us that she and the two poets "walked up to the house and stood some minutes watching the swallows that flew about restlessly, and flung their shadows upon the sunbright walls of the old building; the shadows glanced and twinkled, interchanged and crossed each other, expanded and shrunk up, appeared and disappeared every instant; as I observed to William and Coleridge, seeming more like living things than the birds themselves".

That night they dined at Carlisle and walked upon the city walls, at that time "broken down in places and crumbling away, and most disgusting from filth." Moving on towards Longtown, where they spent the night in the *Graham's Arms* inn, Dorothy reflected on the disappointing impression Carlisle and its environs made on her; "the banks of the river quite flat, and, though the holms are rich, there is not much beauty in the vale from the want of trees."

Next day, they arrived in Scotland, making their way towards Dumfries.

"We enter Scotland by crossing the River Sark; on the Scotch side of the bridge the ground is unenclosed pasturage; it was very green, and scattered over with that yellow flowered plant which we call grunsel; the hills heave and swell prettily enough; cattle feeding; a few cornfields near the river. At the top of the hill opposite is Springfield, a village built by Sir William Maxwell—a dull uniformity in houses, as is usual when all built at one time, or belonging to one individual, each just big enough for two people to live in, and in which a family, large or small as it may happen, is crammed. There the marriages are performed.

"Further on, though almost contiguous, is Gretna Green, upon a hill and among trees. This sounds well, but it is a dreary place; the stone houses dirty and miserable, with broken windows. There is a pleasant view from the churchyard over Solway Firth to the Cumberland mountains. Dined at Annan. On our left as we travelled along appeared the Solway Firth and the mountains beyond, but the near country dreary. Those houses by the roadside which are built of stone are comfortless and dirty; but we peeped into a clay 'biggin' that was very 'canny', and I dare say would be as warm as a swallow's nest in winter. The town of Annan made me think of France and Germany; many of the houses large and gloomy, the size of them outrunning the comforts. One thing which was like Germany pleased me; the shopkeepers expressed their calling by some device or painting; bread-bakers have biscuits, loaves, cakes painted on their window-shutters; blacksmiths horses' shoes, iron tools, etc. etc.; and so on through all trades.

"Reached Dumfries at about nine o'clock–market-day; met crowds of people on the road, and everyone had a smile for us and our car."

The powerful influence Burns had exerted in the formation of Wordsworth's style made them anxious to visit both the last home and the grave of the Scottish poet.

"Went to the churchyard where Burns is buried. A bookseller accompanied us. He showed us the outside of Burns's house, where he had lived the last three years of his life, and where he died. It has a mean appearance, and is in a bye situation, whitewashed; dirty about the doors, as almost all Scotch houses are; flowering plants in the windows.

"Went on to visit his grave. He lies at a corner of the churchyard, and his second son, Francis Wallace, beside him. There is no stone to mark his spot; but a hundred guineas have been collected, to be expended on some sort of monument. 'There,' said the bookseller, pointing to a pompous monument, 'there lies Mr. Such-a-one'–I have forgotten his name–'a remarkably clever man; he was an attorney, and hardly ever lost a cause he undertook. Burns made many a lampoon upon him, and there they rest, as you see'. We looked at the grave with melancholy and painful reflections, repeating to each other his own verses:

Is there a man whose judgment clear
Can others teach the course to steer,
Yet runs himself life's mad career
Wild as the wave?–
Here let him pause, and through a tear
Survey this grave.

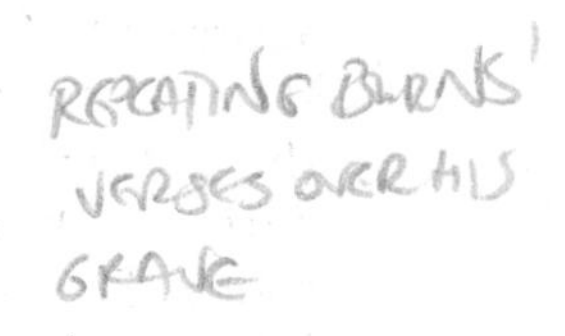

The poor Inhabitant below
Was quick to learn and wise to know,
And keenly felt the friendly glow
And softer flame;
But thoughtless follies laid him low,
And stain'd his name.

"The churchyard is full of grave-stones and expensive monuments in all sorts of fantastic shapes obelisk-wise, pillar-wise etc."

Such was the situation at St. Michael's churchyard in 1803. But it is not the same today; for, as Allan Cunningham tells us, "The body of Burns was not allowed to remain long in this place. To suit the plan of a rather showy mausoleum, his remains were removed into a more commodious spot of the same kirkyard on the fifth July, 1815. The coffin was partly dissolved away; but the dark curly locks of the poet were as glossy, and seemed as fresh, as on the day of his death."

Dorothy noted the Scots custom whereby there was carved "over the graves of married women the maiden name instead of that of the husband, 'spouse' instead of 'wife', and the place of abode preceded by 'in' instead of 'of' ", was followed.

When their guide left them they went back to Burns's house, now a museum, but which was then still occupied by the poet's widow and surviving children.

"Mrs. Burns was gone to spend some time by the sea-shore with her children. We spoke to the servant-maid at the door, who invited us forward, and we sat down in the parlour. The walls were coloured with a blue wash; on one side of the fire was a mahogany desk, opposite to the window a clock, and over the desk a print from the 'Cotter's Saturday Night', which Burns mentions in one of his letters having received as a present. The house was cleanly and neat in the inside, the stairs of stone scoured white, the kitchen on the right side of the passage, the parlour on the left. In the room above the parlour, the poet died, and his son after him in the same room. The servant told us she had lived five years with Mrs. Burns, who was having great sorrow for the death of 'Wallace'. She said that Mrs. Burns's youngest son was at Christs Hospital.

"We were glad to leave Dumfries, which is no agreeable place to them who do not love the bustle of a town, that seems to be rising up to wealth. We could think of little else but poor Burns, and his moving about on that unpoetic ground. In our road to Brownhill, the next stage, we passed Ellisland at a little distance on our right, his farmhouse. We might there have had more pleasure in looking round, if we had been nearer to the spot; but there is no thought surviving in connection with Burns's daily life that is not heart-depressing."

The recent untimely death of a much adored brother poet no doubt had a similar effect on Wordsworth to that which the deaths of the poetic friends listed in his *"Timor mortis conturbat me"* had on William Dunbar. But by 1803 there had been three editions of Dr. James Currie's biography—a fourth appeared that year—which spread the false picture of Burns's last years as "years of decline", during which the poet staggered from one drunken debauch to another, until he toppled into his grave from the effects of alcoholism. Currie was a worthy and interesting man, as R.D. Thornton shows in his study *Dr. James Currie; The Entire Stranger and Robert Burns*. As a firm upholder of that belief so mistakenly called the temperance cause, Currie, perhaps unconsciously, used Burns as a convenient example to back up his "temperance" arguments. It has long since been established beyond dispute that Burns was not a heavy drinker by the standards of his time, and that he died from a form of heart disease brought on in youth by strenuous over-work on his father's ailing farms. The Wordsworths, being themselves frugal people, would no doubt readily accept Currie's presentation of this distorted picture, and in any case had no means of disproving it.

That night they stayed at Brownhill Inn. This was kept by a landlord named Bacon, prompting Burns to improvise:

> *"At Brownhill we always get dainty good cheer*
> *And plenty of bacon each day in the year;*
> *We've a' thing that's nice, and mostly in season–*
> *But why always* Bacon?*–come, tell me a reason?"*

Dorothy, unaware of the existence of this improvisation, wrote:

"I fancied to myself, while I was sitting in the parlour, that Burns might have caroused there, for most likely his rounds extended so far, and this thought gave a melancholy interest to the smoky walls. It was as pretty a room as a thoroughly dirty one could be–a square parlour painted green, but so covered over with smoke and dirt that it looked not unlike green seen through black gauze. There were three windows looking three ways, a buffet ornamented with tea-cups, a super-fine largish looking-glass with gilt ornaments spreading far and wide, the glass spotted with dirt, some ordinary alehouse pictures, and above the chimney-piece a print in a much better style–as William guessed, taken from a painting by Sir Joshua Reynolds–of some lady of quality, in the character of Euphrosyne. 'Ay,' said the servant girl, seeing that we looked at it, 'there's many travellers would give a deal for that, its more admired than any in the house.' We could not but smile; when the rest were such as may be found in the basket of any Italian image and picture hawker.

"William and I walked out after dinner; Coleridge was not well and slept upon the carriage cushions. We made our way to the cottages among the little hills and knots of wood, and then saw what a delightful country this part of Scotland might be made, by planting forest trees. The ground all over heaves and swells like a sea; but for miles there are neither trees nor hedgerows, only 'mound' fences and tracts; or slips of corn, potatoes, clover–with hay between, and barren land; but near the cottages many hills and hillocks covered with wood. We passed some fine trees, and paused under the shade of one close by an old mansion that seemed from its neglected state to be inhabited by farmers. But I must say that many of the 'gentlemen's' houses which we have passed in Scotland have an air of neglect, and even of desolation. It was a beech, in the full glory of complete and perfect growth, very tall, with one thick stem mounting to a considerable height, which was split into four 'thighs', as Coleridge afterwards called them, each in size a fine tree. Passed another mansion, now tenanted by a schoolmaster; many boys playing upon the lawn. I cannot take leave of the country which we passed through today, without mentioning that we saw the Cumberland mountains within half a mile of Ellisland, Burns's house, the last view we had of them. Drayton has prettily described the connection which this neighbourhood has with ours when he makes Skiddaw say

Scurfell[1] *from the sky,*
That Anadale[2] *doth crown, with a most amorous eye,*
Salutes me every day, or at my pride looks grim,
Oft threatning me with clouds, as I oft threatning him.

"These lines recurred to William's memory, and we talked of Burns, and of the prospect he must have had, perhaps from his own door, of Skiddaw and his companions, indulging ourselves in the fancy that we *might* have been personally known to each other, and he have looked upon those objects with more pleasure for our sakes."

Recollecting his feelings long after this experience, and with Currie's strictures possibly still in his mind, William addressed a poem in Burns's own "Standard Habbie" stanza form so-called because it was first used by Francis Robert Sempill of Beltrees for a mock elegy on Habbie Simpson, the town-piper of Kilbarchan, in Renfrewshire, to discountenance that official while he was still very much alive—"To the Sons of Burns, after visiting the grave of their father," in which he gave them some sensible, if poetically flat-footed, advice:

Strong-bodied if ye be to bear
In temperance with less harm beware,
But if your father's wit ye share,
Then, then indeed,
Ye Sons of Burns, for watchful care,
There will be need.

[1] Criffel. [2] Annandale.

Neither of the two other poems inspired by this event, one of which was also written long after the visit, show Wordsworth at anything like his best. But, as so often was William's practice, one of them contains stanzas which versify Dorothy's prose, in this case (unlike the famous "Daffodil" poem) without effecting any improvement in expression or deepening of perception:

I mourned with thousands, but as one
More deeply grieved, for He was gone
Whose light I hailed when first it shone,
And showed my youth
How Verse may build a princely throne
On humble truth.

Alas! where'er the current tends,
Regret pursues and with it blends,–
Huge Criffel's hoary top ascends
By Skiddaw seen,–
Neighbours we were, and loving friends
We might have been;

True friends though diversely inclined;
But heart with heart and mind with mind,
Where the main fibres are entwines,
Through nature's skill,
May even by contraries be joined
More closely still.

The tear will start, and let it flow;
Thou 'poor Inhabitant Below,'
At this dread moment–even so–
Might we together
Have sate and talked where gowans blow,
Or on wild heather.

What treasures would have then been placed
Within my reach; of knowledge graced
By fancy what a rich repast!
But why go on?–
Oh! spare to sweep, thou mournful blast,
His grave grass-grown.

They passed through Thornhill, by the banks of the Nith, turning off through to Vale of Menock towards the remote mining village of Wanlockhead, owned by the Duke of Queensferry. It is to this day a wind-swept place, and the Wordsworths found it even more so then, surrounded, as it was, with isolation:

"Nothing grew upon this ground, or the hills above or below, but heather, yet round about the village—which consisted of a great number of huts, all alike, and all thatched, with a few larger slated houses among them, and a single modern-built one of a considerable size—were a hundred patches of cultivated ground, potatoes, oats, hay and grass. We were struck with the sight of haycocks fastened down with aprons, sheets, pieces of sacking—as we supposed, to prevent the wind from blowing them away. We afterwards found that this practice was very general in Scotland. Every cottage seemed to have its little plot of ground, fenced by a ridge of earth; this plot contained two or three different divisions, kail, potatoes, oats, hay; the houses all standing in lines, or never far apart; the cultivated ground was all together also, and made a very strange appearance with its many greens among the dark brown hills, neither tree nor shrub growing; yet the grass and the potatoes looked greener than elsewhere, owing to the bareness of the neighbouring hills; it was indeed a wild and singular spot—to use a woman's illustration, like a collection of patchwork, made of pieces as they might have chanced to have been cut by the mantua-maker, only just smoothed to fit each other, the different sorts of produce being in such a multitude of plots, and those so small and of such irregular shapes. Add to the strangeness of the village itself, that we had been climbing upwards, though gently, for many miles, and for the last mile and a half up a steep ascent, and did not know of any village till we saw the boys who had come out to play. The air was very cold, and one could not help thinking what it must be in winter when those hills, now 'red brown', should have their three months' covering of snow."

They spent the night in "the house of Mrs. Otto, a widow" at the neighbouring mining village of Leadhills, owned by the Earl of Hopetoun (who, had he been the locally-born poet Allan Ramsay, as lovers of Scottish literature will remember, would have exchanged "all the wealth Hopetoun's high mountains fill" for the love of *The Lass o' Patie's Mill*). It proved to be an informative stay. Dorothy wrote:

"We did not then understand Scotch inns, and were not quite satisfied at first with our accommodations, but all things were smoothed over by degrees; we had a fire lighted in our dirty parlour, tea came after a reasonable waiting; and the fire with the gentle aid of twilight, burnished up the room into cheerful comfort. Coleridge was weary; but William and I walked out after tea. We talked with one of the miners, who informed us that the building which we had supposed to be a school was a library belonging to the village. He said they had got a book into it a few weeks ago, which cost thirty pounds, and that they had all sorts of books. 'What! have you Shakespear?' 'Yes, we have that,' and we found, on further inquiry, that they had a large library, of long standing, that Lord Hopetoun had subscribed liberally to it, and that gentlemen who came with him were in the habit of making larger or smaller donations. Each man who had the benefit of it paid a small sum monthly–I think about fourpence.

"The man we talked with spoke much of the comfort and quiet in which they lived one among another; he made use of a noticeable expression, saying that they were 'very peaceable people considering they lived so much underground',–wages were about thirty pounds a year; they had land for potatoes, warm houses, plenty of coals, and only six hours' work each day, so that they had leisure for reading if they chose. He said the place was healthy, and that the inhabitants lived to a great age; and indeed we saw no appearance of ill-health in their countenances; but it is not common for people working in lead mines to be healthy; and I have since heard that it is not a healthy place. However this may be, they are unwilling to allow it; for the landlady the next morning, when I said to her 'You have a cold climate,' replied, 'Ay, but it is varra *halesome*.' "

Such libraries belonging to self improvement societies in local communities were common in Scotland at the end of the eighteenth century. Burns himself, towards the close of his life, helped in the running of one.

Next day, as Coleridge and the Wordsworths neared

Crawfordjohn, "The air was cold and clear—the sky blue. We walked cheerfully along in the sunshine, each of us alone, only William had the charge of the horse and car, so he sometimes took a ride, which did but poorly recompense him for the trouble of driving. I never travelled with more cheerful spirits than this day. Our road was along the side of a high moor. I can always walk over a moor with a light foot; I seem to be drawn more closely to nature in such places than anywhere else; or rather I feel more strongly the power of nature over me, and am better satisfied with myself for being able to find enjoyment in what unfortunately to many persons is either dismal or insipid. This moor, however, was more than commonly interesting; we could see a long way, and on every side of us were larger or smaller tracts of cultivated land. Some were extensive farms, yet in so large a waste they did but look small, with farm-houses, barns etc., others like little cottages, with enough to feed a cow, and supply the family with vegetables. In looking at these farms we had always one feeling. Why did the plough stop there? Why might not they as well have carried it twice as far? There were no hedgerows near the farms, and very few trees. As we were passing along, we saw an old man, the first we had seen in a Highland bonnet, walking with a staff at a very slow pace by the edge of one of the moorland cornfields; he wore a grey plaid, and his dog was by his side. There was a scriptural solemnity in this man's figure, a sober simplicity which was most impressive. Scotland is the country above all others that I have seen, in which a man of imagination may carve out his own pleasures. There are so many inhabited solitudes, and the employments of the people are so immediately connected with the places where you find them, and their dresses so simple, so much alike, yet, from their being folding garments, admitting of an endless variety, and falling often so gracefully."

This particular virtue of local identity has inevitably disappeared in our age of mass production and improved living standards. Without indulging in facile romanticism at the expense of the social conditions of others, one can perhaps observe that it played a fundamental part in moulding the Scottish character.

After a night at the "large inn" of Douglas Mill, where "a

barefooted lass" looked at them and reported to her mistress, "a remarkably handsome woman", they were shown into "a large parlour" where they ate mutton chops.

On the way to Lanark (which Dorothy always spells with an 'e', in place of the second 'a'), crossing "a moorish tract", they passed a sectarian preacher's stance:

"Not far from the roadside were some benches placed in rows in the middle of a large field, with a sort of covered shed like a sentry-box, but much more like those boxes which the Italian puppet-showmen in London use. We guessed that it was a pulpit or tent for preaching, and were told that a sect met there occasionally, who held that toleration was unscriptural, and would have all religions but their own exterminated. I have forgotten what name the man gave to this sect; we could not learn that it differed in any other respect from the Church of Scotland."

Dorothy was disappointed with her first view of the Clyde. However, they "crossed the river and ascended towards Lanerk, which stands upon a hill. When we were within about a mile of the town, William parted from Coleridge and me, to go to the celebrated waterfalls. Coleridge did not attempt to drive the horse; but led him all the way. We inquired for the best inn, and were told that the New Inn was the best; but they had very 'genteel apartments' at the Black Bull, and made less charges, and the Black Bull was at the entrance of the town, so we thought we would stop there, as the horse was obstinate and weary. But when we came to the Black Bull we had no wish to enter the apartments; for it seemed the abode of dirt and poverty, yet it was a large building. The town showed a sort of French face, and would have done much more, had it not been for the true British tinge of coal-smoke; the doors and windows dirty, the shops dull, the women too seemed to be very dirty in their dress. The town itself is not ugly; the houses are of grey stone, the streets not very narrow, and the market-place decent. The New Inn is a handsome old stone building, formerly a gentleman's house. We were conducted into a parlour, where people had been drinking; the tables were unwiped, chairs in disorder, the floor dirty, and the smell of liquors was most offensive. We were tired, however, and rejoiced in our tea."

Coleridge was unwell, so remained beside a fire in the inn.

William went off to see Bonnington Lynn, one of the Falls of Clyde, but took a wrong turning, and had to be guided to the Linn by a barefooted boy. As a result of this detour he missed Dorothy when she set out to meet him. She, however, came upon David Dale's and Robert Owen's "model" village of New Lanark, and its accompanying cotton mills (later visited and described in the chapter following by Southey,) "the largest and loftiest" she had ever seen. She had "a delicious walk alone through the wood: the sound of the water was very solemn, and even the cotton mills in the fading light of evening had something of the majesty and stillness of natural objects."

Next day, the three of them visited the falls together. Dorothy recorded that she was "much affected by the first view . . . The majesty and strength of the water, for I had never before seen so large a cataract, struck me with astonishment, which died away, giving place to more delightful feelings . . . The waterfall Cora Linn is composed of two falls, with a sloping space, which appears to be about twenty yards between, but is much more. The basin which received the fall is enclosed by noble rocks, with trees, chiefly hazels, birch, and ash growing out of their sides, whenever there is any hold for them; and a magnificent resting-place it is for such a river."

After inspecting the Linn, they "sat upon a bench, placed for the sake of one of these views, whence we looked down upon the waterfall, and over the open country, and saw a ruined tower, called Wallace's Tower, which stands at a very little distance from the fall, and is an interesting object. A lady and gentleman, more expeditious tourists than ourselves, came to the spot; they left us at the seat, and we found them again at another station about the Falls. Coleridge, who is always good-natured enough to enter into conversation with anybody whom he meets in his way, began to talk with the gentleman, who observed that it was a majestic waterfall. Coleridge was delighted with the accuracy of the epithet, particularly as he had been settling in his own mind the precise meaning of the words grand, majestic, sublime, etc., and had discussed the subject with William at some length the day before. "Yes, sir,' says Coleridge, 'it is a majestic waterfall.' 'Sublime and beautiful,' replied his friend. Poor

Coleridge could make no answer, and, not very desirious to continue the conversation, came to us and related the story, laughing heartily."

William later added yet another of his versified versions to the series which eventually appeared as *Memorial of a Tour in Scotland* in 1814, this one, *Composed at Cora Linn,* beginning,

> *Land of the vale! astounding Flood;*
> *The dullest leaf in this thick wood*
> *Quakes—conscious of thy power;*
> *The caves reply with hollow moan;*
> *And vibrates to its central stone,*
> *Yon time-cemented Tower!*

Wallace's connections with Lanark and the surrounding district were of the first importance to Scotland, in that not only did he live in "yon time-cemented Tower," but in 1297, mocked by some of the soldiers of the English garrison as he left church, he sliced the hand from one of them. Escaping to Cartland Crags, he rallied a force of Scots, swept down upon Lanark Castle and overpowered the garrison, slaying the Governor William de Hazelrigg in the course of the action. The battle for Scotland's independence, which ended seventeen years later with the Bruce's victory at Bannockburn, had begun.

Coleridge and the Wordsworths stayed some time at Bonnington Fall, and then went back to the inn at Lanark for lunch.

"The landlord set the first dish upon the table, as is common in England, and we were well waited upon. The first dish was true Scottish—a boiled sheep's head, with the hair singed off; Coleridge and I ate heartily of it; we had barley-broth, in which the sheep's head had been boiled."

After lunch, they arranged for the car to be taken to meet them along the Hamilton road. They themselves had permission from the owner of the grounds in which Cartland Crags were located to visit them. Dorothy found them disappointing:

"We had been told that the Cartland Crags were better worth going to see than the Falls of the Clyde. I did not think so; but I have seen rocky dells resembling this before, with clear water instead of that muddy stream, and never saw anything like the Falls of the Clyde. It would be a delicious spot to have near one's house; one would linger out many a day in the cool shade of the caverns, and the stream would soothe one by its murmuring; still being an old friend, one would not love it the less for its homely face. Even we, as we passed along, could not help stopping for a long while to admire the beauty of the lazy foam, for ever in motion, and never moved away, in a still place of the water, covering the whole surface of it with streaks and lines and ever-varying circles. Wild marjoram grew upon the rocks in great perfection and beauty; our guide gave me a bunch, and said he should come hither to collect a store for tea for the winter, and that it was 'varra halesome'; he drank none else. We walked perhaps half a mile along the bed of the river; but it might *seem* to be much further than it was, owing to the difficulty of the path, and the sharp and many turnings of the glen. Passed two of Wallace's Caves. There is scarce a noted glen in Scotland that has not a cave for Wallace or some other hero."

They rejoined their jaunting car, but left it again to visit the third of the Falls of Clyde (all now somewhat lessened in majesty in that they are harnessed for the provision of electricity), Stonebyres.

"It has not the imposing majesty of Cora Linn; but it has the advantage of being left to itself, a grand solitude in the heart of a populous country, we had a prospect above and below it, of cultivated grounds, with hay-stacks, houses, hills, but the river's banks were lonesome, steep, and woody, with rocks near the fall.

"A little further on, came more into company with the river; sometimes we were close to it, sometimes above it, but always at no great distance; and now the vale became more interesting and amusing. It is very populous, with villages, hamlets, single cottages, or farm-houses embossed in orchards, and scattered over with gentlemen's houses, some of them very ugly, tall and obtrusive, others neat and comfortable. We seemed now to have got into a country where poverty and riches were shaking hands together; pears and apples, of which the crop was abundant, hung over the road, often growing in orchards unfenced; or there might be bunches of broom along the road-side in an interrupted line,

Colonel Thomas Thornton, 1757–1823

Above, Taymouth was associated with all things pleasant by Thornton; *below*, the entrance into Kelso. From Kelso Thornton fished in the Tweed, 'dangerously full of shelves and rapid streams'

that looked like a hedge till we came to it and saw the gaps. Bordering on these fruitful orchards perhaps would be a patch, its chief produce being gorse or broom. There was nothing like a moor or common anywhere; but small plots of uncultivated ground were left high and low, among the potatoes, corn, cabbages, which grew intermingled, now among trees, now bare. The Trough of the Clyde is, indeed, a singular and very interesting region; it is somewhat like the upper part of the vale of Nith but above the Nith is much less cultivated ground–without hedgerows or orchards, or anything that looks like a rich country. We met crowds of people coming from the kirk; the lasses were gaily dressed, often in white gowns, coloured satin bonnets, and coloured silk handkerchiefs, and generally with their shoes and stockings in a bundle hung on their arm. Before we left the river the vale became much less interesting, resembling a poor English country, the fields being large, and unluxuriant hedges.

"It had been dark long before we reached Hamilton, and William had some difficulty in driving the tired horse through the town. At the inn they hesitated about being able to give us beds, the house being brim-full–lights at every window. We were rather alarmed for our accommodations during the rest of the tour, supposing the house to be filled with tourists, but they were in general only regular travellers; for out of the main road from town to town we saw scarcely a carriage, and the inns were empty. There was nothing remarkable in the treatment we met with at this inn, except the lazy inpertinence of the waiter. It was a townish place, with a great larder set out; the house throughout dirty."

Next day, they walked over to Hamilton Palace, the oldest part of which had been built in 1705, much added to in 1803, making it what seemed to Dorothy, "a large building without grandeur, a heavy lumpish mass", and destined to be added to again in 1822, so that it became the largest building in Scotland until that source of wealth which made its Corinthian splendour possible took revenge. Because of undermining, the Palace had to be demolished in 1927.

Alexander, the tenth duke, who built the extensions of 1822, was the son-in-law of the wealthy and eccentric William Beckford, author of the novel *Vathek.* Duke Alexander heired Beckford's library. In addition, the Duke also heired a large collection of pictures bought by his predecessors, one of which was Rubens's *Daniel in the Lions Den,* which Dorothy particularly wanted to see.

The Wordsworths arrived at the Palace only to be met by a surly porter who twice refused them admission. William later relieved his feelings by writing a letter of protest to Lord Archibald Hamilton. Incidentally, on Duke Alexander's death, he was buried in a sarcophagus from Memphis for which he had previously had David Bryce build a magnificent Mausoleum. It is still visited and admired for its wheel mosaic floor in seventy varieties of marble and remarkable echo-throw-back, though the dead Duke no longer rests upon his black marble catafalque but now lies buried in the Bent Cemetery, sarcophagus and all.

On the way from Hamilton to Glasgow, the Wordsworths looked at ruined fourteenth century Bothwell Castle, "the grandest piece of secular architecture that the Middle Ages have bequeathed to us in Scotland", as W. Douglas Simpson called it, "nobly conceived, masterly in design, superbly executed in the finest masonry." Probably the French masons responsible for Château de Courcy were brought over to build Bothwell. Murrays, Douglasses, Ramsays, Bothwells, and Douglasses again, all owned it. It greatly impressed Dorothy:

"The Castle stands nobly, overlooking the Clyde. When we came up to it I was hurt to see that flower-borders had taken place of the natural overgrowings of the ruin, the scattered stones and wild plants. It is a large and grand pile, of red freestone, harmonizing perfectly with the rocks of the river, from which, no doubt, it has been hewn. When I was a little accustomed to the unnaturalness of a modern garden, I could not help admiring the excessive beauty and luxuriance of some of the plants, particularly the purple-flowered clematis, and a broad-leaved creeping plant without flowers, which scrambled up the castle wall along with the ivy, and spread its vine-like branches so lavishly that it seemed to be in its natural situation, and one could not help thinking that, though not self-planted among the ruins of this country, it must somewhere have its natural abode in such places. If Bothwell Castle had not been close to the Douglas mansion we should have been disgusted with the possessor's miserable conception of 'adorning' such a venerable ruin; but it is so very near to the house that of necessity the pleasure grounds must have extended beyond it, and perhaps the neatness of a shaven lawn and the complete desolation natural to a ruin might have made an unpleasing contrast; and besides, being within the precincts of the pleasure grounds, and so very near to the modern mansion of a noble family, it has forfeited in some degree its independent majesty, and becomes a tributary to the mansion; its solitude being interrupted, it has no longer the same command over the mind in sending it back into past times, or excluding the ordinary feelings which we bear about us in daily life. We had then only to regret that the castle and house were so near to each other; and it was impossible not to regret it; for the ruin presides in state over the river, far from city or town, as if it might have had a peculiar privilege to preserve its memorials of past ages and maintain its own character and independence for centuries to come.

"We sat upon a bench under the high trees, and had beautiful views of the different reaches of the river above and below. On the opposite bank, which is finely wooded with elms, and other trees, are the remains of an ancient priory, built upon a rock; and rock and ruin are so blended together that it is impossible to separate the one from the other. Nothing can be more beautiful than the little remnants of this holy place; elm trees—for we were near enough to distinguish them by their branches—grow out of the walls, and overshadow a small but very elegant window. It can scarcely be conceived what a grace the castle and priory impart to each other; and the river Clyde flows on smooth and unruffled below, seeming to my thoughts more in harmony with the sober and stately images of former times, than if it had roared over a rocky channel, forcing its sound upon the ear. It blended gently with the warbling of the smaller birds and chattering of the larger ones that had made their nests in the ruins. In this fortress the chief of the English nobility were confined after the battle of Bannockburn. If a man is to be a prisoner, he scarcely could have a more pleasant place to solace his captivity."

The Douglas classical mansion to which Dorothy refers, quarried from a square north-east tower of the Castle by a

Red Douglas owner, has unfortunately been demolished in our own century. Here, while a visitor, Scott wrote his poem *Young Lochinvar.*

On Monday 22nd August, the Wordsworths arrived at Glasgow, to stay at one of the most famous of Glasgow's eighteenth-century inns. Moving towards the City at walking pace they had ample opportunity of absorbing the distant prospect, and the approaches:

"The suburbs of Glasgow extend very far, houses on each side of the highway–all ugly, and the inhabitants dirty. The roads are very wide; and everything seems to tell of the neighbourhood of a large town. We were annoyed by carts and dirt, and the road was full of people, who all noticed our car in one way or other; the children often sent a hooting after us.

"Wearied completely, we at last reached the town, and were glad to walk, leading the car to the first decent inn, which was luckily not far from the end of the town. William, who gained most of his road-knowledge from ostlers, had been informed of this house by the ostler at Hamilton; it proved quiet and tolerably cheap, a new building–the Saracen's Head. I shall never forget how glad I was to be landed in a little quiet back-parlour, for my head was beating with the noise of carts which we had left, and the wearisomeness of the disagreeable objects near the highway; but with my first pleasant sensations also came the feeling that we were not in an English inn–partly from its half-unfurnished appearance, which is common in Scotland, for in general the deal wainscots and doors are unpainted, and partly from the dirtiness of the floors. Having dined, William and I walked to the post-office, and after much seeking found out a quiet timber-yard wherein to sit down and read our letter. We then walked a considerable time in the streets, which are perhaps as handsome as streets can be, which derive no particular effect from their situation in connexion with natural advantages, such as rivers, sea, or hills. The Trongate, an old street, is very picturesque–high houses, with an intermixture of gable fronts towards the street. The New Town is built of fine stone, in the best style of the very best London streets at the west end of the town, but, not being of brick, they are greatly superior. One thing must strike every stranger in his first walk through Glasgow—an appearance of business and bustle, but no coaches or gentlemen's carriages; during all the time we walked in the streets I only saw three carriages, and these were travelling chaises. I also could not but observe a want of cleanliness in the dress and outside of the whole mass, as they moved along. We returned to the inn before it was dark. I had a bad headache, and was tired, and we all went to bed soon."

Next day, Dorothy explored further, beginning with Glasgow Green:

"A cold morning. Walked to the bleaching-ground[1], a large field bordering on the Clyde, the banks of which were perfectly flat, and the general face of the country is nearly so in the neighbourhood of Glasgow. This field, the whole summer through, is covered with women of all ages, children, and young girls spreading out their linen, and watching it while it bleaches. The scene must be very cheerful on a fine day, but it rained when we were there, and though there was linen spread out in all parts, and great numbers of women and girls were at work, yet there would have been many more on a fine day, and they would have appeared happy, instead of stupid and cheerless. In the middle of the field is a wash-house, whither the inhabitants of this large town, rich and poor, send or carry their linen to be washed. There are two very large rooms, with each a cistern in the middle for hot water; and all round the rooms are benches for the women to set their tubs upon. Both the rooms were crowded with washers; there might be a hundred, or two, or even three; for it is not easy to form an accurate notion of so great a number; however, the rooms were large, and they were both full. It was amusing to see so many women, arms, head, and face all in motion, all busy in an ordinary household employment, in which we are accustomed to see, at the most, only three or four women employed in one place. The women were very civil. I learned from them the regulations of the house; but I have forgotten the particulars. The substance of them is, that 'so much' is to be paid for each tub of water, 'so much' for a tub, and the privilege of washing for a day, and, 'so much' to the general overlookers of the linen, when it is left to be bleached. An old man and woman have

[1] *Glasgow Green*

this office, who were walking about, two melancholy figures.

"The shops at Glasgow are large, and like London shops, and we passed by the largest coffee-room I ever saw. You look across the piazza of the Exchange, and see to the end of the coffee-room, where there is a circular window, the width of the room. Perhaps there might be thirty gentlemen sitting on the circular bench of the window, each reading a newspaper. They had the appearance of figures in a fantoccine, or men seen at the extremity of the opera-house, diminished into puppets.

"I am sorry I did not see the High Church:[1] both William and I were tired, and it rained very hard after we had left the bleaching-ground; besides, I am less eager to walk in a large town than anywhere else; so we put it off, and I have since repented of my irresolution.

"Dined, and left Glasgow at about three o'clock, in a heavy rain."

Some schoolboys were fascinated by the unusual sight of the Wordsworth jaunting car as they drove out westwards through the City, the boys longing to jump aboard it:

"At last, though we were seated, they made several attempts to get on behind; and they looked so pretty and wild, and at the same time so modest, that we wished to give them a ride, and there being a little hill near the end of the town, we got off, and four of them who still remained, the rest having dropped into their homes by the way, took our places, and indeed I would have walked two miles willingly, to have had the pleasure of seeing them so happy. When they were to ride no longer, they scampered away, laughing and rejoicing."

William and Dorothy drove along the North bank of the Clyde to Dumbarton, admiring Erskine House, then the seat of Lord Blantyre, and the prospect down-river. Dorothy and William thought the views reminded them of the views on the Thames in Kent, "which though greatly superior in richness and softness, are much inferior in grandeur."

They reached the inn in Dumbarton just before it became dark, "having pushed on briskly that we might have start of a traveller at the inn, who was following us as fast as he could in a gig."

Even so, they had a moment of anxiety on arrival.

[1] *Glasgow Cathedral*

"Every front room was full, and we were afraid we should not have been admitted. They put us into a little parlour, dirty, and smelling of liquors, the table uncleaned, and not a chair in its place; we were glad, however, of our sorry accommodations.

"While tea was preparing we lolled at our ease, and though the room-window overlooked the stable-yard, and at our entrance there appeared to be nothing but gloom and unloveliness, yet while I lay stretched upon the carriage cushions on three chairs, I discovered a little side peep which was enough to set the mind at work. It was no more than a smoky vessel lying at anchor, with its bare masts, a clay hut and the shelving bank of the river, with a green pasture above. Perhaps you will think that there is not much in this, as I describe it: it is true; but the effect produced by these simple objects, as they happened to be combined, together with the gloom of the evening, was exceedingly wild. Our room was parted by a slender partition from a large dining-room, in which were a number of officers and their wives, who, after the first hour, never ceased singing, dancing, laughing, or loud talking. The ladies sang some pretty songs, a great relief to us. We went early to bed; but poor Coleridge could not sleep for the noise at the street door; he lay in the parlour below stairs. It is no uncommon thing in the best inns of Scotland to have shutting-up beds in the sitting-rooms."

Next day, they inspected the rock on which Dumbarton Castle stands:

"The rock of Dumbarton is very grand when you are close to it, but at a little distance, under an ordinary sky, and in open day, it is not grand, but curiously wild. The castle and fortifications add little effect to the general view of the rock, especially since the building of a modern house, which is white-washed, and consequently jars, wherever it is seen, with the natural character of the place. There is a path up to the house, but it being low water we could walk round the rock, which we resolved to do. On that side next the town green grass grows to a considerable height up the rock, but wherever the river borders upon it, it is naked stone. I never saw rock in nobler masses, or more deeply stained by time and weather; nor is this to be wondered at, for it is in the very eye of sea-storms and land-storms, of mountain winds and water winds. It is of all colours, but a rusty yellow predominates. As we walked along, we could not but look up continually, and the mass above being on every side so huge, it appeared more wonderful than when we saw the whole together.

"We sat down on one of the large stones which lie scattered near the base of the rock, with sea-weed growing amongst them. Above our heads the rock was perpendicular for a considerable height, nay, as it seemed, to the very top, and on the brink of the precipice a few sheep, two of them rams with twisted horns, stood, as if on the look-out over the wide country. At the same time we saw a sentinel in his red coat, walking backwards and forwards between us and the sky, with his forelock over his shoulder. The sheep, I suppose owing to our being accustomed to see them in similar situations, appeared to retain their real size, while, on the contrary, the soldier seemed to be diminished by the distance till he almost looked like a puppet moved with wires for the pleasure of children, or an eight years' old drummer in his stiff, manly dress beside a company of grenadiers. I had never before, perhaps, thought of sheep and men in soldiers' dresses at the same time, and here they were brought together in a strange fantastic way. As will be easily conceived, the fearlessness and stillness of those quiet creatures, on the brow of the rock, pursuing their natural occupations, contrasted with the restless and apparently unmeaning motions of the dwarf soldier, added not a little to the general effect of this place, which is that of wild singularity, and the whole was aided by a blustering wind and a gloomy sky. Coleridge joined us, and we went up to the top of the rock.

"The road to a considerable height is through a narrow cleft, in which a flight of steps is hewn; the steps nearly fill the cleft, and on each side the rocks form a high and irregular wall; it is almost like a long sloping cavern, only that it is roofed by the sky. We came to the barracks; soldiers' wives were hanging out linen upon the rails, while the wind beat about them furiously—there was nothing which it could not set in motion but the garments of the women and the linen upon the rails; the grass—for we had now come to green grass—was close and smooth, and not one pile an inch above another, and neither tree nor shrub. The standard pole stood erect without a flag. The rock has two summits, one much broader and higher than the other. When we were near to the top of the lower eminence we had the pleasure of finding a little garden of flowers and vegetables belonging to the soldiers. There are three distinct and very noble prospects—the first up the Clyde towards Glasgow—Dunglass Castle, seen on its promontory—boats, sloops, hills, and many buildings; the second, down the river to the sea—Greenock and Port Glasgow, and the distant mountains at the entrance of Loch Long; and the third extensive and distant view is up the Leven, which here falls into the Clyde, to the mountains of Loch Lomond. The distant mountains in all these views were obscured by mists and dingy clouds, but if the grand outline of any one of the views can be seen, it is sufficient recompence for the trouble of climbing the rock of Dumbarton."

Passing through the Vale of Leven, they paid the customary tribute at the monument to the Scottish novelist, Tobias Smollett, at Bonhill, and reached the shores of Loch Lomond. Luss was their destination. As they reached the water's edge they came to "just such a place as we had wanted to see. The road was close to the water, and a hill, bare, rocky, or with scattered copses rose above it. A deep shade hung over the road, where some little boys were at play; we expected a dwelling-house of some sort ; and when we came nearer, saw three or four thatched huts under the trees, and at the same moment felt that it was a paradise. We had before seen the lake only as one wide plain of water; but here the portion of it which we saw was bounded by a high and steep, heathy and woody island opposite, which did not appear like an island, but the main shore, and framed out a little oblong lake apparently not so broad as Rydale-water, with one small island covered with trees, resembling some of the most beautiful of the holms of Windermere, and only a narrow river's breadth from the shore. This was a place where we should have liked to have lived, and the only one we had seen near Loch Lomond. How delightful to have a little shed concealed under the branches of the fairy island! The cottages and the island might have been made for pleasure of each other. It was but like a natural garden, the distance was so small; nay, one could not have forgiven any one living there, not compelled to daily labour, if he did not connect it with his dwelling by some feeling of domestic attachment, like what he has for the orchard where his children play. I thought, what a place for William! he might row himself over with twenty strokes of the oars, escaping from the business of the house, and as safe from intruders, with his boat anchored beside him, as if he had locked himself up in the strong tower of a castle. We were unwilling to leave this sweet spot; but it was so simple, and therefore so rememberable, that it seemed almost as if we could have carried it away with us. It was nothing more than a small lake enclosed by trees at the ends and by the way-side, and opposite by the island, a steep bank on which the purple heath was seen under low oak coppice-wood, a group of houses over-shadowed by trees, and a bending road. There was one remarkable tree, an old larch with hairy branches, which sent out its main stem horizontally across the road, an object that seemed to have been singled out for injury where everything else was lovely and thriving, tortured into that shape by storms, which one might have thought could not have reached it in that sheltered place.

"We were now entering into the Highlands. I believe Luss is the place where we were told that country begins; but at these cottages I would have gladly believed that we were there, for it was like a new region. The huts were after the Highland fashion, and the boys who were playing wore the Highland dress and philabeg."

The inn at Luss, then as now, was "a nice-looking white house by the roadside." But in more than a century and a half, its standards of hospitality have improved. When Coleridge and the Wordsworths arrived: "no person came out till we had shouted a considerable time. A barefooted lass showed me up-stairs, and again my hopes revived; the house was clean for a Scotch inn, and the view very pleasant to the lake, over the top of the village—a cluster of thatched houses among the trees with a large chapel in the midst of them. Like most of the Scotch kirks which we had seen, this building resembles a big house; but it is a much more pleasing building than they generally are, and has one of our rustic belfries, not unlike that at Ambleside, with two bells hanging in the open air. We chose one of the back rooms to sit in, being more snug, and they looked upon a very sweet prospect–a stream tumbling down a cleft or glen on the hill-side, rocky coppice ground, a rural lane, such as we have from house to house at Grasmere, and a few out-houses. We had a poor dinner, and sour ale; but as long as the people were civil we were contented.

Coleridge was not well, so he did not stir out, but William and I walked through the village to the shore of the lake. When I came close to the houses, I could not but regret a want of loveliness correspondent with the beauty of the situation and the appearance of the village at a little distance; not a single ornamented garden. We saw potatoes and cabbages, but never a honeysuckle. Yet there were wild gardens, as beautiful as any that man cultivated, overgrowing the roofs of some of the cottages, flowers and creeping plants. How elegant were the wreaths of the bramble that had 'built its own bower' upon the riggins in several parts of the village; therefore we had chiefly to regret the want of gardens, as they are symptoms of leisure and comfort, or at least of no painful industry. Here we first saw houses without windows, the smoke coming out of the open window-places; the chimneys were like stools with four legs, a hole being left in the roof for the smoke, and over that a slate placed upon four sticks–sometimes the whole leaned as if it were going to fall. The fields close to Luss lie flat to the lake, and a river, as large as our stream near the church at Grasmere, flows by the end of the village, being the same which comes down the glen behind the inn; it is very much like our stream–beds of blue pebbles upon the shores.

"We walked towards the head of the lake, and from a large pasture field near Luss, a gentle eminence had a very interesting view back upon the village and the lake and islands beyond. We then perceived that Luss stood in the centre of a spacious bay, and that close to it lay another small one, within the large, where the boats of the inhabitants were lying at anchor, a beautiful natural harbour. The islands, as we look down the water, are seen in great beauty. Inch-ta-vanach, the same that framed out the little peaceful lake which we had passed in the morning, towers above the rest. The lake is very wide here, and the opposite shores not being lofty the chief part of the permanent beauty of this view is among the islands, and on the near shore, including the low promontories of the bay of Luss, and the village; and we saw it under its dullest aspect—the air cold, the sky gloomy, without a glimpse of sunshine.

"On a splendid evening, with the light of the sun diffused over the whole islands, distant hills, and the broad expanse of the lake, with its creeks, bays, and little slips of water among the islands, it must be a glorious sight.

"Up the lake there are no islands; Ben Lomond terminates the view, without any other large mountains; no clouds were upon it, therefore we saw the whole size and form of the mountain, yet it did not appear to me so large as Skiddaw does from Derwent-water. Continued our walk a considerable way towards the head of the lake, and went up a high hill, but saw no other reach of the water. The hills on the Luss side become much steeper, and the lake, having narrowed a little above Luss, was no longer a very wide lake where we lost sight of it.

"Came to a bark hut by the shores, and sate for some time under the shelter of it. While we were here a poor woman with a little child by her side begged a penny of me, and asked where she could 'find quarters in the village.' She was a travelling beggar, a native of Scotland, had often 'heard of that water,' but was never there before. This woman's appearance, while the wind was rustling about us, and the waves breaking at our feet, was very melancholy: the waters looked wide, the hills many, and dark, and far off—no house but at Luss. I thought what a dreary waste must this lake be to such poor creatures, struggling with fatigue and poverty and unknown ways!

"We ordered tea when we reached the inn, and desired the girl to light us a fire; she replied 'I dinna ken whether she'll gie fire' meaning her mistress. We told her we did not wish her mistress to give fire, we only desire her to let *her* make it and we would pay for it. The girl brought the tea-things, but no fire, and when I asked if she was coming to light it, she said 'her mistress was not varra willing to gie fire.' At last, however, on our insisting upon it, the fire was lighted: we got tea by candlelight, and spent a comfortable evening. I had seen the landlady before we went out, for, as had been usual in all the country inns, there was a demur respecting beds, notwithstanding the house was empty, and there were at least half-a-dozen spare beds. Her countenance corresponded with the unkindness of denying us a fire on a cold night, for she was the most cruel and hateful-looking woman I ever saw. She was overgrown with fat, and was sitting with her feet and legs in a tub of water for the dropsy—probably brought on by whisky-drinking. The sympathy which I felt and expressed for her, on seeing her in this wretched condition—for her legs were swollen as thick as mill-posts—seemed to produce no effect; and I was obliged, after five minutes' conversation to leave the affair of the beds undecided. Coleridge had some talk with her daughter, a smart lass in a cotton gown, with a bandeau round her head, without shoes and stockings. She told Coleridge with some pride that she had not spent all her time at Luss, but was then fresh from Glasgow.

"It came on a very stormy night; the wind rattled every window in the house, and it rained heavily. William and Coleridge had bad beds, in a two-bedded room in the garrets, though there were empty rooms on the first floor, and they were disturbed by a drunken man, who had come to the inn when we were gone to sleep."

Next morning, "the sky was bright blue with quick-moving clouds, the hills cheerful, lights and shadows vivid and distinct. The village looked exceedingly beautiful . . . the stream glittering near it, while it flowed under trees through the level fields to the lake."

A boatman rowed them out to Inch-ta-vanach, and they climbed its highest point.

"We had not climbed far before we were stopped by a sudden burst of prospect, so singular and beautiful that it was like a flash of images from another world. We stood with our backs to the hill of the island, which we were ascending, and which shut out Ben Lomond entirely, and all the upper part of the lake, and we looked towards the foot of the lake, scattered over with islands without beginning and without end. The sun shone, and the distant hills were visible, some through sunny mists, others in gloom with patches of sunshine; the lake was lost under the low and distant hills, and the islands lost in the lake, which was all in motion with travelling fields of light, or dark shadows under rainy clouds."

Walking to a different part of the island, the prospect changed.

"Beyond we had the same intricate view as before, and could discover Dumbarton rock with its double head. There being a mist over it, it had a ghost-like appearance—as I observed to William and Coleridge, something like the Tor of Glastonbury from the Dorsetshire hills. Right before us, on the flat island mentioned before, were several small single trees or shrubs, growing at different distances from each other, close to the shore, but some optical delusion had detached them from the land on which they stood, and they had the appearance of so many little vessels sailing along the coast of it. I mention the circumstances, because, with the ghostly image of Dumbarton Castle, and the ambiguous ruin on the small island, it was much in the character of the scene, which was throughout magical and enchanting—a new world in its great permanent outline and composition, and changing at every moment in every part of it by the effect of sun and wind, and mist and shower and cloud, and the blending lights and deep shades which took place of each other, traversing the lake in every direction. The whole was indeed a strange mixture of soothing and restless images, of images inviting to rest, and others hurrying the fancy away into an activity still more pleasing than repose. Yet, intricate and homeless, that is without lasting abiding-place for the mind, as the prospect was, there was no perplexity; we had still a guide to lead us forward."

They drove on to Tarbet. On the way, Dorothy studied Ben Lomond, and concluded that "there was something in this mountain which disappointed me—a want of massiveness and simplicity, perhaps from the top being broken into three distinct stages", a deficiency not present about "the famous Cobbler, near Arrochar, the rocks on the summit distinct in shape as if they were buildings raised up by man, or uncouth images of some strange creature".

Their immediate purpose was to visit the Trossachs—and this before Scott had made them famous with *The Lady of the Lake*—so at the inn in Tarbet, where they were to spend the night, they tried to get some information.

"After tea we made inquiries respecting the best way to go to Loch Ketterine;[1] the landlord could give but little

[1] *Loch Katrine: I have retained all Dorothy's archaic spellings.*

information, and nobody seemed to know anything distinctly of the place, though it was but ten miles off. We applied to the maid-servant who waited on us: she was a fine-looking young woman, dressed in a white bed-gown, her hair fastened up by a comb, and without shoes and stockings. When we asked her about the Trossachs she could give us no information, but on our saying, 'Do you know Loch Ketterine?' she answered with a smile, 'I should know that loch, for I was bred and born there'. After much difficulty we learned from her that the Trossachs were at the foot of the lake, and that by the way we were to go we should come upon them at the head, should have to travel ten miles to the foot of the water, and that there was no inn by the way. The girl spoke English very distinctly; but she had few words, and found it difficult to understand us. She did not much encourage us to go, because the roads were bad, and it was a long way, 'and there was no putting-up for the like of us'. We determined, however, to venture, and throw ourselves upon the hospitality of some cottager or gentleman. We desired the landlady to roast us a couple of fowls to carry with us. There are always plenty of fowls at the doors of a Scotch inn, and eggs are as regularly brought to table at breakfast as bread and butter".

The three of them made a perilous crossing of Loch Lomond in a leaking over-laden rowing-boat, inspected Rob Roy's Caves which, as Dorothy observed, "are not caves at all, but some fine rocks on the brink of the lake, in the crevices of which a man might hide himself cunningly enough", then crossed the hilly road which leads from Loch Lomond to Loch Katrine. It was an exhausting journey.

"Pursued the road, a mountain horse-track, till we came to a corner of what seemed the head of the lake, and there sate down completely tired, and hopeless as to the rest of our journey. The road ended at the shore, and no houses were to be seen on the opposite side except a few widely parted huts, and on the near side was a trackless heath. The land at the head of the lake was but a continuation of the common we had come along, and was covered with heather, intersected by a few straggling foot-paths.

Coleridge and I were faint with hunger, and could go no further till we had refreshed ourselves, so we ate up one of our fowls, and drank of the water of Loch Ketterine; but William could not be easy till he had examined the coast, so he left us, and made his way along the moor across the head of the lake. Coleridge and I, as we sate, had what seemed to us but a dreary prospect—a waste of unknown ground which we guessed we must travel over before it was possible for us to find a shelter. We saw a long way down the lake; it was all moor on the near side; on the other the hills were steep from the water, and there were large coppice-woods, but no cheerful green fields, and no road that we could see; we knew, however, that there must be a road from house to house; but the whole lake appeared a solitude—neither boats, islands, nor houses, no grandeur in the hills, nor any loveliness in the shores. When we first came in view of it we had said it was like a barren Ulswater—Ulswater dismantled of its grandeur, and cropped of its lesser beauties. When I had swallowed my dinner I hastened after William, and Coleridge followed me. Walked through the heather with some labour for perhaps half a mile, and found William sitting on the top of a small eminence, whence we saw the real head of the lake, which was pushed up into the vale a considerable way beyond the promontory where we now sate. The view up the lake was very pleasing, resembling Thirlemere below Armath. There were rocky promontories and woody islands, and, what was most cheering to us, a neat white house on the opposite shore; but we could see no boats, so, in order to get to it we should be obliged to go round the head of the lake, a long and weary way.

After Coleridge came up to us, while we were debating whether we should turn back or go forward, we espied a man on horseback at a little distance, with a boy following him on foot, no doubt a welcome sight, and we hailed him. We should have been glad to have seen either man, woman or child at this time, but there was something uncommon and interesting in this man's appearance, which would have fixed our attention wherever we had met him. He was a complete Highlander in dress, figure, and face, and a very fine-looking man, hardy and vigorous though past his prime. While he stood waiting for us in his bonnet and plaid which never look more graceful than on horseback, I forgot our errand, and only felt glad that we were in the Highlands. William accosted him with, 'Sir, do you speak English?' He replied, 'A little'. He spoke however, sufficiently well for our purpose, and very distinctly, as all Highlanders do who learn English as a foreign language; but in a long conversation they want words; he informed us that he himself was going beyond the Trossachs, to Callander, that no boats were kept to 'let'; but there were two gentlemen's houses at this end of the lake, one of which we could not yet see, it being hidden from us by a part of the hill on which we stood. The other house was that which we saw opposite to us; both the gentlemen kept boats, and probably might be able to spare one of their servants to go with us. After we had asked many questions, which the Highlander answered with patience and courtesy, he parted from us, going along a sort of horse-track, which a foot-passenger, if he once get into it, need not lose if he be careful.

"When he was gone we again debated whether we should go back to Tarbet, or throw ourselves upon the mercy of one of the two gentlemen for a night's lodging. What we had seen of the main body of the lake made us little desire to see more of it; the Highlander upon the naked heath, in his Highland dress, upon his careful-going horse, with the boy following him, was worth it all; but after a little while we resolved to go on, ashamed to shrink from adventure."

They had begun their journey that day about eleven o'clock in the morning. They reached the "gentleman's house" between five and six in the evening. Half a dozen people were working in the field surrounding the house when William spoke to one who appeared to be in charge of them. Dorothy, reporting the encounter, could not perhaps appreciate the astonishment which the sight of two poets and a young woman would arouse in the minds of these isolated Gaelic-speaking people as her brother began to explain why they had come.

"All drew near him, staring at William as nobody could have stared but out of sheer rudeness, except in such a lonely place. He told his tale, and inquired about boats; there were no boats, and no lodging nearer than Callander, ten miles beyond the foot of the lake. A laugh was on every face when William said we were come to see the Trossachs; no doubt they thought we had better have stayed at our own homes.

William endeavoured to make it appear not so very foolish, by informing them that it was a place much celebrated in England, though perhaps little thought of by them, and that we only differed from many of our countrymen in having come the wrong way in consequence of an erroneous direction.

"After a little time the gentleman said we should be accommodate with such beds as they had, and should be welcome to rest in their house if we pleased. William came back for Coleridge and me; the men all stood at the door to receive us, and now their behaviour was perfectly courteous. We were conducted into the house by the same man who had directed us hither on the other side of the lake, and afterwards we learned that he was the father of our hostess. He showed us into a room up-stairs, begged we would sit at our ease, walk out, or do just as we pleased. It was a large square deal wainscoted room, the wainscot black with age, yet had never been painted: it did not look like an English room, and yet I do now know in what it differed, except that in England it is not common to see so large and well-built a room so ill-furnished: there were two or three large tables, and a few old chairs of different sorts, as if they had been picked up one did not know how, at sales, or had belonged to different rooms of the house ever since it was built. We sat perhaps three-quarters of an hour, and I was about to carry down our wet coffee and sugar and ask leave to boil it, when the mistress of the house entered, a tall fine-looking woman, neatly dressed in a dark-coloured gown, with a white handkerchief tied round her head; she spoke to us in a very pleasing manner, begging permission to make tea for us, an offer which we thankfully accepted. Encouraged by the sweetness of her manners, I went down-stairs to dry my feet by the kitchen fire; she lent me a pair of stockings, and behaved to me with the utmost attention and kindness. She carried the tea-things into the room herself, leaving me to make tea, and set before us cheese and butter and barley cakes. These cakes are as thin as our oat-bread, but, instead of being crisp, are soft and leathery, yet we, being hungry, and the butter delicious, ate them with great pleasure, but when the same bread was set before us afterwards we did not like it.

"After tea William and I walked out; we amused ourselves with watching the Highlanders at work: they went leisurely about everything, and whatever was to be done, all followed, old men, and young, and little children. We were driven into the house by a shower, which came on with the evening darkness, and the people leaving their work paused at the same time. I was pleased to see them a while after sitting round a blazing fire in the kitchen, father and son-in-law, master and man, and the mother with her little child on her knee. When I had been there before tea I had observed what a contrast there was between the mistress and her kitchen, she did not differ in appearance from an English country lady; but her kitchen, roof, walls, and floor of mud, was all black alike; yet now, with the light of a bright fire upon so many happy countenances, the whole room made a pretty sight.

"We heard the company laughing and talking long after we were in bed; indeed I believe they never work till they are tired. The children could not speak a word of English: they were very shy at first; but after I had caressed the eldest, and given her a red leather purse, with which she was delighted, she took hold of my hand and hung about me, changing her side-long looks for pretty smiles. Her mother lamented they were so far from school, they should be obliged to send the children down into the Lowlands to be taught reading and English. Callender, the nearest town, was twenty miles from them, and it was only a small place: they had their groceries from Glasgow."

Mrs. Macfarlane, their hostess, assured them they would sleep on blankets "fresh from the fauld", and in the morning brought them in whey, the best Dorothy had ever tasted, before they got up. For breakfast, they had tea with "plenty of butter and barley-cakes, and fresh baked oaten cakes . . . kneaded with cream", and a cheese was laid on the table. Over the meal, they listened to tales of Rob Roy, he "being as famous here as ever Robin Hood was in the Forest of Sherwood; *he* also robbed from the rich, giving to the poor, and defending them from oppression."

Thanking their kind hostess and her family, they left the sheep farm to walk three miles, where, they had been told, a man would row them to the Trossachs. On the way, they passed a burial ground near a white house. "It was in a sloping green field among woods", Dorothy noted, "and within sound of the beating of the water against the shore, if there were but a gentle breeze to stir it: I thought if I lived in that house, and my ancestors and kindred were buried there, I should sit many an hour under the walls of this plot of earth, where all the household would be gathered together."

They arrived at the boatman's hut while he was out working in the fields, so they sheltered round his fire.

"This was the first genuine Highland hut we had been in. We entered by the cow-house, the house-door being within, at right angles to the outer door. The woman was distressed that she had a bad fire, but she heaped up some dry peats and heather, and, blowing it with her breath, in a short time raised a blaze that scorched us into comfortable feelings. A small part of the smoke found its way out of the hole of the chimney, the rest through the open window-places, one of which was within the recess of the fireplace, and made a frame to a little picture of the restless lake and the opposite shore, seen when the outer door was open. The woman of the house was very kind: whenever we asked her for anything it seemed a fresh pleasure to her that she had it for us; she always answered with a sort of softening down of the Scotch exclamation, 'Hoot!' 'Ho!' yes, ye'll get that', and hied to her cupboard in the spence.' "

Coleridge was afraid that he might catch cold in the boat, so decided to walk round the end of the loch. William fell asleep in the bottom of the boat. It was thus on Dorothy's gaze that the loveliness of the Trossachs in Autumn first made its impact.

"After turning a rocky point we came to a bay closed in by rocks and steep woods, chiefly of full-grown birch. The lake was elsewhere ruffled, but at the entrance of this bay the breezes sunk, and it was calm: a small island was near, and the opposite shore, covered with wood, looked soft through the misty rain. William, rubbing his eyes, for he had been asleep, called out that he hoped I had not let him pass by anything that was so beautiful as this; and I was glad to tell him that it was but the beginning of a new land. After we had left this bay we saw before us a long reach of woods and rocks and rocky points, that promised other bays more beautiful than what we had passed . . .

"The second bay we came to differed from the rest; the hills retired a short space from the lake, leaving a few level fields between, on which was a cottage embosomed in trees: the bay was defended by rocks at each end, and the hills behind made a shelter for the cottage, the only dwelling, I believe, except one, on this side of Loch Ketterine. We now came to steeps that rose directly from the lake, and passed by a place called in the Gaelic the Den of the Ghosts,[1] which reminded us of Lodore; it is a rock, or mass of rock, with a stream of large black stones like the naked or dried-up bed of a torrent down the side of it; birch-trees start out of the rock in every direction, and cover the hill above, further than we could see. The water of the lake below was very deep, black, and calm. Our delight increased as we advanced, till we came in view of the termination of the lake, seeing where the river issues out of it through a narrow chasm between the hills.

"Here I ought to rest, as we rested, and attempt to give utterance to our pleasure: but indeed I can impart but little of what we felt. We were still on the same side of the water, and, being immediately under the hill, within a considerable bending of the shore, we were enclosed by hills all round, as if we had been upon a smaller lake of which the whole was visible. It was an entire solitude; and all that we beheld was the perfection of loveliness and beauty.

"We had been through many solitary places since we came into Scotland, but this place differed as much from any we had seen before, as if there had been nothing in common between them; no thought of dreariness or desolation found entrance here; yet nothing was to be seen but water, wood, rocks, and heather, and bare mountains above. We saw the mountains by glimpses as the clouds passed by them, and were not disposed to regret, with our boatman, that it was not a fine day, for the near objects were not concealed from us, but softened by being seen through the mists. The lake is not very wide here, but appeared to be much narrower than it really is, owing to the many promontories, which are pushed so far into it that they are much more like islands than promontories. We had a longing desire to row to the outlet and look up into the narrow passage through which the river went; but the point where we were to land was on

[1] *Goblins' Cave*

the other side, so we bent our course right across, and just as we came in sight of two huts, which have been built by Lady Perth as a shelter for those who visit the Trossachs, Coleridge hailed us with a shout of triumph from the door of one of them, exulting in the glory of Scotland".

They walked through the pass at the foot of Loch Katrine, and saw Loch Achray.

"At the opening of the pass we climbed up a low eminence, and had an unexpected prospect suddenly before us–another lake, small compared with Loch Ketterine, though perhaps four miles long, but the misty air concealed the end of it. The transition from the solitary wildness of Loch Ketterine and the narrow valley or pass to this scene was very delightful: it was a gentle place, with lovely open bays, one small island, corn fields, woods, and a group of cottages. This vale seemed to have been made to be tributary to the comforts of man, Loch Ketterine for the lonely delight of Nature, and kind spirits delighting in beauty. The sky was grey and heavy,–floating mists on the hill-sides, which softened the objects, and where we lost sight of the lake it appeared so near to the sky that they almost touched one another, giving a visionary beauty to the prospect. While we overlooked this quiet scene we could hear the stream rumbling among the rocks between the lakes, but the mists concealed any glimpse of it which we might have had".

On their way back, it rained heavily, and they were wet and very tired when eventually they arrived back at the Macfarlanes' sheep farm.

"The good woman had provided, according to her promise, a better fire than we had found in the morning; and indeed when I sate down in the chimney-corner of her smoky biggin' I thought I had never been more comfortable in my life. Coleridge had been there long enough to have a pan of coffee boiling for us, and having put our clothes in the way of drying, we all sate down, thankful for a shelter. We could not prevail upon the man of the house to draw near the fire, though he was cold and wet, or to suffer his wife to get him dry clothes till she had served us, which she did, though most willingly, not very expeditiously. A Cumberland man of the same rank would not have had such a notion of what was fit and right in his own house, or if he had, one would have accused him of servility; but in the Highlander it only seemed like politeness, however erroneous and painful to us, naturally growing out of the dependence of the inferiors of the clan upon their laird; he did not, however, refuse to let his wife bring out the whisky-bottle at our request: 'She keeps a dram', as the phrase is; indeed, I believe there is scarcely a lonely house by the wayside in Scotland where travellers may not be accommodated with a dram. We asked for sugar, butter, barley-bread, and milk, and with a smile and a stare more of kindness than wonder, she replied, 'Ye'll get that', bringing each article separately.

"We caroused our cups of coffee, laughing like children at the strange atmosphere in which we were: the smoke came in gusts, and spread along the walls and above our heads in the chimney, where the hens were roosting like light clouds in the sky. We laughed and laughed again, in spite of the smarting of our eyes, yet had a quieter pleasure in observing the beauty of the beams and rafters gleaming between the clouds of smoke. They had been crusted over and varnished by many winters, till, where the firelight fell upon them, they were as glossy as black rocks on a sunny day cased in ice. When we had eaten our supper we sate about half an hour, and I think I had never felt so deeply the blessing of a hospitable welcome and a warm fire".

On Sunday 28th August, they set out over the hill road back to Loch Lomond, in heavy rain. In the ferry house at Inversnaid, they dried their clothes while they waited for the boat to come back with a party of churchgoers. The ferryman's sister, who received them along with her sister-in-law, made a memorable impression on them.

"One of the girls was exceedingly beautiful; and the figures of both of them, in grey plaids falling to their feet, their faces only being uncovered, excited our attention before we spoke to them; but they answered us so sweetly that we were quite delighted, at the same time that they stared at us with an innocent look of wonder. I think I never heard the English language sound more sweetly than from the mouth of the elder of these girls, while she stood at the gate answering our inquiries, her face flushed with the rain; her pronunciation was clear and distinct: without difficulty, yet slow, like that of a foreign speech".

Not long after William returned home from the Scottish tour, the recollection of that girl inspired his poem *To a Highland Girl. At Inversneyde upon Loch Lomond,*

Sweet Highland Girl, a very shower
Of beauty is thy earthly dower!
Twice seven consenting years have shed
Their utmost bounty on thy head:
And these grey rocks; this household lawn;
These trees, a veil just half withdrawn;
This fall of water, that doth make
A murmur near the silent Lake;
This little Bay, a quiet road
That holds in shelter thy abode;
In truth together ye do seem
Like something fashion'd in a dream;
Such forms as from their covert peep
When earthly cares are laid asleep!
Yet, dream and vision as thou art,
I bless thee with a human heart:
God shield thee to thy latest years!
I neither know thee nor thy peers;
And yet my eyes are filled with tears. . .

That night, back at Tarbet, they asked to have "a broiled fowl, a dish very common in Scotland, to which the mistress replied, 'Would not a boiled one do as well?' " When the fowl made its appearance, "it proved a cold one that had been stewed in the broth at dinner".

Next morning, Dorothy and Coleridge set out on foot to go to Arrochar, on Loch Long, while William followed with the horse and jaunting car. Over lunch, the landlord of the New Inn told them that he was fully booked for the night, so they left Arrochar at four o'clock in the afternoon. Coleridge accompanied them for a little way, and then decided that he wanted to go back to Tarbet and make for Edinburgh. (After he left the Wordsworths, he in fact made his own way on foot as far north as Glencoe.) Dorothy and William were used to his bouts of ill health and his increasing fits of waywardness: but as they travelled together round the northern shore of Loch Long, into Glencoe, though "the stillness of the mountains, the motion of the waves, the streaming torrents, the sea-birds, the fishing-boats were all melancholy", they were aware that their reactions were subjective ones.

"Our thoughts were full of Coleridge, and when we were enclosed in the narrow dale, with a length of winding road before us, a road that seemed to have insinuated itself into the very heart of the mountains–the brook, the road, bare hills, floating mists, scattered stones, rocks, and herds of black cattle being all that we could see–I shivered at the thought of his being sickly and alone, travelling from place to place".

As they reached the summit of "Rest and be Thankful", the rain blew itself out, and they were able to enjoy the view down the valley out of which they had just climbed. As they descended into Glen Kinglas:

"We now saw the western sky, which had hitherto been hidden from us by the hill–a glorious mass of clouds uprising from a sea of distant mountains, stretched out in length before us, towards the west–and close by us was a small lake or tarn. From the reflection of the crimson clouds the water appeared of deep red, like melted rubies, yet with a mixture of a grey or blackish hue: the gorgeous light of the sky, with the singular colour of the lake, made the scene exceedingly romantic; yet it was more melancholy than cheerful. With all the power of light from the clouds, there was an overcasting of the gloom of evening, a twilight upon the hills".

At Cairndow, they were well received, and given Loch Fyne herring for breakfast next morning before they set out for Inveraray. Dorothy admired the approaching prospect of the place.

"Our road wound round the semicircular shore, crossing two bridges of lordly architecture. The town looked pretty when we drew near to it in connexion with its situation, different from any place I had ever seen, yet exceedingly like what I imaged to myself from representations in raree-shows, or pictures of foreign places–Venice, for example–painted on the scene of a play-house, which one is apt to fancy are as cleanly and gay as they look through the magnifying-glass of the raree-show or in the candle-light dazzle of a theatre. At the door of the inn, though certainly the buildings had not that delightful outside which they appeared to have at a distance, yet they looked very pleasant. The range bordering

on the water consisted of little else than the inn, being a large house, with very large stables, the county gaol, the opening into the main street into the town, and an arched gateway, the entrance into the Duke of Argyle's private domain".

Dorothy dismissed Inveraray Castle, the work of Roger Morris and Robert Mylne, which contained, and still does, not only interesting pictures but Highland reliques of the kind she would have liked to see, rather too cursorily.

"Walked through avenues of tall beech-trees, and observed some that we thought even the tallest we had ever seen; but they were all scantily covered with leaves, and the leaves exceedingly small—indeed, some of them, in the most exposed situations, were almost bare, as if it had been winter. Travellers who wish to view the inside of the Castle send in their names, and the Duke appoints the time of their going; but we did not think that what we should see would repay us for the trouble, there being no pictures, and the house, which I believe has not been built above half a century, is fitted up in the modern style. If there had been any reliques of the ancient costume of the castle of a Highland chieftain, we should have been sorry to have passed it.

"Sate after dinner by the fireside till near sunset, for it was very cold, though the sun shone all day. At the beginning of this our second walk we passed through the town, which is but a doleful example of Scotch filth. The houses are plastered or rough-cast, and washed yellow—well built, well sized, and sash-windowed, bespeaking a connexion with the Duke, such a dependence as may be expected in a small town so near to his mansion; and indeed he seems to have done his utmost to make them comfortable, according to our English notions of comfort: they are fit for the houses of people living decently upon a decent trade; but the windows and doorsteads were as dirty as in a dirty by-street of a large town, making a most unpleasant contrast with the comely face of the buildings towards the water, and the ducal grandeur and natural festivity of the scene. Smoke and blackness are the wild growth of a Highland hut: the mud floors cannot be washed, the door-steads are trampled by cattle, and if the inhabitants be not very cleanly it gives one little pain; but dirty people living in two-storied stone houses, with dirty sash windows, are a melancholy spectacle anywhere, giving the notion either of vice or the extreme of wretchedness".

Today, the "extreme of wretchedness" long since alleviated by an improved social conscience, Inveraray is now rightly regarded as a splendid piece of Georgian planning, its broad Main Street uncompromisingly Scottish in character and a worthy monument to the vision of the third Duke of Argyll, who commissioned both castle and the town as it now stands. The church at the head of Main Street is presently without its steeple, which Dorothy thought elegantly "overtopped" the town. It was dismantled when heavy traffic during the Second World War was thought to have dangerously weakened it. It is much to be hoped that the restoration of the town, being undertaken in our own day on a Government grant, will eventually include the rebuilding of this steeple.

From Inveraray, the Wordsworths set out for Loch Awe. They stopped at Cladich so that their horse should have "a sixpenny feed of miserable corn", while they had "skimmed milk, oat-bread, porridge, and blue milk cheese", then got a man to row them out onto the loch. Afterwards, they came upon Kilchurn Castle, at that time still islanded but now surrounded merely by marsh. A Campbell stronghold, it was built about 1440 by Sir Colin Campbell, the founder of the Breadalbane family, and added to in the seventeenth and eighteenth centuries. It was offered as a garrison to the Hanoverian troops. In 1879, the same gale that blew down the Tay Bridge brought down one of its tower tops, so it was more impressive when the Wordsworths saw it than it is today.

Dorothy remarked: "We were very lucky in seeing it after a great flood; for its enchanting effect was chiefly owing to its situation in the lake, a decayed palace rising out of the plain of waters! . . . William, addressing himself to the ruin, poured out these verses". "These verses were his *Address to Kilchurn Castle,* which begin.

Child of loud-throated War! the mountain Stream
Roars in thy hearing; but thy hour of rest
Is come, and thou art silent in thy age;
Save when the wind sweeps by and sounds are caught
Ambiguous, neither wholly thine nor theirs . . .

A gentleman who rode on "a beautiful white pony" overtook them, advised them to travel to Glencoe by way of Loch Etive. This they decided to do.

Next day, as they approached the Pass of Awe, Dorothy noticed "a sight always painful to me—two or three women, each creeping after her single cow, while it was feeding on the slips of grass between the corn-grounds".

Getting their horse and jaunting car over the mouth of Loch Etive provided them with an alarming adventure.

"Four or five men came over with the boat; the horse was unyoked, and being harshly driven over rough stones, which were as slippery as ice, with slimy seaweed, he was in terror before he reached the boat, and they completed the work by beating and pushing him by main force over the ridge of the boat, for there was no open end, or plank, or any other convenience for shipping either horse or carriage. I was very uneasy when we were launched on the water. A blackguard-looking fellow, blind of one eye, which I could not but think had been put out in some strife or other, held him by force like a horse-breaker, while the poor creature fretted and stamped with his feet against the bare boards, frightening himself more and more with every stroke; and when we were in the middle of the water I would have given a thousand pounds to have been sure that we should reach the other side in safety. The tide was rushing violently in, making a strong eddy with the stream of the loch, so that the motion of the boat and the noise and foam of the waves terrified him still more, and we thought it would be impossible to keep him in the boat, and when we were just far enough from the shore to have been all drowned he became furious, and, plunging desperately, his hind-legs were in the water, then, recovering himself, he beat with such force against the boat-side that we were afraid he should send his feet through. All the while the men were swearing terrible oaths, and cursing the poor beast, redoubling their curses when we reached the landing-place, and whipping him ashore in brutal triumph.

"We had only room for half a heartful of joy when we set foot on dry land, for another ferry was to be crossed five miles further. We had intended breakfasting at this house if it had been a decent place; but after this affair we were glad to pay the men off and depart, though I was not well and needed refreshment. The people made us more easy by assuring us that we might easily swim the horse over the next ferry. The first mile or two of our road was over a peat-moss; we then came near to the sea-shore, and had beautiful views backwards towards the Island of Mull and Dunstaffnage Castle, and forward where the sea ran up between the hills".

The ferrying of the horse was an operation not to be repeated, they decided when they reached Loch Creran: "a large irregular sea loch, with low sloping banks, coppice woods, and uncultivated grounds, with a scattering of corn fields; as it appeared to us, very thinly inhabited: mountains at a distance. We found only women at home at the ferry-house. I was faint and cold, and went to sit by the fire, but, though very much needing refreshment, I had not heart to eat anything there—the house was so dirty, and there were so many wretchedly dirty women and children; yet perhaps I might have got over the dirt, though I believe there are few ladies who would not have been turned sick by it, if there had not been a most disgusting combination of laziness and coarseness in the countenances and manners of the women, though two of them were very handsome. It was a small hut, and four women were living in it: one, the mother of the children and mistress of the house; the others I supposed to be lodgers, or perhaps servants; but there was no work amongst them. They had just taken from the fire a great pan full of potatoes, which they mixed up with milk, all helping themselves out of the same vessel, and the little children put in their dirty hands to dig out of the mess at their pleasure. I thought to myself, how light the labour of such a house as this! Little sweeping, no washing of floors, and as to scouring the table, I believe it was a thing never thought of.

"After a long time the ferryman came home; but we had to wait yet another hour for the tide. In the meanwhile our horse took fright in consequence of his terror at the last ferry, ran away with the car, and dashed out umbrellas, greatcoats, etc.: but luckily he was stopped before any serious mischief was done. We had determined, whatever it cost, not to trust ourselves with him again in the boat; but sending him round the lake seemed almost out of the question, there being no road, and probably much difficulty in going round with a horse; so after some deliberation with the ferryman it was agreed that he should swim over. The usual place of ferrying was very broad, but he was led to the point of a peninsula at a little distance. It being an unusual affair–indeed, the people of the house said that he was the first horse that had ever swum over–we had several men on board, and the mistress of the house offered herself as an assistant: we supposed for the sake of a share in eighteen-pennyworth of whisky which her husband called for without ceremony, and of which she and the young lasses, who had helped to push the boat into the water, partook as freely as the men. At first I feared for the horse: he was frightened, and strove to push himself under the boat; but I was soon tolerably easy, for he went on regularly and well, and after from six to ten minutes swimming landed in safety on the other side. Poor creature! he stretched his nostrils and stared wildly while the man was trotting him about to warm him, and when he put him into the car he was afraid of the sound of the wheels."

By lunch-time, they had reached Portnacroish.

"It is a small village–a few huts and an indifferent inn by the side of the loch. Ordered a fowl for dinner, had a fire lighted, and went a few steps from the door up the road, and turning aside into a field stood at the top of a low eminence, from which, looking down the loch to the sea through a long vista of hills and mountains, we beheld one of the most delightful prospects that, even when we dream of fairer worlds than this, it is possible for us to conceive in our hearts. A covering of clouds rested on the long range of the hills of Morven, mists floated very near to the water on their sides, and were slowly shifting about: yet the sky was clear, and the sea, from the reflection of the sky, of an ethereal or sapphire blue, which was intermingled in many places, and most by gentle graduations, with beds of bright dazzling sunshine; green islands lay on the calm water, islands far greener, for so it seemed, than the grass of other places; and from their excessive beauty, their unearthly softness, and the great distance of many of them, they made us think of the islands of the blessed in the Vision of Mirza–a resemblance more striking from the long tract of mist which rested on the top of the steeps of Morven."

When they arrived at Ballachulish inn, where they had the

usual difficulty in persuading the landlady to light a fire for them, they discovered that Coleridge had been there three days before them. By moonlight, Ballachulish appeared "exceedingly wild". In the morning, Dorothy was disappointed, having mistaken "cornfields for naked rocks", and thought the hills more lofty than they really were.

On Saturday, 3rd September, having risen at six o'clock and taken "a basin of milk" for breakfast, they set out for Glencoe: "a delightful morning, the road excellent, and so we were in good spirits, happy that we had no more ferries to cross". But their difficulties with the horse were not yet over; for, as they walked up the shore of Loch Leven:

"We travelled close to the water's edge, and were rolling along a smooth road, when the horse suddenly backed, frightened by the upright shafts of a roller rising from behind the wall of a field adjoining the road. William pulled, whipped, and struggled in vain; we both leapt upon the ground, and the horse dragged the car after him, he going backwards down the bank of the loch, and it was turned over, half in the water, the horse lying on his back, struggling in the harness, a frightful sight! I gave up everything; thought that the horse would be lamed, and the car broken to pieces. Luckily a man came up in the same moment, and assisted William in extricating the horse, and, after an hour's delay, with the help of strings and pocket-handkerchiefs, we mended the harness and set forward again, William leading the poor animal all the way, for the regular beating of the waves frightened him, and any little gushing stream that crossed the road would have sent him off. The village where the blacksmith lived was before us—a few huts under the mountains, and, as it seemed, at the head of the loch; but it runs further up to the left, being narrowed by a hill above the village, near which, at the edge of the water, was a slate quarry, and many large boats with masts, on the water below, high mountains shutting in the prospect, which stood in single, distinguishable shapes, yet clustered together—simple and bold in their forms, and their surfaces of all characters and all colours—some that looked as if scarified by fire, others green; and there was one that might have been blasted by an eternal frost, its summit and sides for a considerable way down being as white as hoar-frost at eight o'clock on a winter's morning. No clouds were on the hills; the sun shone bright, but the wind blew fresh and cold.

"When we reached the blacksmith's shop, I left William to help to take care of the horse, and went into the house. The mistress, with a child in her arms and two or three running about, received me very kindly, making many apologies for the dirty house, which she partly attributed to its being Saturday; but I could plainly see that it was dirt of all days. I sate in the midst of it with great delight, for the woman's benevolent, happy countenance almost converted her slovenly and lazy way of leaving all things to take care of themselves into a comfort and a blessing.

"It was not a Highland hut, but a slated house built by the master of the quarry for the accommodation of his blacksmith —the shell of an English cottage, as if left unfinished by the workmen, without plaster, and with floor of mud. Two beds, with not over-clean bedclothes, were in the room. Luckily for me, there was good fire and a boiling kettle. The woman was very sorry she had no butter; none was to be had in the village: she gave me oaten and barley bread. We talked over the fire; I answered her hundred questions, and in my turn put some to her. She asked me, as usual, if I was married, how many brothers I had, etc. etc. I told her that William was married, and had a fine boy; to which she replied, 'And the man's a decent man too'. Her next-door neighbour came in with a baby on her arm, to request that I would accept of some fish, which I broiled in the ashes."

After the blacksmith, in whose house they sheltered, had repaired their damaged harness, they visited the Ballachulish slate quarries, and climbed a hill nearby in order to get a view up Loch Leven, not then scarred by the aluminium plant whose industrial dominance lends such an un-highland aspect to the town of Kinlochleven.

At the entrance to Glencoe, they went a little out of their way "to look at a nice white house belonging to the laird of Glen Coe, which stood sweetly in a green field under the hill near some tall trees and coppice woods. At this house the horrible massacre of Glen Coe began, which we did not know when we were there; but the house must have been rebuilt since that time."

Moving into the glen, they made for the inn of Kingshouse,

William Wordsworth,
1770–1850

Dorothy Wordsworth,
1771–1855

Above, Gretna Green: 'a dreary place,' decided Dorothy Wordsworth; *below*, Hamilton, where the Wordsworths found a dirty inn with an impertinent waiter

where once again they found that Coleridge had been there before them, this time the previous night. Dorothy depicts an untamed wildness which the spendid new road, built in 1935, along which the modern car-tourist speeds in even the wettest weather, has somewhat softened. Her account of the journey, and of the reception which she and William encountered at this now comfortable hotel, preserves a vivid impression of the loneliness of the Highlands a century and a half ago.

"Our road frequently crossed large streams of stones, left by the mountain-torrents, losing all appearance of a road. After we had passed the tarn the glen became less interesting, or rather the mountains, from the manner in which they are looked at; but again, a little higher up, they resume their grandeur. The river is, for a short space, hidden between steep rocks: we left the road, and, going to the top of one of the rocks, saw it foaming over with stones, or lodged in dark black dens; birch-trees grew on the inaccessible banks, and a few old Scotch firs towered above them. At the entrance of the glen the mountains had been all without trees, but here the birches climb very far up the side of one of them opposite to us, half concealing a rivulet, which came tumbling down as white as snow from the very top of the mountain. Leaving the rock, we ascended a hill which terminated the glen. We often stopped to look behind at the majestic company of mountains we had left. Before us was no single paramount eminence, but a mountain waste, mountain beyond mountain, and a barren hollow or basin into which we were descending.

"We parted from our companion at the door of a whisky hovel, a building which, when it came out of the workmen's hands with its unglassed windows, would, in that forlorn region, have been little better than a howling place for the winds, and was now half unroofed. On seeing a smoke, I exclaimed, 'Is it possible any people can live there?' when at least half a dozen, men, women, and children, came to the door. They were about to rebuild the hut, and I suppose that they, or some other poor creatures, would dwell there through the winter, dealing out whisky to the starved travellers. The sun was now setting, the air very cold, the sky clear; I could have fancied that it was winter-time, with hard frost. Our guide pointed out King's House to us, our resting-place for the night. We could just distinguish the house at the bottom of the moorish hollow or basin—I call it so, for it was nearly as broad as long—lying before us, with three miles of naked road winding through it, every foot of which we could see. The road was perfectly white, making a dreary contrast with the ground, which was of a dull earthy brown. Long as the line of road appeared before us, we could scarcely believe it to be three miles—I suppose owing to its being unbroken by any one object, and the moor naked as the road itself, but we found it the longest three miles we had yet travelled, for the surface was so stony we had to walk most of the way.

"The house looked respectable at a distance—a large square building, cased in blue slates to defend it from storms—but when we came close to it the outside forewarned us of the poverty and misery within. Scarce a blade of grass could be seen growing upon the open ground; the heath-plant itself found no nourishment there, appearing as if it had but sprung up to be blighted. There was no enclosure for a cow, no appropriated ground but a small plot like a church yard, in which were a few starveling dwarfish potatoes, which had, no doubt, been raised by means of the dung left by travellers' horses: they had not come to blossoming, and whether they would either yield fruit or blossom I know not. The first thing we saw on entering the door was two sheep hung up, as if just killed from the barren moor, their bones hardly sheathed in flesh. After we had waited a few minutes, looking about for a guide to lead us into some corner of the house, a woman, seemingly about forty years old, came to us in a great bustle, screaming in Erse, with the most horrible guinea-hen or peacock voice I ever heard, first to one person, then another. She could hardly spare time to show us upstairs, for crowds of men were in the house—drovers, carriers, horsemen, travellers, all of whom she had to provide with supper, and she was, as she told us, the only woman there.

"Never did I see such a miserable, such a wretched place,—long rooms with ranges of beds, no further furniture except benches, or perhaps one or two crazy chairs, the floors far dirtier than an ordinary house could be if it were never washed,—as dirty as a house after a sale on a rainy day, and the rooms being large, and the walls naked, they looked as if more than half the goods had been sold out. We sate shivering in one of the large rooms for three quarters of an hour before the woman could find time to speak to us again; she then promised a fire in another room, after two travellers, who were going a stage further, had finished their whisky, and said we should have supper as soon as possible. She had no eggs, no milk, no potatoes, no loaf-bread, or we should have preferred tea. With length of time the fire was kindled, and, after another hour's waiting, supper came,—a shoulder of mutton so hard that it was impossible to chew the little flesh that might be scraped off the bones, and some sorry soup made of barley and water, for it had no other taste.

"After supper, the woman, having first asked if we slept on blankets, brought in two pair of sheets, which she begged that I would air by the fire, for they would be dirtied below-stairs. I was very willing, but behold! the sheets were so wet, that it would have been at least a two-hours' job before a far better fire than could be mustered at King's House,—for, that nothing might be wanting to make it a place of complete starvation, the peats were not dry, and if they had not been helped out by decayed wood dug out of the earth along with them we should have had no fire at all. The woman was civil, in her fierce, wild way. She and the house, upon that desolate and extensive Wild, and everything we saw, made us think of one of those places of rendezvous which we read of in novels—Ferdinand Count Fathom or Gil Blas—where there is one woman to receive the booty, and prepare the supper at night. She told us that she was only a servant, but that she had now lived there five years, and that, when but a 'young lassie', she had lived there also. We asked her if she had always served the same master, 'Nay, nay, many masters, for they were always changing'. I verily believe that the woman was attached to the place like a cat to the empty house when the family who brought her up are gone to live elsewhere. The sheets were so long in drying that it was very late before we went to bed. We talked over our day's adventures by the fireside, and often looked out of the window towards a huge pyramidal mountain[1] at the entrance of Glen Coe. All between, the dreary waste was clear, almost, as sky, the moon shining full upon it. A rivulet ran amongst

LITERARY PERCEPTION

[1] *Buchal, the Shepherd of Etive*

stones near the house, and sparkled with light: I could have fancied that there was nothing else, in that extensive circuit over which we looked, that had the power of motion".

Next morning they left early, and climbed the Black Mount, passing "neither tree nor shrub for miles". They ate a wretched breakfast at Inveroran "the butter not eatable, the barley-cakes fusty, the oat-bread so hard I could not chew it, and there were only four eggs in the house, which they had boiled as hard as stones". Dorothy wished herself an artist when, in the middle of the meal, she had occasion to go to the kitchen in search of service.

"About seven or eight travellers, probably drovers, with as many dogs, were sitting in a complete circle round a large peat-fire in the middle of the floor, each with a mess of porridge, in a wooden vessel, upon his knee; a pot, suspended from one of the black beams, was boiling on the fire; two or three women pursuing their household business on the outside of the circle, children playing on the floor. There was nothing uncomfortable in this confusion: happy, busy, or vacant faces, all looked pleasant; and even the smoky air, being a sort of natural indoor atmosphere of Scotland, served only to give a softening, I may say harmony, to the whole."

At Tyndrum, which they reached about two o'clock, they fared rather better.

"We had a moorfowl and mutton-chops for dinner, well cooked, and a reasonable charge. The house was clean for a Scotch inn, and the people about the doors were well dressed. In one of the parlours we saw a company of nine or ten, with the landlady, seated round a plentiful table,—a sight which made us think of the fatted calf in the alehouse pictures of the Prodigal Son. There seemed to be a whole harvest of meats and drinks, and there was something of festivity and picture-like gaiety even in the fresh-coloured dresses of the people and their Sunday faces. The white table-cloth, glasses, English dishes, etc., were all in contrast with what we had seen at Inveroran: the places were but about nine miles asunder, both among hills . . . "

Three hours later, they "bowled downwards through a pleasant vale" to Luib, where they had a bad supper, an "uncivil" servant, and were overcharged. By the River Dochart they walked and rode to Killin, where they spent a night, then set out to cover the fourteen miles to Kenmore, on Loch Tay.

"We travelled through lanes, wood, or open fields, never close to the lake, but always near it, for many miles, the road being carried along the side of a hill, which rose in an almost regularly receding steep from the lake. The opposite shore did not much differ from that down which we went, but it seemed more thinly inhabited, and not so well cultivated. The sun shone, the cottages were pleasant, and the goings-on of the harvest—for all the inhabitants were at work in the corn fields—made the way cheerful. But there is an uniformity in the lake which, comparing it with other lakes, made it appear tiresome. It has no windings: I should even imagine, although it is so many miles long, that, from some points not very high on the hills, it may be seen from one end to the other. There are few bays, no lurking-places where the water hides itself in the land, no outjutting points or promontories, no islands; and there are no commanding mountains or precipices. I think that this lake would be the most pleasing in spring-time, or in summer before the corn begins to change colour, the long tracts of hills on each side of the vale having at this season a kind of patchy appearance, for the corn fields in general were very small, mere plots, and of every possible shade of bright yellow. When we came in view of the foot of the lake we perceived that it ended, as it had begun, in pride and loveliness."

Dorothy's enthusiasm for waterfalls was rather less fulsome than that of Mrs. Murray. However, when they left Kenmore next morning, Dorothy recorded that they "turned out of our way to the Falls of Moness, a stream tributary to the Tay, which passes through a narrow glen with very steep banks. A path like a woodman's track has been carried through the glen, which, though the private property of a gentleman, has not been taken out of the hands of Nature, but merely rendered accessible by this path, which ends at the waterfalls. They tumble from a great height, and are indeed very beautiful falls, and we could have sate with pleasure the whole morning beside the cool basin in which the waters rest, surrounded by high rocks and overhanging trees."

At Aberfeldy, they looked for the "birks . . . . spoken of in some Scotch songs", but did not find them; hardly surprising, since these birches were merely a poetic translation by Burns from Abergeldie because of Aberfeldy's more harmonious name.[1] Aberfeldy, however, has since provided itself with well-advertised birks for the benefit of later tourists.

By Logierait, they made their way to Faskally, which they reached in twilight with their horse even wearier than themselves. They were directed to a small inn.

"It proved to be rather better than a common cottage of the country; we seated ourselves by the fire, William called for a glass of whisky, and asked if they could give us beds. The woman positively refused to lodge us, though we had every reason to believe that she had at least one bed for me; we entreated again and again in behalf of the poor horse, but all in vain; she urged, though in an uncivil way, that she had been sitting up the whole of one or two nights before on account of a fair, and that now she wanted to go to bed and sleep; so we were obliged to mount our car in the dark, and with a tired horse we moved on, and went through the Pass of Killicrankie, hearing only the roaring of the river, and seeing a black chasm with jagged-topped black hills towering above. Afterwards the moon rose, and we should not have had an unpleasant ride if our horse had been in better plight, and we had not been annoyed, as we were almost at every twenty yards, by people coming from a fair held that day near Blair—no pleasant prognostic of what might be our accommodation at the inn, where we arrived between ten and eleven o'clock, and found the house in an uproar; but we were civilly treated, and were glad, after eating a morsel of cold beef, to retire to rest, and I fell asleep in spite of the noisy drunkards below stairs, who had outstayed the fair."

Next day, they visited the grounds of Blair Castle, rested on a heather seat where Burns, when the Duke of Athole's guest a few years before, had also sat, and surveyed the castle, which Dorothy thought at that time "a large irregular pile, not handsome, but I think may have been picturesque, and even noble, before it was docked of its battlements and whitewashed".

[1] Burns wrote in his copy of *The Scots Musical Museum* that he composed his song on August 30th, 1787 "standing under the falls of Aberfeldy, at or near Moness". Two stanzas of the Abergeldie original, collected by David Herd in 1776, are also printed in the *Museum.*

Then they rode to the Falls of Bruar, three miles away, about which Burns had written a poem making the water advise its owner to plant trees to beautify its banks; advice the Duke subsequently took.

"After having gone for some time under a bare hill, we were told to leave the car at some cottages, and pass through a little gate near a brook which crossed the road. We walked upwards at least three quarters of a mile in the hot sun, with the stream on our right, both sides of which to a considerable height were planted with firs and larches intermingled—children of poor Burn's song; for his sake we wished that they had been the natural trees of Scotland, birches, ashes, mountain-ashes, etc.; however, sixty or seventy years hence they will be no unworthy monument to his memory."

In order to see Killiecrankie by daylight, they retraced their steps, spent a night in the neighbourhood, and visited it before breakfast. Dorothy thought it: "A very fine scene; the river Garry forcing its way down a deep chasm between rocks, at the foot of high rugged hills covered with wood, to a great height. The Pass did not, however, impress us with awe, or a sensation of difficulty or danger, according to our expectations; but, the road being at a considerable height on the side of the hill, we at first only looked into the dell or chasm. It is much grander seen from below, near the river's bed".

The memory of it, stimulated by the then present danger of a French invasion, a month later inspired William to write:

Six thousand Veterans practised in War's game,
Tried men, at Killicrankie were array'd
Against an equal host that wore the Plaid,
Shepherds and herdsmen. Like a whirlwind came
The Highlanders; the slaughter spread like flame,
And Garry, thundering down his mountain road,
Was stopp'd, and could not breathe beneath the load
Of the dead bodies. 'Twas a day of shame
For them whom precept and the pedantry
Of cold mechanic battle do enslave.
Oh! for a single hour of that Dundee
Who on that day the word of onset gave:
Like conquest might the men of England see,
And her Foes find a like inglorious grave.

Dunkeld, which they reached at three o'clock that afternoon, Dorothy thought:

"... a pretty, small town, with a respectable and rather large ruined abbey, which is greatly injured by being made the nest of a modern Scotch kirk, with sash windows–very incongruous with the noble antique tower,– a practice which we afterwards found is not uncommon in Scotland."

The cathedral, built over two centuries between 1318 and 1501, was reduced to a roofless ruin sixty years later during the Reformation. The little houses which make up its environs have been admirably restored by the National Trust for Scotland during the present century.

From Dunkeld, the Wordsworths made for Crieff, passing through Amulree and the Sma' Glen, in which Ossian, according to one tradition, is reputed to be buried. Dorothy wrote: "... we crossed a bridge, and the road led us down the glen, which had become exceedingly narrow, and so continued to the end: the hills on both sides heathy and rocky, very steep, but continuous; the rocks not single or overhanging, not scooped into caverns or sounding with torrents: there are no trees, no houses, no traces of cultivation, not one outstanding object. It is truly a solitude, the road even making it appear still more so: the bottom of the valley is mostly smooth and level, the brook not noisy: everything is simple and undisturbed, and while we passed through it the whole place was shady, cool, clear, and solemn. At the end of the long valley we ascended a hill to a great height, and reached the top, when the sun, on the point of setting, shed a soft yellow light upon every eminence. The prospect was very extensive; over hollows and plains, no towns, and few houses visible–a prospect, extensive as it was, in harmony with the secluded dell, and fixing its own peculiar character of removedness from the world, and the secure possession of the quiet of nature more deeply in our minds". William, brooding on the Ossian tradition, later wrote:

In this still place remote from men
Sleeps Ossian, in the Narrow Glen,
In this still place where murmurs on

But one meek streamlet, only one.
He sung of battles and the breath
Of stormy war, and violent death,
And should, methinks, when all was pass'd,
Have rightfully been laid at last
Where rocks were rudely heap'd, and rent
As by a spirit turbulent;
Where sights were rough, and sounds were wild,
And everything unreconciled,
In some complaining, dim retreat
Where fear and melancholy meet;
But this is calm; there cannot be
A more entire tranquillity.

Does then the bard sleep here indeed?
Or is it but a groundless creed?
What matters it? I blame them not
Whose fancy in this lonely spot
Was moved, and in this way express'd
Their notion of its perfect rest.
A convent, even a hermit's cell
Would break the silence of this Dell;
It is not quiet, is not ease,
But something deeper far than these;
The separation that is here
Is of the grave; and of austere
And happy feelings of the dead:
And therefore was it rightly said
That Ossian, last of all his race,
Lies buried in this lonely place.

So strong an impression had the Trossachs made on the Wordsworths that they decided to revisit the district, soon to be transformed into a place romantically sought out by lovers of Scott's poetry. By Loch Earn and Glen Ogle, they came to Loch Lubnaig, noting the one-time home of James "Abyssinian" Bruce as they travelled through the Pass of Leny to Callander, where they arrived "wet and cold and glad of a good fire" as the darkness closed in.

Once again they enjoyed the hospitality of the Macfarlane family, once again marvelled at the varying loveliness of the Trossachs. This time, one of their excursions was up Glen Falloch. They climbed a mountain above the glen, and looked down on a scene of activity below.

"I observed that the people were busy bringing in the hay before it was dry into a sort of 'fauld' or yard, where they intended to leave it, ready to be gathered into the house with the first threatening of rain, and if not completely dry brought out again. Our guide bore me in his arms over the stream, and we soon came to the foot of the mountain. The most easy rising, for a short way at first, was near a naked rivulet which made a fine cascade in one place. Afterward, the ascent was very laborious, being frequently almost perpendicular.

"It is one of those moments which I shall not easily forget, when at that point from which a step or two would have carried us out of sight of the green fields of Glenfalloch, being at a great height on the mountain, we sate down, and heard, as if from the heart of the earth, the sound of torrents ascending out of the long hollow glen. To the eye all was motionless, a perfect stillness. The noise of waters did not appear to come this way or that, from any particular quarter: it was everywhere, almost, one might say, as if 'exhaled' through the whole surface of the green earth. Glenfalloch, Coleridge has since told me, signifies the Hidden Vale; but William says, if we were to name it from our recollections of that time, we should call it the Vale of Awful Sound."

On another occasion, during an evening walk, they met two women, also out walking.

"One of them said to us in a friendly, soft tone of voice, 'What! you are stepping westward?' I cannot describe how affecting this simple expression was in that remote place, with the western sky in front, yet glowing with the departed sun."

This chance encounter gave rise to one of William's most successful Scottish poems:

"What! you are stepping westward?" Yea,
'Twould be a wildish destiny
If we, who thus together roam

In a strange land, and far from home,
Were in this place the guests of chance:
Yet who would stop, or fear to advance,
Though home or shelter he had none,
With such a sky to lead him on?

The dewy ground was dark and cold,
Behind all gloomy to behold,
And stepping westward seem'd to be
A kind of heavenly destiny;
I liked the greeting, 'twas a sound
Of something without place or bound;
And seem'd to give me spiritual right
To travel through that region bright.

The voice was soft; and she who spake
Was walking by her native Lake;
The salutation was to me
The very sound of courtesy;
Its power was felt, and while my eye
Was fix'd upon the glowing sky,
The echo of the voice enwrought
A human sweetness with the thought
Of travelling through the world that lay
Before me in my endless way.

Another excursion took them to a burial ground in Glengyle where they had been told Rob Roy was buried. They searched in vain for his tombstone; hardly surprisingly, since he was, in fact, buried at Kirkton of Balquhidder. However, this experience gave rise to William's poem in honour of Rob Roy beginning:

A famous man is Robin Hood,
The English Ballad-singer's joy,
And Scotland has a thief as good,
An outlaw of as daring mood;
She has her brave Rob Roy!

It is a lively ballad, catching something of the outlaw's swagger as it recounts his practice of robbing the rich to help the poor.

And thus among these rocks he lived
Through summer heat and winter snow;
The Eagle, he was lord above,
And Rob was lord below.

Dorothy recounts William's most famous Scottish poem, *To a Highland Girl,* while she is describing their walk above Loch Voil. But in fact the poem, written in 1805, two years later, was touched off by a sentence in Thomas Wilkinson's *Tour in the Highlands,* more so, Wordsworth's biographer Mary Moorman suggests, "than by the recollection of a particular incident in their own tour". There would be nothing odd about a writer's remark recalling an image or an incident and fleshing it into another's poem, for this is how the creative process often works. The girl sang in Gaelic, the language constantly in the Wordsworths' ears while they were in the Highlands, and the poem, with its familiar beginning

Behold her, single in the field,
Yon solitary Highland Lass . . .

contains, in its third stanza, one of the most emotive images in English poetry:

Will no one tell me what she sings?
Perhaps the plaintive numbers flow
For old, unhappy far-off things,
And battles long ago . . .

Near Loch Lubnaig, they lodged at an inn, hoping "that it should not prove wretched indeed". As was her wont, Dorothy soon got into conversation with the landlady:

"This woman whose common language was the Gaelic, talked with me a very good English, asking many questions, yet without the least appearance of an obtrusive or impertinent curiousity; and indeed I must say that I never, in those women with whom I conversed, observed anything on which

I could put such a construction. They seemed to have a faith ready for all; and as a child when you are telling them stories, asks for 'more, more', so they appeared to delight in being amused without effort of their own minds. Among other questions she asked me the old one over again, if I was married; and when I told her that I was not, she appeared surprised, and, as if recollecting herself, said to me, with a pious seriousness and perfect simplicity, 'To be sure, there is a great promise for virgins in Heaven'; and then she began to tell how long she had been married, that she had had a large family and much sickness and sorrow, having lost several of her children. We had clean sheets and decent beds."

On Wednesday, September 14th, they passed through Callander and Doune, on their way to Stirling.

"Long before we reached the town of Stirling, saw the Castle, single, on its stately and commanding eminence. The rock or hill rises from a level plain . . . The surrounding plain appears to be of a rich soil, well cultivated. The crops of ripe corn were abundant. We found the town quite full; not a vacant room in the inn, it being the time of the assizes: there was no lodging for us, and hardly even the possibility of getting anything to eat in a bye-nook of the house. Walked up to the Castle. The prospect from it is very extensive, and most exceedingly grand on a fine evening or morning, with the light of the setting or rising sun on the distant mountains, but we saw it at an unfavourable time of day, the mid-afternoon, and were not favoured by light and shade. The Forth makes most intricate and curious turnings, so that it is difficult to trace them, even when you are overlooking the whole. It flows through a perfect level, and in once place cuts its way in the form of a large figure of eight. Stirling is the largest town we had seen in Scotland, except Glasgow. It is an old irregular place; the streets towards the Castle on one side very steep. On the other, the hill or rock rises from the fields. The architecture of a part of the Castle is very fine, and the whole building in good repair: some parts indeed, are modern. At Stirling we bought Burn's Poems in one volume, for two shillings."

Seeing in the distance the Carron Ironworks, they noticed that "the sky above them was red with a fiery light". As they passed Falkirk, they encountered many Highland drovers setting out home for the North after attending the Falkirk Cattle-Tryst. That night they lodged in a private house at Linlithgow.

At Edinburgh, they stayed at the White Hart inn in the Grassmarket, which, though not in the fashionable New Town, had the advantage of being "not noisy and cheap".

The modern motorised traveller, easily deflected from his exploratory intent by a few drops of rain, misses much that his hardier ancestors enjoyed. Next morning, in rain and with a mist which obscured the Forth, the Wordsworth's explored Edinburgh.

"We set out upon our walk, and went through many streets to Holyrood House, and thence to the hill called Arthur's Seat, a high hill, very rocky at the top, and below covered with smooth turf, on which sheep were feeding. We climbed up till we came to St. Anthony's Well and Chapel, as it is called, but it is more like a hermitage than a chapel—a small ruin, which from its situation is exceedingly interesting, though in itself not remarkable. We sate down on a stone not far from the chapel, overlooking a pastoral hollow as wild and solitary as any in the heart of the Highland mountains: there, instead of the roaring of torrents, we listened to the noises of the city, which were blended in one loud indistinct buzz,—a regular sound in the air, which in certain moods of feeling, and at certain times, might have a more tranquillizing effect upon the mind than those which we are accustomed to hear in such places. The Castle rock looked exceedingly large through the misty air: a cloud of black smoke overhung the city, which combined with the rain and mist to conceal the shapes of the houses—an obscurity which added much to the grandeur of the sound that proceeded from it. It was impossible to think of anything that was little or mean, the goings-on of trade, the strife of men, or every-day city business:—the impression was one, and it was visionary; like the conceptions of our childhood of Bagdad or Balsora when we have been reading the Arabian Nights' Entertainments. Though the rain was very heavy we remained upon the hill for some time, then returned by the same road by which we had come, through green flat fields, formerly the pleasure-grounds of Holyrood House, on the edge of which stands the old roofless chapel, of venerable architecture. It is a pity that it should be suffered to fall down, for the walls appear to be yet entire. Very near to the chapel is Holyrood House, which we could not but lament has nothing ancient in its appearance, being sash-windowed and not an irregular pile. It is very like a building for some national establishment,–a hospital for soldiers or sailors . . .

"We walked industriously through the streets, street after street, and, in spite of wet and dirt, were exceedingly delighted. The old town, with its irregular houses, stage above stage, seen as we saw it, in the obscurity of a rainy day, hardly resembles the work of men, it is more like a piling up of rocks, and I cannot attempt to describe what we saw so imperfectly, but must say that, high as my expectations had been raised, the city of Edinburgh far surpassed all expectation."

Next day, they set out for Roslin, past Hawthornden, "the house of Drummond the poet, whither Ben Jonson came on foot from London to visit his friend", and so to Lasswade, "before Mr. and Mrs. Walter Scott had risen, and waited some time in a large sitting-room. Breakfasted wtih them, and stayed till two o'clock, and Mr. Scott accompanied us back almost to Roslin, having given us directions respecting our future journey, and promised to meet us at Melrose two days after

"We ordered dinner on our return to the inn, and went to view the inside of the Chapel of Roslin, which is kept locked up, and so preserved from the injuries it might otherwise receive from idle boys; but as nothing is done to keep it together, it must in the end fall. The architecture within is exquisitely beautiful. The stone both of the roof and walls is sculptured with leaves and flowers, so delicately wrought that I could have admired them for hours, and the whole of their groundwork is stained by time with the softest colours. Some of those leaves and flowers were tinged perfectly green, and at one part the effect was most exquisite: three or four leaves of a small fern, resembling that which we call adder's tongue, grew round a cluster of them at the top of a pillar, and the natural product and the artificial were so intermingled that at first it was not easy to distinguish the living plant from the other, they being of an equally determined green, though the fern was of a deeper shade."

Something has since been done to keep Roslin Chapel together, with its Prentice Pillar, a unique monument to the decorative sculptor's art.

That night, at Peebles, on the Tweed, they found "a comfortable old-fashioned public-house" which had "a neat parlour" in which they drank tea and spent a good night.

"After breakfast walked up the river to Neidpath Castle, about a mile and a half from the town. The castle stands upon a green hill, overlooking the Tweed, a strong square-towered edifice, neglected and desolate, though not in ruin, the garden overgrown with grass, and the high walls that fenced it broken down. The Tweed winds between green steeps, upon which, and close to the river side, large flocks of sheep pasturing; higher still are the grey mountains; but I need not describe the scene, for William has done it better than I could do in a sonnet which he wrote the same day; the five last lines, at least, of his poem will impart to you more of the feeling of the place than it would be possible for me to do:

Degenerate Douglass! thou unworthy Lord
Whom mere despite of heart could so far please,
And love of havoc (for with such disease
Fame taxes him) that he could send forth word
To level with the dust a noble horde,
A brotherhood of venerable trees,
Leaving an ancient Dome and Towers like these
Beggar'd and outraged! Many hearts deplored
The fate of those old trees; and oft with pain
The Traveller at this day will stop and gaze
On wrongs which Nature scarcely seems to heed;
For shelter'd places, bosoms, nooks, and bays,
And the pure mountains, and the gentle Tweed,
And the green silent pastures yet remain.

"I was spared any regret for the fallen woods when we were there, not then knowing the history of them. The soft low mountains, the castle, and the decayed pleasure-grounds, the scattered trees which have been left in different parts, and the road carried in a very beautiful line along the side of the hill, with the Tweed murmuring through the unfenced green pastures spotted with sheep, together composed an harmonious scene, and I wished for nothing that was not there".

The despoiler of the trees was the fourth Duke of Queensberry, the notorious hard-drinking gambler nicknamed "Old Q".

Moving along the Tweed, they admired "several old halls yet inhabited," but particularly one house with "an allegorical air", now the oldest inhabited house in Scotland, on which Dorothy later commented:

"We have since heard that it was the residence of Lord Traquair, a Roman Catholic nobleman, of a decayed family."

There was no time to visit Yarrow, in Selkirkshire, giving rise to William's poem *Yarrow Revisited,* with its conclusion that there is virtue in the frugality which preserves some of life's delights for future enjoyment:

If care with freezing years should come,
And wandering seem but folly,
Should we be loth to stir from home,
And yet be melancholy,
Should life be dull and spirits low,
'Twill soothe us in our sorrow
That earth has something yet to show–
The bonny Holms of Yarrow'.

They rose early next day, and by Gala Water, rode to Melrose before breakfast, noting the change that was coming upon "the village of Galashiels, pleasantly situated on the bank of the stream; a pretty place it once has been, but a manufactory is established there; and a townish bustle and ugly stone houses are fast taking place of the brown-roofed thatched cottages, of which a great number yet remain, partly overshadowed by trees."

Scott took them round Melrose Abbey.

"He pointed out many pieces of beautiful sculpture in obscure corners which would have escaped our notice. The Abbey has been built of a pale red stone; that part which was first erected of a very durable kind, the sculptured flowers and leaves and other minute ornaments being as perfect in many places as when first wrought. The ruin is of considerable extent, but unfortunately it is almost surrounded by insignificant houses, so that when you are close to it you see it entirely separated from many rural objects, and even when viewed from a distance the situation does not seem to be particularly happy, for the vale is broken and disturbed, and the Abbey at a distance from the river, so that you do not look upon them as companions of each other, and surely this is a national barbarism: within these beautiful walls is the ugliest church that was ever beheld—if it had been hewn out of the side of the hill it could not have been more dismal; there was no neatness, nor even decency, and it appeared to be so damp, and so completely excluded from fresh air, that it must be dangerous to sit in it; the floor is unpaved, and very rough. What a contrast to the beautiful and graceful order apparent in every part of the ancient design and workmanship!"

Melrose, begun in 1136, suffered badly in the War of Independence, and was sacked again by the Earl of Hertford in 1544. Its fifteenth-century decorative work is among the finest in Scotland. Scott's superintendence of the repair of the Abbey in 1822 was paid for by his friend the Duke of Buccleuch, who gave it to the nation, the "ugliest church" being by then removed.

Dryburgh Abbey was then owned by the eccentric eleventh Earl of Buchan, whose ancestors had built their house from some of the Abbey's stones.

"The ruins of Dryburgh are much less extensive than those of Melrose, and greatly inferior both in the architecture and stone, which is much mouldered away. Lord Buchan has trained pear-trees along the walls, which are bordered with flowers and gravel walks, and he has made a pigeon-house, and a fine room in the ruin, ornamented with a curiously-assorted collection of busts of eminent men, in which lately a ball was given; yet, deducting for all these improvements, which are certainly much less offensive than you could imagine, it is a very sweet ruin, standing so enclosed in wood, which the towers overtop, that you cannot know that it is not in a state of natural desolation till you are close to it. The opposite bank of the Tweed is steep and woody, but unfortunately many of the trees are firs. The old woman followed us after the fashion of other guides, but being slower of foot than a younger person, it was not difficult to slip away from the scent of her poor smoke-dried body. She was sedulous in pointing out the curiosities, which, I doubt not, she had a firm belief were not be surpassed in England or Scotland."

Scott was to be buried in Dryburgh Abbey in 1832, and later his son-in-law and biographer John Gibson Lockhart; later still, Field Marshall Earl Haig, commander of the British forces in the First World War.

While the Wordsworths were at Dryburgh, the rain came on so heavily that they decided to miss out Kelso and go straight to Jedburgh, where Scott was involved in Court business.

"We gave in our passport—the name of Mr. Scott, the Sheriff—and were very civilly treated, but there was no vacant room in the house except the Judge's sitting-room, and we wanted to have a fire, being exceedingly wet and cold. I was conducted into that room, on condition that I would give it up the moment the Judge came from Court. After I had put off my wet clothes I went up into a bedroom, and sate shivering there, till the people of the inn had procured lodgings for us in a private house."

Scott sat with them for two hours, and recited part of his new poem *The Lay of the Last Minstrel.* Dorothy did not set down her reaction, but as we know from a later letter of William's neither of them was much impressed with the poem's merits, feeling that rhythmically it derived too much from Coleridge's *Christabel.* The old woman who was their hostess so impressed William that long afterwards she inspired a poem, that beginning "Aye! twine thy brows with fresh spring flowers".

Jedburgh Abbey, explored while waiting for Scott to finish his cases, seemed to Dorothy "much less beautiful" than Melrose.

"After Mr. Scott's business in the Courts was over, he walked with us up the Jed—'sylvan Jed' it has been properly called by Thomson—for the banks are yet very woody, though wood in large quantities has been felled within a few years. There are some fine red scars near the river, in one or two of which we saw the entrances to caves, said to have been used as places of refuge in times of insecurity.

Walked up to Ferniehurst, an old hall, in a secluded

situation, now inhabited by farmers; the neighbouring ground had the wildness of a forest, being irregularly scattered over with fine old trees. The wind was tossing their branches, and sunshine dancing among the leaves, and I happened to exclaim, 'What a life there is in trees!' on which Mr. Scott observed that the words reminded him of a young lady who had been born and educated on an island of the Orcades, and came to spend a summer at Kelso and in the neighbourhood of Edinburgh. She used to say that in the new world into which she was come nothing had disappointed her so much as trees and woods; she complained that they were lifeless, silent, and, compared with the grandeur of the ever-changing ocean, even insipid. At first I was surprised, but the next moment I felt that the impression was natural. Mr. Scott said that she was a very sensible young woman, and had read much. She talked with endless rapture and feeling of the power and greatness of the island without any probability of quitting it again.

The valley of the Jed is very solitary immediately under Ferniehurst; we walked down the river, wading almost up to the knees in fern, which in many parts overspread the forest-ground. It made me think of our walks at Alfoxden, and of *our own* park—though at Ferniehurst there is no park at present—and the slim fawns that we used to startle from their couching-places among the fern at the top of the hill. We were accompanied on our walk by a young man from the Braes of Yarrow, an acquaintance of Mr. Scott's,[1] who, having been much delighted with some of William's poems which he had chanced to see in a newspaper, had wished to be introduced to him; he lived in the most retired part of the dale of Yarrow, where he had a farm: he was fond of reading, and well informed, but at first meeting as shy as any of our Grasmere lads, and not less rustic in his appearance."

That evening, they had "dinner sent from the inn, and a bottle of wine, that we might not disgrace the Sheriff, who supped with us . . . stayed late, and repeated some of his poem."

Next day, they took leave of the old woman at whose house they had lodged.

"She had been out to buy me some pears, saying that I must take away some 'Jedderd' pears. We learned afterwards that

[1] *Scott's retainer Will Laidlaw*

Jedburgh is famous in Scotland for pears, which were first cultivated there in the gardens of the monks.

Mr. Scott was very glad to part from the Judge and his retinue, to travel with us in our car to Hawick; his servant drove his own gig. The landlady, very kindly, had put up some sandwiches and cheese-cakes for me, and all the family came out to see us depart. Passed the monastery gardens, which are yet gardens, where there are many remarkably large old pear-trees. We soon came into the vale of Teviot, which is open and cultivated, and scattered over with hamlets, villages, and many gentlemen's seats, yet, though there is no inconsiderable quantity of wood, you can never, in the wide and cultivated parts of the Teviot, get rid of the impression of barrenness, and the fir plantations, which in this part are numerous, are for ever at war with simplicity. One beautiful spot I recollect of a different character, which Mr. Scott took us to see a few yards from the road. A stone bridge crossed the water at a deep and still place, called Horne's Pool, from a contemplative school-master, who had lived not far from it, and was accustomed to walk thither, and spend much of his leisure near the river. The valley was here narrow and woody. Mr. Scott pointed out to us Ruberslaw, Minto Crags, and every other remarkable object in or near the vale of Teviot, and we scarcely passed a house for which he had not some story."

They arrived at what is now the Tower Hotel, in Hawick, and "did not go out in the evening".

Next morning: "Before breakfast, walked with Mr. Scott along a high road for about two miles, up a bare hill. Hawick is a small town. From the top of the hill we had an extensive view over the moors of Liddisdale, and saw the Cheviot Hills. We wished we could have gone with Mr. Scott into some of the remote dales of this country, where in almost every house he can find a home and a hearty welcome. But after breakfast we were obliged to part with him, which we did with great regret: he would gladly have gone with us to Langholm, eighteen miles further. Our way was through the vale of Teviot, near the banks of the river."

The Wordsworths passed Branxholm Hall, which, because it featured in Scott's *Lay*, they looked at with special interest. They met "the Edinburgh coach with several passengers, the only stage-coach that had passed us in Scotland". But they failed to find the old stump of trees said by Scott to be the place of execution of Johny Armstrong, the Border reiver whom James V hanged and who, posthumously, got the better of that monarch by becoming the subject of one of the best of the Border Ballads.

As they climbed beyond the upper reaches of the Teviot, they saw "a single stone house a long way before us, which we conjectured to be, as it proved, Moss Paul, the inn where we were to bait. The scene, with this single dwelling, was melancholy and wild, but not dreary, though there was no tree or shrub; the small streamlet glittered, the hills were populous with sheep; but the gentle bending of the valley, and the correspondent softness in the forms of the hills, were of themselves enough to delight the eye. At Moss Paul we fed our horse;–several travellers were drinking whisky. We neither ate nor drank, for we had, with our usual foresight and frugality in travelling, saved the cheese-cakes and sandwiches which had been given us by our countrywoman at Jedburgh the day before. After Moss Paul we ascended considerably, then went down other reaches of the valley, much less interesting, stony and barren. The country afterwards not peculiar, I should think, for I scarcely remember it.

"Arrived at Langholm at about five o'clock. The town, as we approached, from a hill, looked very pretty, the houses being roofed with blue slates, and standing close to the river Esk, here a large river, that scattered its waters wide over a stony channel. The inn neat and comfortable–exceedingly clean: I could hardly believe we were still in Scotland."

Next morning, Saturday, September 24th, they "rose very early", and travelled along the banks of the Esk, to Longtown. The day became a fine one, and as they caught sight of Solway Moss, to the west, which they had crossed on their way north, they "did not look along the white line of the road without some emotion". But they had "the fair prospect of the Cumberland mountains full in view, with the certainty, barring accidents, of reaching our own dear home the next day".

They breakfasted at the Graham's Arms Hotel (now less possessive in its nomenclature) and reached Carlisle by the evening. Next day, Sunday September 25th, "a beautiful autumnal day", they "breakfasted at a public-house by the road-side; dined at Threlkeld", and "arrived home between eight and nine o'clock", where they found "Mary in perfect health, Joanna Hutchinson"–Mary's sister–"with her, and little John asleep in the clothes basket by the fire".

As the jaunting car jogged along between Dalston and Grasmere, William celebrated his return to the domestic scene with a sonet:

"FLY, some kind spirit, fly to Grasmere Vale!
Say that we come, and come by this day's light
Glad tidings!–spread them over field and height,
But, chiefly, let one Cottage hear the tale!
There let a mystery of joy prevail,
The kitten frolic with unruly might,
And Rover whine as at a second sight
Of near-approaching good, that will not fail:
And from that Infant's face let joy appear;
Yea, let our Mary's one companion child,
That hath her six weeks' solitude beguiled
With intimations manifold and dear,
While we have wander'd over wood and wild–
Smile on its Mother now with bolder cheer!"

There were to be other Scottish holidays. On July 10th, 1813, William and his wife Mary, their son, John, then ten, and Sara Hutchinson set out upon an excursion in the same Irish jaunting car which William and Dorothy had used in 1803. Johnny rode on a black pony. Mary had by now lost two of her children, and the tour was intended to restore her spirits.

From Carlisle, the travellers went to Brampton, from where they visited Lannercost Priory. Their way north then took them through Eskdale, where Johnny was left at the Miss Malcolms' farm to attend a village school. They called at Robert Owen's model village of New Lanark, where, according to Sara's notes, they watched the workers "disporting themselves in their gay clothes by the side of the river"–presumably it was a Sunday–and then spent five nights in Glasgow. They went through Helensburgh, up Loch Long, down Loch Lomond to Luss, and through Drymen to Aberfoyle, from where they crossed over to the Trossachs, accepting with cheerful fortitude the same sort of varying hospitality they had received in the various Highland houses at which they lodged ten years before, and a great deal of wet weather. They then drove north, through Glencoe, up Loch Linnhe to Inverness and Beauly, coming south through Blair Atholl to Edinburgh, which they reached on 28th August. William walked up Corstorphine Hill, in the company of Scott's friend R.D. Gillies. The Wordsworths drove through Peebles to Traquair. At the Manse of Traquair they met the poet and novelist James Hogg, the "Ettrick Shepherd", who acted as their guide on a visit to the Braes of Yarrow, which William had left unvisited in 1803. To mark this occasion, Wordsworth wrote his second Yarrow poem. After admiring St. Mary's Loch, they breakfasted with Mrs. Scott and her daughter Sophia, the future Mrs. Lockhart, Scott himself being away. They also dined with Lord Buchan at Dryburgh, then returned over Moss Paul to pick up Johnny.

William came twice again to Scotland; in 1831 and in 1833. In mid-September 1831, Sir Walter Scott invited him to Abbotsford. Wordsworth, with his daughter Dora as his companion, travelled by carriage by way of Carlisle and Hawick. He was suffering from an infection of the eyelid—a complaint which recurred during his latter years—and wore a shade.

Father and daughter arrived at Abbotsford on September 19th to be Scott's guests for three days. Scott had by this time suffered a stroke, but although paralysed, he still enjoyed entertaining. Although Wordsworth had never thought highly of Scott's poetry, and was no enthusiast for novels of any kind, he greatly admired Scott, the man. Now, Wordsworth was shocked by the physical change he found in him, recalling how, when Scott and Lockhart visited him in the Lake District some years before, Scott had declared: "I mean to live till I am *eighty*, and shall write as long as I can."

Scott took William and Dora by carriage to Newark and Yarrow, a visit resulting in the composition of Wordsworth's third and last Yarrow poem, *Yarrow Revisited.* An unknown artist has made a lithograph of the two elderly poets together by the banks of the river. On the way back to Abbotsford, Wordsworth was deeply moved by the sight of the sun sinking red behind the Eildon Hills, and the realisation that the life of the great man who so loved the Border scene was also sinking.

Taking farewell of Scott, William and Dora drove to Edinburgh. They visited Roslin Chapel on a day of lashing rain, the poet composing a sonnet inside it as he remembered the earlier visit with his sister almost thirty years before. As they moved west and north to Callander, William walked beside the carriage, "scarcely less than twenty miles a day," he said afterwards. By slow stages they made their way to Bonawe, on the shores of Loch Etive, where their old horse, Naso, had a well-earned rest. At Oban, they went aboard the new steamer which sailed twice weekly from Glasgow to Mull. Rain and the lateness of the season made the landing at Staffa impossible, so they returned to Bonawe, and began the homeward journey with hired horses (Naso being left to be "wintered" at Bonawe) William composed sonnets steadily throughout the journey.

This series of poems, later published under the title *Yarrow Revisited,* lacked the grandeur of the pieces which made up his *Memorials of a Tour in Scotland,* the results of the 1803 visit, published in 1814. One sonnet from the later group, however, pays high tribute to Scott in music of noble dignity:

A trouble, not of clouds, or weeping rain,
Nor of the setting sun's pathetic light
Engendered, hangs o'er Eildon's triple height.

Scott was about to set out upon his Italian journey in search of health, a journey which he curtailed because he was anxious to die at home.

Wordsworth asks that:

Blessings and prayers in nobler retinue
Than sceptred King or laurelled conqueror knows
Follow this wondrous Potentate.

In 1833, the year after Scott's death, Wordsworth, with his old friend Crabb Robinson and Johnny, made another visit to Scotland, this time sailing from Whitehaven to Douglas, Isle of Man, and from Douglas to Greenock. Another steamer took them from Greenock to Oban. This tour, lasting only a fortnight, produced some further sonnets for the volume of

1835, including a sonnet on Ailsa Craig and one entitled *Steamboats, Viaducts and Railways,* in which the poet concludes that as part of "Nature's lawful offspring" and "Man's Art," these new "preserves" in the landscape should be welcomed–

> *In spite of all that Beauty may discover*
> *In your harsh features.*

Dorothy Wordsworth made only one return visit to Scotland, in 1822, with her sister-in-law, Johanna Hutchinson. They drove by coach to Edinburgh, arriving, according to her Journal, on September 16th[1]. The two women spent two days exploring the City. Unlike the beautifully-written earlier Journal, the account of her travels of 1822 is merely in note form, making somewhat jerky reading. Her description of her walk up the High Street gives some impression of its unpolished style:

"Up High Street–women in crowds–all the Babies surely brought out of doors to be nursed–and every nurse with her company gathered round her. The women very coarse, but no rudeness–children at play on their knees and running about in the middle of the crowded street with bare legs and feet. What horrible alleys on each side of the High Street, especially downwards like Passes in Quarries of dark-coloured stone. I ventured down one, and hastened back to escape from the spitting of two children who were leaning out of an upper window, and would no doubt have attained the utmost point of pleasure in their sport could they but have hit my Bonnet. Up to the Castle Hill–mist clearing away. To Tea with Mrs. Wilson[2] in Queen Street. Her eldest orphan Grandchild a beautiful Girl. Margaret Ferrier checked in her growth and delicate–amiable, accomplished and devoted to learning, understands Latin and Greek. Conducted back to the Black Bull by Mrs. W's maid at ten o'clock. Starlight night–streets very quiet, yet many shops open."

Dorothy and Johanna drove to Newhaven, to board the little paddle-steamer which then sailed up the Forth to Alloa,

[1] *But she made an error of one day at the beginning of her Journal, according to its editor, E. de Selincourt, and so presumably arrived on the 15th of September; an error continued throughout her dating.*

[2] *The mother of John Wilson ("Christopher North").*

for Stirling. After visiting Stirling Castle, they went by coach to Castlecary, from where a horse-drawn "track-boat" on the Forth and Clyde Canal brought them into Glasgow. They seated themselves at what Dorothy called "the Gentry end" of the boat, which they regretted, the weather being too good to tempt them to use the "very pretty Cabin supplied with books", and the steering end at half the price being "just as comfortable and much more amusing."

Dorothy took notes as they glided gently, though not very slowly along, for the horses trotted briskly.

"Scene at the steerage end very pretty, of which 'the Quality' on the lower Deck see nothing. A soldier at the Boat's head–scarlet shawls and cloaks–blue ribbands and mixture of gay colours–something that reminds me of Bruges; but we want the Nuns, the Priest and the Flemish Girl with her flowers. The people talk cheerfully, yet all appears quiet–no swearing–no smoking–little Babies a pleasant accompaniment on a fine day like this. I have not heard a cry from one of them, and it is pleasant to observe what amusement they give. The Fiddler is now below, and his music is much less harsh. The country open, yet not flat, nor bare of trees, generally cultivated, though not rich. Town with a tower (I have not noted down its name) long in view. Now the Spire of Kirkintiller,[1] a pretty object is before us. The Canal altogether pleasing. It mostly winds gently, resembling a River in a flat country–the banks frequently not unpicturesque–scars that resemble rocks where coals have been dug out often produce an agreeable effect in connexion with other objects. Two Lasses in pink bedgowns, while they watch a Baby that is sprawling on the ground, are spreading their linen at the top of a steep green Bank. Our handsome Boatman throws an apple to each–graceful waving of thanks–and they stand to look after us. An old woman coming along the path dances forward to the music of our fiddle, claps her hands to the tune and smiles merrily upon us.

Ye play not for me,
But mine is your glee!

[1] *Kirkintilloch*

Such might be the sentiment of the old woman. "Blow the horn, Willy!" says the Captain. A drawbridge is uplifted–Town and Spire to the right We have passed several steamboats with large companies on board, whom we have always greeted with a brisk tune from the fiddle. Landed at the suburbs of Glasgow at 4 o'clock."

They stayed at the Eagle Inn in Maxwell Street, explored the town, and next morning rose early to catch the Dumbarton steamer at the Broomielaw.

"Hurried away to reach the Steam-boat at 6, and arrived 10 minutes before the Boat was ready, tho' the horn was clamorously sounding to summon the Passengers. What a labouring of smoke in the harbour from many steam-boats! one, close to ours, taking in its cargo, and crew, chiefly mechanics and peasants. Women's white caps very lively, with a few scarlet shawls, among the grimly-attired men. We move swiftly forward carrying with us our own beating, rushing sound and black volume of smoke. The morning rather foggy, and still, while the prospect to the west brightens before us, a dense cloud hangs over Glasgow. The Clyde (it being low water) hitherto, as we have come along, has resembled the Canal, though much wider, and the immediate banks not so pretty. Fast we glide away–heaving and labouring below–and smoking above. Suddenly appears the Rock of Dumbarton . . . We land beneath the Rock–low water–and we have to walk over sea-weed and slippery stones. The rock very wild–scattered fragments interesting to me from recollections. Screaming birds overhead–sea gulls below . . . The distance to Balloch 5 miles."

A coach connected the Dumbarton steamer with the "Marion", which was waiting for them at Balloch, on Loch Lomond. As the boat paddled past Inversnaid, Dorothy noticed a girl standing on the threshold, and her mind went back, as so often on this tour, to the excursion of 1803.

"We are not near enough to distinguish whether her person be awkward or graceful, or her face pretty; but I cannot fancy her so fair as our Highland Girl. Poor thing. I ask myself in vain what is become of her? And that little Babe that squalled the harder while its Grandame rocked, as if to stifle its cries. Brought up in toil and hardship, is it still struggling on? or, with the aged woman, sleeping in the quiet grave? The white waterfall drops into the Lake as before; and the small Bay is calm while the middle of the Lake is stirred by breezes; but we have long left the sea-like region of the Isles and low hills. Our Highland Musician tunes his pipes as we approach Rob Roy's Caves. The grandeur of nature strangely mixed up with stage effects; but it is good acting–not of the Surrey Theatre. An old Highlander, with long grey locks, bonnet, and plaid, is seated on one of the crags. Boys at different heights with bags of fresh-gathered nuts. Every passenger leaves the Boat, and what a scramble among rocks and trees! The Piper in his Tartan Robes is still playing a rouzing tune. All press forward to Rob Roy's cave, as it is called, pass through in succession, the Cave being so small that not more than two or three can enter at once, and having an outlet at the other side. We flatter ourselves we make a wiser choice in not entering at all; for they profess to have no motive but to say they have been in Rob Roy's Caves because Sir Walter Scott has made them so much talked about; and, when they come out, dashing the dust off their clothes, the best they can say is "Well!" there is nothing to be seen; but it is worth while, if only to say that one has been there!"

The inn at Tarbet, which on their tour together William and Mary had found better than what it had been when William and Dorothy stayed there in 1803, turned out to be once more "a villainous Inn, that for scolding and dirt, and litter and damp, surely cannot be surpassed through all Scotland."

From Tarbet, they drove over to Arrochar, from where they decided to go on to Inveraray. They managed to get themselves places on a gentleman's private cart that was making the journey, and spent the first day crossing "Rest and Be Thankful" to reach Cairndow in the early evening, the ladies sitting on the cart, the gentleman walking in front of it.

"Now sitting in an upper room at Cairndow–the exterior of the house just the same as when I was here before (I suppose they now white-wash every year) but within much smarter. Carpets covering every floor, but you find these everywhere, even at the villainous Inn at Tarbet, which we have just escaped from. We now sit in a quiet cleanly bedroom–for the carpets here do not seem to be a cover for dirt—tea comfortably set out—civil attendants, and nothing wanting. In the kitchen there is a fine blazing coal fire. A lovely baby, the landlady's child, not nursed by herself. Still there is an unintelligible number of women; but they are peaceable—no scolding as at Tarbet. This room is even expensively furnished, two washing-stands, tables mahogany, handsome mirror, not dim or sullied. 10 o'clock—prepare for bed."

Next day, after crossing the head of Loch Shira by ferryboat, Dorothy and Johanna set out along the northern shore of Loch Fyne. A heavy shower of rain forced them to seek shelter.

"I shelter under a Bank, Joanna passes me, fearful of the damp, and when it was nearly over I followed, and found her standing within the threshold of a cottage with the mistress of the house, who looked melancholy, and I perceived a tear on her cheek. Three or four very pretty children were crowded together beside them. Joanna said to me 'There is a corpse within,' and the mistress desired me to enter. I did so, leaving my companion in the outer room. A cheerful fire was in the centre of the small black apartment, and at one end lay the body of a child covered with a clean linen cloth. The mother of the child (the mistress's sister) seated at the head of the bier. The house was very small, yet another woman, nursing her child, was of the family, and there were at least four belonging to the mistress herself. Cakes were baking on the girdle—a little bare-footed girl came and cowered over the smoke and flame; and the sorrowing mother, seeing no one else at liberty, suspends her last duties to the dead to turn the cakes, and goes back again to her place. While I was seated by this humble fire-side, musing on poverty and peace, on death and the grave, the mistress of the house repaired to an inner room, and brought out a basin of milk, which she courteously offered me. I begged some of her warm bread, and would fain have kept my seat; but the smoke was not to be endured, so I returned to Joanna with my milk and bread. The mistress and children followed. I asked for a spoon, and she went back to her inner apartment, and after waiting a little while, as if to give her spoons an extra cleaning, brought me two, saying I might take which I liked, the larger or smaller. The shower was over, and giving a few halfpence to the little-ones we departed. We could not have presented money to the good woman of this cottage as a recompense for what she had given us: we should have felt it almost like an insult offered to human nature. Her kindness seemed to proceed from habitual good-will and hospitality; and the solemn event, which had happened but the day before, and the humble state and decency, with which the body had been watched, seemed to make the interior of the hut a sacred place. There was an expression of thoughtful melancholy on every countenance except those of the children, who seemed to be chiefly intent upon looking at us. It appeared that the child now lying dead, had long been languishing; but they knew not what ailed it, the Doctor living far off; so that it was too expensive, as the woman said, to call him in; but it was our questions which called forth that observation; for I daresay it was a thing never thought of. These poor people in lonely places have a few simple remedies, which they resort to, and when they fail are spared much of the anxiety and perplexity which we are tormented with, who know more of the various diseases that beset all periods of life, and can call in medical help at our pleasure."

Dunderave Castle (spelt by Dorothy *Dunderawe*) built by the Clan MacNachtan of Glen Shira in 1560 (despite the date 1598 carved above the door), was a shell when Dorothy and Johanna turned off the road at the promontary on which it stands.

"An inscription over the door, which we could not wholly make out," wrote Dorothy. The inscription reads "I.M.A.N. Behold the end. Be nocht Vyser nor the Hiest. I hop in God," the initials being these of the last MacNachtan to bring a bride to the place and those of his wife, while the last sentence is the motto of the Clan. She went on: "Walls of the Fort not shattered, but decaying. A small publick-house under the shadow of it." The Castle was later to be used by the novelist Neil Munro as the prototype for *Doom Castle*. Fortunately, the decay was arrested by Sir Robert Lorimer who restored the castle in 1911.

At Inveraray, Dorothy found things "still pretty much the same as in 1803." They walked in the grounds of the Castle, and attended the English service in the church, having missed the earlier Gaelic service by taking a longer walk than they had intended.

They sailed back to Glasgow, calling at Tarbert, Loch Fyne,

before passing through the Kyles of Bute to Rothesay, and so up-river to Dunoon, Greenock and Glasgow. Dorothy's notes form one of the earliest accounts of such a trip to survive, and so deserve to be quoted in full. The steamer at Inveraray pier sounded its horn before five o'clock in the morning.

"Monday morning before sunrise, on board the steam-boat —western shore now very woody, low rocky belt at the water's edge—a cluster of hills and ridges—rocky point—woody point—and the top of the hills dark purple heather, with wandering sheep—two wreaths of smoke. Pretty white cots now seen as spots at a distance, which I passed in my walk yester morning. A part of the town of Inveraray still visible. The mountains of Kinglas, and those beyond Cairndow very beautiful in long perspective . . . The sun yet unseen himself, shines on the western hills . . . The eastern shore hitherto of little interest—not populous, nor rich, the outlines unraised. It begins to improve. A large rocky island, yet with fine pasturage, and spotted with sheep. Sea-gulls flying about, and covering a small rock in the water, like comfits on a cake . . . Then the opening of the Canal from the Sound of Jura (6 or 7 miles distant.) We take in passengers and luggage from the pier, chiefly peasantry—the women look anxiously till their panniers are stowed, or, fancying the important charge less endangered in their own care, they descend with their burthens—baskets of eggs, fowls, etc. The pier crowded with gazers, men, women and children—a bustling scene! and our end of the vessel is now pretty well covered with people and their luggage. Bundles of all sorts and sizes—a lot of chickens, tied by the legs, is lying at my feet. The water now is spread out in great majesty. The mountain Island of Arran, beautiful in form and outline, soft as a cloud yet perfectly distinct, is before us. On the western shore (to our right) the steeps are covered with low woods—a road follows the shore, and pretty one-arched bridges cross the outlets of little streams that contribute their mite to the sea. Still woody—the grey arch of a bridge—thatched cottages in shelter beside it—woods retiring and climbing up the steeps. Not a boat now moving on the wide expanse of calm water—not one but ours, which sends its black rolling fleeces over the gentry's heads, while the sky above our end of the boat is of a bright clear blue. I sit aloft on a bundle placed at the top of a box—my neighbours two women who can hardly speak twenty

Robert Southey, 1774–1843

Above, Perth, considered 'a good city' by Southey; *below*, in Lanark Southey met the industrialist Robert Owen, whose model village for his cotton workers is seen here

words of English. One of them wears a tattered cloak that has been scarlet. An old man with a huge hamper of chickens is going to Greenock—a perfect tramper grown over with hair, his clothes hang loosely about him. I hear him say that he had walked twenty miles this morning with that burthen before he took boat at Tarbet. The men are greatly amused with his stories—he is all fun and rags. It is his business to travel from house to house in the Highlands, picking up fowls and eggs and any other marketable commodities. An old woman near him, whose store is but a small basket of eggs, inquires of him how they are selling, and his reply makes her look grave.

"A silver cloud now rests upon the mountain Island of Arran—its rocky ridgy top clear, above the white mantle. We tend eastward and Loch Riden with mountain head appears in view. Water here very wide;—but we hurry away to the Kyles of Bute, the heathy and rocky shores of that island to our right hand. Arran, the glory of these Isles, now a little behind us. A few poor fields are won from the wastes of Bute (a hilly ridge), and we see a few huts. The shores of Argyleshire to the left are much more varied. Large tracts of arable ground. Much of the corn secured in stacks, yet reapers are still busy . . . Rothesay, though but a small town, has every appearance of a busy sea port, strong quays, merchandise in the harbour, large Inns fronting the water with inviting inscriptions legible from the steam-boat, some hundred yards distant. Many of our company land, to take a run or a walk on the pier; and some, doubtless, for refreshment at the Inns. Our Cairndow companions leave us, and we see them sailing away towards the southern part of the Island. Near Rothesay, a beautiful view of Loch Striven—simple, flowing lines of mountains—one white house at the end. Resting shadows and vivid sunshine. When we have left Bute, and are upon the broad Firth of Clyde, looking back we see the mountains of Arran rising above the Isle of Bute—the shores pleasant on each side—fertile lands, villages, and sometimes a church tower. The town of Greenock seen long before we reach it, rapidly though we travel. A very large place, large buildings near the shore. Shipping in Harbour. Now we have busy work. Many of the Highland crew depart with their hampers, baskets and bundles. A big-boned porter greets a bare headed and bare-footed girl, whose charge has been a weighty basket of eggs, with "God bless thy bonny face," and lifting up her load hies with it over the plank and she follows him. Boys and men, the moment we drew under the wall, hurried on board with apples, pears and cakes to sell; and shops of eatables on the shore were innumerable. At the sound of the horn, passengers, who had landed, hurried back to the boat, and the hawkers were off with their stores. The sail from Greenock to Port Glasgow, as delightful as glorious prospects of mountains and gently-varied shores could make it, while we glided over unruffled waters beneath a bright blue sky. But at Port Glasgow the magnificence and stately grandeur surpassed all we had seen before. So indeed it seemed, yet this might in part be owing to our reaching that port just before the time of sunset. I was surprized to see such an appearance of a large town, with the bustle and traffic of a great sea-port . . . It is not possible to conceive any earthly spectacle more beautiful than the water, mountains, and glowing sky to the west in our approach to Dumbarton—and to the east, the Rock, now rising out of the full swolen waters (for it was high tide) had, in addition to its peculiar wildness, a character of stately beauty of which it bore no impression when we approached from Glasgow at low water before the sun had dispersed the morning clouds and haziness. The river too, all the way up, was much finer, being full to its banks. Met and passed several steam-boats and vessels of various kinds . . . Landed at Glasgow in the twilight—great bustle in the harbour—puffing of steam-boats—masts of ships all along the shore. Taverns, houses and shops, a row fronting the water. Among many claimants a little boy without shoes and stockings offered to carry our luggage, and conduct us to the Eagle. We took him into our service, and as darkness was coming on and Joanna's pace was not to be hurried, I left her and her guide to find my way to the Bookseller's shop where places were to be taken for Lanark. Lamp light was begun; and before I reached the Trongate twilight was gone, and the shops shining in full splendour. Streets very busy—not with carriages, but people—posting away, like the Londoners, as if they had more business than time."

From Glasgow, Dorothy and Johanna visited the Falls of Clyde, and noted the increase in the acreage given over to the cultivation of fruit in the Clyde valley. They called at New Lanark, and were shown over one of Robert Owen's schools by his sister.

From Lanark, they travelled by Crawford and Elvanfoot to Moffat, and from there to Boreland, Burnfoot, Langholm, and down the valley of the Eden to Longtown.

William Wordsworth, as everyone knows, became a Government servant (much to the disgust of the young Keats), as a Distributor of Stamps for his part of the country. As his poetic fame increased and his circumstances became easier, he made more frequent trips to London and to the Continent, until advancing age confined him to his beloved Lake District, a seer whose poetry inspired the young but whose conservative opinions (though more thoroughly argued out by their holder than is commonly supposed) upset many of those who warmed to the poet's earlier revolutionary fervour. His closing years were saddened by the death of Johanna in 1843; by the marriage of his daughter Dora to the unstable Edward Quillinan and her death in 1847 six years later; and by the death of John's son Edward in 1845, and of John's wife Isabella in 1848. A more prolonged sorrow was the serious illness of his sister Dorothy in 1829, an illness from which she never recovered, and which, within a few years, left her in a permanent condition of selfish and childish querulousness. a sore trial to Wordsworth's wife Mary, the last of that generation of the family to survive. Wordsworth himself died in April, 1850, Dorothy in January, 1855, and Mary, by then blind, in January, 1859.

Wordsworth's Scottish poems, included in his collected works even during his lifetime, are his tribute to a nation whose greatest poet had been a formative influence, and for whose greatest novelist he developed a profound affection. Dorothy's Journal of the 1803 tour, carefully composed and written for "the sake of a few friends", was first published in 1874, edited by Principal Shairp of Edinburgh University. All Dorothy Wordsworth's Journals were republished in 1952, edited by E. de Selincourt. Her *Journal* of 1803 remains one of the most delightful travel-books about Scotland ever written.

6

Robert Southey:
Laureate with Engineer

The year 1819 was an auspicious one for English letters. Shelley was busy with *Prometheus Unbound* and *The Cenci*, and Keats was at work upon *Hyperion*. It was also the year in which Robert Southey, the Poet Laureate, made a journey into Scotland in the company of the great Scots engineer Thomas Telford, who himself had an interest in poetry.

Southey, born at Bristol in 1774, was the son of an unsuccessful draper, and had been brought up at Bath by his mother's half-sister from the age of three. After four years at Westminster School, he was expelled for writing an essay against flogging, *The Flagellant*, in the school magazine. His uncle, a British chaplain at Lisbon who had paid for Southey's schooling, now tried, unsuccessfully, to get his charge admitted to Oxford. With some difficulty, the future laureate was eventually entered at Balliol.

His enthusiasm for the French Revolution inspired him to produce, in 1793, *Joan of Arc*, the first of his long series of dull epic poems. The following year Coleridge visited Oxford and Southey became obsessed with Coleridge's idea of founding a "pantisocracy", or American Utopia, in which the male members were to earn their living from the soil on the banks of the Susquehanna, while their wives looked after the house and reared the children. Back at Bristol, Robert Lovell was drawn into their dreams. Lovell was married to Sara Fricker, whose sister later married Coleridge. Southey became engaged to a third sister, Edith, who made it plain that she would not be a party to any idealistic "pantisocracy". He married shortly before accompanying his uncle to Portugal. On his return, after a short period at Gray's Inn, Southey took a cottage at Bristol, then another at Burton, in

Hampshire. A further trip to Portugal, this time with his wife, followed. Then in 1801, at the invitation of Coleridge, Southey paid his first visit to the Lake District. After a short spell as private secretary to the Chancellor of the Exchequer for Ireland, Isaac Corry, Southey and his wife settled at Greta Hall, Keswick, with the Coleridges and Mrs. Lovell. Southey was a devoted family man. When Coleridge deserted his wife and children, without hesitation Southey took on the additional responsibility of providing for them too, although he was never a rich man.

He amassed a fine library, became an authority on Portugal (though he failed to complete what was to have been his definitive history of that country), and produced epic after epic–*Madoc and Metrical Tales and Other Poems* in 1805, *The Curse of Kehana* in 1810, and *Roderick, the Last of the Goths*, in 1814–as well as excellent prose works like that rambling miscellany *The Doctor*, which contained Southey's immortal tale for children "The Three Bears", and in 1813, *The Life of Nelson*, a model of all that a short biography should be, and which has become a classic.

This was the year in which Sir Walter Scott was offered the Laureateship in succession to a nonentity called Pye. Scott declined it, but used his influence to get Southey appointed. Six more peaceful and industrious years passed during which, day after day, Southey sat in his study overlooking Derwentwater writing assiduously. Then his friend John Rickman, Clerk Assistant of the House of Commons and Secretary to the Commissioners for the Caledonian Canal, suggested to Thomas Telford that the Poet Laureate might accompany them both on the great Scots engineer's forthcoming tour of inspection of the work in progress in his native land for which he was then responsible.

So on Monday, August 16th, 1819, Southey boarded the Carlisle Mail for Edinburgh, admiring "the New Courts at Carlisle, one on each side the entrance of the City from the South", and noting that Lord Lonsdale interfered with the architect's original intention of uniting them by "an arch supporting a cupola" on the grounds that unnecessary cost would have been incurred.

During that first day's journey, he admired the "quiet sober character" of the Eskdale scenery: "a somewhat melancholy kind of beauty in accord with autumn, evening, and declining life: green hills high enough to assume something of a mountainous sweep and swell: green pastures where man has done little, but where little more seems to be wanting."

He was the only passenger on the coach. As it was dark when he reached Hawick, he made tea for himself "in a comfortless room". At five o'clock on the morning of the 17th, he reached Edinburgh, to find that "even at that early hour there was a busy greens-market in the High Street. Upon enquiry I learned that every thing must be cleared away before eight o'clock–a good, wise regulation."

He managed to get into MacGregor's Hotel in Princes Street, where Rickman and his wife were staying, and sat down to wait "till the guests of the house were stirring."

He spent his first day in Edinburgh calling on friends and their relations, and on the publisher Blackwood, who gave him a copy of Christopher North's newly-published and highly diverting account of Edinburgh manners, *Peter's Letters to his Kinsfolk*.

In the afternoon, Telford arrived from Glasgow, and Southey recorded:

"There is so much intelligence in his countenance, so much frankness, kindness and hilarity about him, flowing from the never-failing well-spring of a happy nature, that I was on cordial terms with him in five minutes."

Thomas Telford was seventeen years Southey's senior, born the son of a shepherd in Eskdalemuir, Dumfriesshire, in 1757. He was largely self-educated, having picked up some French, German and Latin while working as a stonemason. His verse-letter to Burns, signed "Eskdale Tam", if hardly distinguished poetically, shows not only a certain mastery of language, but an awareness of the "feel" of the current Scots vernacular literary idiom.

Building canals and enlarging houses as surveyor and engineer for the County of Salop (Shropshire), he soon established the reputation of being one of the most able civil engineers of his day, a reputation endorsed when, in 1806, the King of Sweden called him in to advise on the construction of the series of locks which provide a kind of water staircase on the upper reaches of the River Göta, which, through the Gothenburg Canal, links Gothenburg, on the sea coast, and Stockholm. Two years later he received a diamond ring from Alexander I for services rendered to the Russian Government.

In Scotland, where he was adviser to the two Commissions for canals and roads that had been set up by 1803, his works were numerous, the most spectacular being the road from Carlisle to Glasgow, which only recently has given place to a dual carriageway incorporating large stretches of Telford's original highway. There was also the Caledonian Canal, along with numerous other roads and bridge-works actively under construction in the year 1819.

The party was not due to leave for another day or two, so Southey further explored Edinburgh. One morning, he looked out of his window, and wrote:

"The view from this hotel in the morning, when the fires are just kindled, is probably the finest smoke-scape that can anywhere be seen. Well may Edinburgh be called Auld Reekie! and the houses stand so one above another, that none of the smoke wastes itself upon the desert air before the inhabitants have derived all the advantage of its odour and smuts. You might smoke bacon by hanging it out of the window."

He visited Holyrood, looked at the portraits of Scottish kings, fabulous and genuine, and decided that while Mary, Queen of Scots was thought beautiful by Scottish standards, "anywhere else such a countenance would only be called good-looking, and that rather by courtesy than by right."

The High Street he thought odd and characteristic. "The Windes, down which an English eye may look, but into which no English nose would willingly venture, for stinks older than the Union are to be found there—show at once how a Porteous mob might rise like Myrmidons from the earth and presently disappear again."

He was equally critical of the New Town, which made him wonder at "the enormous lengths of the streets in the New Town, where there is neither protection nor escape from the severe winds to which Edinburgh is exposed." He also commented on the Scots custom of numbering houses "across the street, the odd numbers on one side, the even on the other—a convenient arrangement after one has found it out."

On a hot afternoon, he took a coach to Leith and walked across the Links, "for the chance of seeing the golf-players; but the weather was too hot for them." There being still some time before dinner, he "got into a bathing machine, and left some of my superfluous heat in the Forth."

At five o'clock on the morning of Friday August 20th, he rose, packed his trunk, and set out with Telford and his party by coach. At Linlithgow, Southey admired the Church, "a venerable structure", and the Palace, but thought the town as a whole "decayed, dirty and dolorous". After a good breakfast of fresh boiled salmon the party set off "thro' a fertile and highly cultivated country" for Falkirk and Stirling.

The view from Stirling Castle fully equalled his expectations, and the Castle itself interested him greatly. But he had something about which to complain.

"The general want of cleanliness . . . . The houses seem to have been white washed when they were built, and never since that time; and they look the worse because the windows are not casements, but in wooden frames, which when the panes . . . . are broken are seldom mended; the hole is either patched with paper, or stuffed with a clout, or pieced, or left with no other covering than what the spiders may be pleased to make." He also disliked the girls, smartly dressed, but going about "in the filthy bare-foot fashion of the country, a custom to which nothing could ever reconcile our English feelings."

From Stirling, the party headed for Callander; but just beyond Doune, one of the horses stumbled and fell, dragging the postillion down with him. Fortunately the boy was unhurt, but the incident gave Southey the chance to recount the story of the traveller who suddenly found himself on "a sort of Devil's bowling-green", and who called out in alarm "What's the matter?" only to get the calm reply: "Perthshire–we're in Perthshire, sir". Alone among the Highland counties Perthshire, for some reason, refused to allow the Commissioner for roads to interfere in its affairs. Its roads were then among the worst in Scotland.

Nowadays we have perhaps come to believe that the reluctance of some Highland hotel keepers to serve meals to travellers other than at regular hours has the force of Scots tradition behind it. Such, however, is not the case, for in coaching days early departures and late arrivals were a daily occurrence. Southey and Telford arrived at their inn at Callander at nine o'clock, and one hour later sat down to hot and cold salmon and lamb chops, washed down by "good bottled porter, but no twopenny, which everybody would have liked better," a reflection of the English preference for light ale.

Next day they set out for Loch Katrine. For a Lake Poet, and one whose study looked out upon water, Southey's reactions to Loch Vennacher and Loch Achray were singularly casual. He commented upon an inn which had been "a farmhouse till Walter Scott brought the Trosachs (*sic*) and Loch Katrin (*sic*) into fashion," and reflected that if its owner "has a proper sense of its obligations, he will set up the sign of Walter Scott's head."

The party sailed up the loch, disembarking at a vantage point where Southey noted: "The higher and greater part is not interesting; the lower end is unequalled by anything I have ever seen."

He found it incredible that the Duke of Montrose should in the previous year have sold "the woods on Benvenue, which was then completely clothed with fine trees, for the paltry sum of 200£," thereby incurring "the obloquy and the disgrace of disfiguring, as far as it was in his power to disfigure the most beautiful spot in the whole island of Great Britain."

Southey, like Wordsworth, understandably made comparison with his own Lake District—the Pass resembled the Gorge of Borrowdale, though it was "upon a large scale and better wooded," while Benvenue resembled "Helvellin as seen from Ullswater" although on the whole Southey took a kinder view of Scotland's scenery than his fellow laker.

Early next day, a Sunday, they travelled through the Pass of Leny to the head of Loch Earn, passing on the way a house where James ("Abyssinian") Bruce "used to have his summer residence while he was preparing his travels for the press." Southey, who had reviewed various editions of Bruce's book, found it "one of the most interesting spots that I have seen."

After breakfast, they moved on to Killin, part of the way

being along General Wade's road, whom "as bound by duty, and by rhyme, we blest", then to Kenmore by that "noble piece of water", Loch Tay.

Aberfeldy was reached next day. Southey commented favourably on the "fine views of Lord Bredalbane's house and park and of the fine valley of the Tay", but thought Aberfeldy itself "a place which might preferably be called Aberfilthy, for marvellously foul it is."

Southey found "the approach to Dunkeld peculiarly fine. The cathedral, which tho' grievously injured, has escaped with less injury than many others from the brutality of Calvinistic reformers, is most happily placed with the river in front, and some noble woods on a rising ground behind . . . . The bridge is one of Telford's works, and one of the finest in Scotland. The Duke (of Athol) was at the expence, Government aiding him with 5,000£. There are five arches, the dimensions of the middle arches of Westminster Bridge; and besides these there are two upon the land."

Southey records an interesting detail about the construction of the bridge, which no doubt he got from Telford.

"It was built on dry ground, formerly the bed of the river; for the Braan, which enters a little above the town, had brought down gravel enough to force the Tay out of its old channel. When the bridge was completed the original bed was cleared and made the channel again; by this means the building was carried on with greater ease, and at much less expence."

The Cathedral, which had "a crack down the tower" when Southey saw it, still stands, and the little houses in the precinct have been carefully restored by the National Trust for Scotland. Telford's bridge also still stands, skilfully widened to take the burden of twentieth-century traffic.

Before setting out for Perth next morning, Southey "re-crost the bridge, and proceeded along the side of what formerly was Birnam Wood, of locomotive celerity," adding "it seems now to have taken its final departure."

At Perth, Southey sought out "Dr. Woods, a delightful old man", who set him "at ease concerning one of the tumours on my head which has just begun to supperate, having been there more than ten years without annoying me before. He says it will discharge itself, and recommends a poultice at night, and some simple ointment on a piece of lint by day. The former part of his advice it is impossible to follow while I am travelling. But I laid in lint and ointment, and must trust to Mr. Telford's kindness to apply them; we are generally quartered in a double bedded room."

This medical visit prevented Southey from seeing as much of Perth as he had hoped, though he saw enough to reckon it, "a good city". At three in the afternoon, the party left Perth to drive through the Carse of Gowrie to Dundee. The fields were full of reapers. Southey commented on "the land all in open cultivation of the best kind and now in the best season and happiest state."

Next day, Wednesday, 25th August, Southey rose early and went with Telford to inspect the "huge floating dock, and the finest graving dock I ever saw." With the earth thus excavated, ground formerly covered by the tide was to be raised. The town wanted Telford to build them fifteen piers on this reclaimed land, but Telford declared three to be enough, saying that "the creation of fifteen new Scotch Peers was too strong a measure."

Inspired by this sight, Southey confessed to the artist's romantic and usually secret admiration for the lot of the practical man.

"Telford's is a happy life: everywhere making roads, building bridges, forming canals, and creating harbours–works of sure, solid permanent utility; everywhere employing a great number of persons, selecting the most meritorious and putting them forward in the world, in his own way."

Southey went on to reveal how Telford set about road-making.

"The plan upon which he proceeds . . . . is this: first to level and drain, then, like the Romans, to lay a solid pavement of large stones, the round or broad end downwards, as close as they can be set; the points are then broken off, and a layer of stones to about the size of walnuts, laid over them, so that the whole are bound together; over all a little gravel if it be at hand, but this, is not essential."

Southey inspected "the Cathedral"–St. Mary's does not, in fact, have this status–"an extraordinary mass of buildings of all ages; the tower, which is the oldest part, being connected by a modern interpolation to a portion of intermediate date or dates." He also commented on the unpleasant odour of flax, the ingredient of Dundee's jute-making industry being at that time still in part home grown.

At half past four in the afternoon they set out for Arbroath, getting a good view of Dundee as they looked back, as well as a glimpse of St. Andrews across the water "at a great distance". At Arbroath, Southey had just light enough left to see the Abbey, "which must have been a magnificent building before the beastly multitude destroyed it", and to reflect that it was the sight of these ruins which made John Wesley exclaim: "God deliver us from reforming mobs!"

Years before, Southey had written one of the ballads by which he is still popularly remembered, *The Inchcape Rock*. Now, he was able to look on "the Inchcape or Bell Rock Light House (or Sir Ralph the Rover's rock)" and note that it is "visible from the town, two revolving lights, one very bright, the other less so, being red: they are about three minutes in revolving," an accurate observation which perhaps illustrates how far from his romanticism of twenty years before the Poet Laureate had travelled.

Moving up the coast, Southey noted "pigeon houses in the fields of singular construction–slender but not narrow buildings, with a shelving roof in front, and a straight wall on the back from the summit of the roof." These dovecots kept seventeenth and eighteenth century East Coast lairds supplied with birds for their tables. After having crossed the North Esk, Southey again noted "the stench of the flax . . . . abominable in these parts, so bad indeed that the odour from fields manured with putrid fish-offal, seemed tolerable in comparison."

At Bervie, "an ugly town", Southey was introduced to two of Telford's *aides de camps,* Mr. Gibb and John Mitchell, whom Telford had found as a working mason near Inverness, and had trained so that he was now overseer of the roads under the management of the Commissioners. Mitchell was nicknamed the "Tartar" because of "his cast of countenance", and the fact that he travelled somewhere between six and nine thousand miles on horseback a year.

Bervie pier, which cost "less than 2,000£", was in process of construction. Southey investigated the mechanics and the financing of the operation.

"The stones are lifted by a crane, with strong iron cramps or pinchers; and an iron rail-road is in use, which is carried from pier to pier, wherever it is wanted. They use pudding-stone being the nearest material; of all stone it is the worst for working, but it is hard and durable, and when in its place will do as well as if it were granite or marble. Mr. Farquahar, the Lord of the soil, who has made about 150,000£ as a Civilian, advances that half the cost which Government requires as the condition of its aid with the other. Without national aid the work would not have been undertaken, tho' in such a place and county it is the first step towards improvement."

The party then moved on to Stonehaven, passing the very extensive ruin of Dunottar, where the regalia of Scotland was taken for security during the Cromwellian wars before being buried in the old parish kirkyard of Kineff when George Ogilvie, Dunottar's defender, could no longer hold out against the English soldiers.

"What a blessing that such places are only ruins," Southey exclaimed; "and how different is the feeling which such ruins excite from that which depresses the heart at Aberbrothock, Melrose and Glastonbury!"

That night at ten, and again at breakfast next morning, Friday, August 27th, Southey and his companions ate "Findon haddocks, which Mr. Telford would not allow us to taste at Dundee, nor till we reached Stonehaven, lest this boasted dainty of Aberdeen should be disparaged by a bad specimen. The fish is very slightly salted, and as slightly smoked by a peat fire, after which the sooner they are eaten the better."

Thus regaled, they set out for Aberdeen "in one of those mists which had a right to wet Rickman and myself, as Englishmen, to the skin", passing through "peat-mosses succeeded by wastes where poor heather grew among the stones. Yet even in this unpromising land, great improvements are going on. The owners of the soil encourage the settlers by giving them a few pounds wherewith to erect a hut, and letting them the land for a few years rent free."

This was the system which Burns's father (whose people came from the North East) found so ruinous, completed improvements in due course leading to a demand for higher rent.

In old Aberdeen Southey inspected the exterior of King's College and the Cathedral of St. Machar, admiring the "air of quietness and permanence—of old times; long walls well built in four days; a few old trees, and houses standing separately, each in its garden", an "air" which still invests the place today in spite of the expansion of the University.

It formed a marked contrast to New Aberdeen, which then had a population of forty thousand, being all "bustle, business and improvement". Union Street was new with "many houses still building". The extension to Smeaton's pier at the quay was Telford's work, and the special executive concern of Gibb. Having paid his respects to the tomb of James Beattie, author of that once popular poem *The Minstrel,* in the Town's East and West Churches, Southey went down to inspect the harbour.

"A ship was entering under full sail—*The Prince of Waterloo*—she had been to America, had discharged her cargo at London, and we now saw her reach her own port in safety—a joyous and delightful sight. The Whalers are come in, and there is a strong odour of train oil, which would rejoice the heart of a Greenlander, and really even to us it was perfume after the flax."

Southey spent the day scanning the sights and sounds of Aberdeen, a city which well lends itself to this sort of enjoyment, and jotted down in crisp sentences some of his impressions:

"The Cryer here summons the people not by bell, but by beat of drum. I saw a beggar in the street reading his bible. At the Inn they cut off the crust of the loaf, and made their bread and butter with only the soft part of the loaf—a bad practise; showing that they know not what good bread and butter is. Melted butter seems not to be used with vegetables—what in honest old English used to be called garden-stuff.... But garden-stuff itself is of late introduction into Scotland.... The Findon haddocks are regularly brought at breakfast and tea. They have little glass decanters for whiskey of all sizes, down to a gill."

In spite of the growth of manufactured goods, in Southey's day local variants not only in food and drink, but also in building customs and materials were still to be found:

"The sash windows have generally two brass handles at bottom for lifting them by."

There was also the steady exploitation of local building materials. Southey spoke of "the fine granite which this neighbourhood supplies", adding:

"The Scotch regard architectural beauty in their private houses, as well as in their public edifices, much more than we do; partly perhaps because their materials are so much better. For as for making fine buildings with brick, you might as easily make a silk purse out of a sow's ear."

Next day, after admiring King's College, with its tower, "better than that at Edinburgh, St. Giles because the Scotch Crown is made the crest of the open work, instead of forming the open work itself", Southey proceeded by way of "the fine old bridge over the Don" to Old Meldrum, where, at the inn, they had a peat fire in their room. Southey graphically captures the atmosphere of many a small-town inn of the day.

"My bed room was as small as a ship's cabin; and a small jug, the same which held my poor Scotch allowance of water, was placed under the sash window to prop it up! A good breakfast as usual in Scotland, with Findon haddocks, eggs, sweatmeats (preserved blackcurrants formed one) and honey."

And so on in the morning to Turriff, passing Fyvie Castle on the way. At Turriff, "the best house in the place is a Lawyer's—proof how the profession flourishes in Scotland. Watchmakers as well as booksellers seem much more numerous than in England; there are three in this little place". He found Banff, "except where the odour of herrings prevailed (which is no bad odour), a clean, fresh town, open to the sea breezes and the country air". Southey was taken to see the Earl of Fife's Duff House, built by Robert Adam; with its library at the top of the house commanding a fine view of the bridge over the River Deveron and of the North Sea, "bright and blue in the sunshine." Here, as at Macduff, Telford was building a pier.

Passing through Portsoy, "a neat thriving little place, where a good proportion of the houses have gardens, and several are prettily clothed with creepers and fruit trees", the travellers reached Cullen where, after "a magnificent breakfast (fresh herrings of the finest kind being added here to the usual abundance of good things)", they walked down to the pier.

Here, the pier, which was to cost four thousand pounds, was well enough advanced to allow the fishing boats to use it, and Southey brings the busy scene on that long-ago morning vividly alive for us:

"When I stand upon it at low water, seeing the tremendous rocks with which the whole shore bristled, and the open sea to which it is exposed, it was with a proud feeling that I saw the finest talents in the world employed by the British Government in work of such unostentatious, but great, immediate, palpable and permanent utility. Already the excellent effects are felt. The fishing vessels are just come in, having caught about 300 barrels of herrings during the night. All hands were busy. Some in clearing from the nets the fish which were caught by the gills; some in shovelling them with a long and broad wooden shovel into baskets; women walked more than knee deep into the water to take these baskets on their backs, while under sheds erected for protection in hot weather, girls and women out of number were employed in ripping out the gills and entrails, some others in strewing salt over them, and others again in taking them from the troughs into which they were thrown after this operation, and packing them into barrels. Others were spreading the nets to dry . . . . Air and ocean also were alive with flocks of sea fowl, dipping every minute for their share in the herring fishery. . . . A heap of dog-fish was lying on the pier . . . ."

The herring, it seems, were selling at twenty five shillings the barrel, and were "chiefly sent to the West Indies, for the slaves".

Similar harbours were under construction up and down the East Coast, paid for by the Government "from the remainder of the rents of the forfeited estates"—forfeited by those who had come "out" on the Jacobite side during the risings of 1715 and 1745—"the whole of which rents (till the estates were restored)" being "designed to be appropriated to the improvement of Scotland."

At Fochabers, Southey looked at the Duke of Gordon's "great ugly house", and discovered the sense of injustice felt by the villagers at having to pay a shilling a pound for their salmon when the Duke, who let his fishing rights for seven thousand pounds a year, "a sum almost incredible", insisted on being supplied at sixpence the pound. Southey, nicknamed by his travelling companions "The Wolf" because of his interest in food and voracious appetite, opined that "They spoil their fish very commonly in Scotland by cutting it in slices fit for boiling, and boiling it in that form."

Elgin induced him to admire its fine-arched bridge over the Spey, and "groan over the brutal spirit of mob-reformation" as he looked on the ruined Cathedral. "We went on the roof–one of the symptoms which I perceive in myself of declining life is that such places make me giddy, and I can no longer rely upon myself among crags and steep places as I used to do."

Of Elgin itself, still today well preserved in spite of Victorian depredations, Southey said: "The city has an ancient air, and an appearance of decay about it . . . . A bell rings here at eight o'clock, and an abominable drum is beaten at nine."

Early travellers in Scotland frequently complained of the bad food and diet they had to put up with at our inns. Southey found more sophisticated fault with the inn at Elgin.

"All possible faults of bedmaking were exemplified to a nicety in my bed last night. The under sheet was spread over the bolster instead of being wrapped round it; the upper one too short, so that it scarcely turned over the blanket; the bed or mattrass (I know not which it ought to be called) hard, higher in the middle than at the side, and sloping in an inclined plane to the foot. Nevertheless I slept well."

Rothes was the next place to be reached, a village of "three long streets . . . . all composed of new cottages, neatly built, of one floor each, side by side, and with a mournful uniformity such as immediately told you they had not risen in the natural course of happy and enterprizing industry, but had been built at once by the Lord of the soil, and planted as a colony." Southey nevertheless remarks that conditions in Scotland have so far improved that everywhere except Aberfeldy he found a built-in lavatory, or "commodity", as he calls it.

Craigalachie, Telford's bridge with a span of a hundred and fifty feet, excited Southey's attention. He tells us that the whole cost of the bridge, including the approaches, was eight thousand two hundred pounds, and that it was planned, cast and erected in twelve months.

At Ballendalloch Castle, once owned by that General Grant who "lost the fairest opportunity of success offered during the whole American war", and then owned by Macpherson Grant, the member of Parliament for Sutherlandshire, Southey looked at a portrait of General Wade, Telford's military road-building predecessor–who operated almost a century before in an attempt to pacify the Highlands–"with a blue velvet robe over his breast-plate–and a wig! the countenance mild and pleasing, by no means deficient in intellect, but not indicating a strong mind."

Here, at lunch, Southey tasted sheep's-head broth and found it "rather better than hodge-podge: the flavour of the burnt wool hardly differs from what might be better obtained by burnt cheese."

On the way along the Spey to Grantown, Southey noted Telford's custom that "a road be always defined, if it be only by a line of turf on either side where nothing more is needed; for this defining presents any excuse if the road is not kept in order by the Contractors."

Grantown's regularity arose from the same cause as that at Rothes, both being laid out by a Grant of Rothiemurchus. Here, the inn, kept by a retired army sergeant and his "vulgar handsomish" wife from Portsmouth, was furnished with cheap military prints "in true Portsmouth taste". But Southey and Telford dried themselves at a "beautiful peat fire . . . . I never saw coal or wood build up a finer body of fire", and after tea with scones and a mutchkin of whisky, retired for the night.

On the road to Forres and Nairn, Southey noticed that the few inhabitants of the countryside were "black as peat stacks in their appearance, the peat stack in reality generally forming part of the edifice–peat stack, peat sty, and peat house being altogether: the roofs are also covered with turf, or peat, on which grass and heather grow comfortably, and probably the better because of the smoke which warms the soil."

At Forres, he examined a monument purporting to show the spot at which the witches who prophesised to Macbeth were burned alive. After dining at Forres, Southey and Telford crossed the heath where the encounter was said to have taken place, and where, on arrival, Southey found awaiting him a diploma making him an Honorary Member of the Literary Society of Banff, the seal of this society being a beehive and the motto, Alveum Accipite. Because of a noisy initiation ceremony of the local Masons, neither Southey nor Telford were able to get much sleep in their double-bedded room.

They travelled next day through Nairn to Inverness, passing Cawdor Castle. They arrived on Fair Day, and the streets were filled with women.

Southey had been troubled throughout the trip by the tumour on the side of his head, so he visited an Inverness surgeon by the name of Kennedy, who gave him some ointment to relieve a suppuration in it.

We are reminded of the comparatively recent development by Lowland standards of Inverness as a town when Southey observes:

"Sixty years ago, there were no shops in Inverness. Booths were at that time erected in the streets, as they are now at fair-time. And still at fairs, and on market days, altho' there are numerous shops and good ones, men stand in the streets with pieces of cloth or linen under their arms for sale."

On this occasion, however, the stay in Inverness was a brief one, and Southey and his friends continued North as far as Beauly, making a detour into Strathglas to see the Falls of Kilmorack.

"On the one side, a lad was angling, knee deep in the water; on the other a woman was beating linen in the river—a practice which makes washing a cleanly and picturesque operation. Sometimes a dozen salmon have been caught here in the course of a single night merely by laying branches along the shelves of rock, to catch them if they fail in the leap, and prevent them from falling into the water. Lord Lovat once disposed some boiling kettles about these falls in such a manner that he served his guests with fish which had leapt from the river into the pot."

At Beauly, where he looked at the Cathedral, "rather an extensive ruin", Southey had "a decent dinner of salted ling, eggs, mutton chops, and excellent potatoes, with ginger-beer, and good port wine at what appeared no better than an English alehouse . . . . kept by an Irishman, who speculates in road-making."

Crossing Connal Bridge, which, like Lovat Bridge, was one of Telford's constructions and cost six thousand five hundred pounds, they moved on to Dingwall, reminding Southey by its name of "the Icelandic capital Thingvalla." However, this capital of Rosshire, which exported timber and grain and imported lime and coal through two basins cut by Telford in the river Peffer at a cost of three thousand eight hundred pounds, seemed to Southey, "a vile place" whose recent paving induced him to remark that "such a mark of civilisation" ill accorded with "the general aspect of the place".

Invergordon seemed to him "an ugly village, in an important situation", since it was the point at which "the ferry communicates with the Black Isle, and so, by another ferry with Fort George, thus saving a day's journey. Piers for the use of this ferry, here and on the opposite coast, are nearly finished; the cost of both will be 1628£." A reminder of the unpleasant nature of travel in the Highlands before Telford began his work is provided by Southey's remark: "Before these were begun passengers were sometimes obliged to mount their horses nearly a quarter of a mile from the shore, and ride mid-leg deep in the water."

They rode round Cromarty Bay after breakfast one morning, and arrived at Tain, "a neater town than Dingwall". Southey found that "the Tainites entertain a great contempt for Dornoch, the capital of Sutherland, which is on the opposite side of the bay." The landlord reinforced this opinion, saying that "as for himself he would not set his foot in such a place", and Telford's lieutenant, Mitchell, concurred, claiming that "The church yard's made a common thoroughfare for men and cattle, without any regard to decency, and the fair is held among the tombs."

On the way to Bonar Bridge, Southey saw the recently established mail coach to Thurso, "a Diligence, drawn by two horses and carrying three inside", and the Iron Age broch of Dunaliskaig. Accommodation could not be found at Bonar Bridge for all the party, so Southey stayed at Kincardine, where he inspected the kirkyard, concluding that: "There is something affecting in the Scottish custom of calling a woman by the name of her husband while she lives, but designating her upon her tombstone by her family name, as if death restored her to her own kin."

Next day, Monday, September 16th, the travellers set out on the last northern lap of their journey. They passed through Spinningdale, "so named with double reference to the site and to himself, by David Dale of New Lanark, the well-known father-in-law of the better known Robert Owen. He thought that a manufactory of the wool of the country might be established with advantage here, where there was command of water, a navigable firth close at hand, and labour cheap". After investing twenty thousand pounds in the scheme, however, Dale found that the Yorkshire manufacturers could undercut him, and so the earliest of many schemes imposed from outside and designed to bring industry to the Highlands failed, though the stone cottages originally built to house the spinners were better than the usual Highland homes of the time.

Fleet Mound, now known simply as The Mound, the northernmost point of their journey, gave them a sight of Dunrobin Castle, the seat of the Sutherland family, and, "far off, the Ord of Caithness, and the mountains in that county".

A wall nearly a thousand yards in length with flood-gates shut by the tide as it rose was constructed by Telford in the narrow estuary of the Fleet, as a result of which land which formerly flooded had been reclaimed.

At this time, the Highlands, whose social structure, with its strong clan loyalties, had been so severely racked by the risings of 1715 and 1745, and whose pacification had led to the preliminary road works of Wade and was now in part the cause and source of some of the finance for Telford's numerous projects, was about to be racked again by a crisis with more far-reaching consequences than the death-throes of the Stuart cause. Since the 'Forty Five', and the subsequent dismantling of the clan system by the Government in London, the Highland landowners had increasingly orientated themselves towards the South. Many of their children were educated at English schools and universities, and so grew up without any feeling for the old loyalties. When, early in the 19th century, it became apparent that sheep would produce more profit from their lands than the rents of crofters, some landlords cruelly evicted, and to all intent forcibly deported, whole families to Nova Scotia and Canada.

Southey was apparently made aware of such excesses, which became a shameful feature of the Clearance, as the burning of thatched roofs to drive out the families reluctant to leave their homesteads, and although he was naturally appalled at the housing conditions prevalent throughout the Highland countryside, he was moved to indignation and compassion:

"There is at this time a considerable ferment in the country concerning the management of the M[arquis] of Stafford's estates:[1] they comprize nearly 2/5ths of the county of Sutherland, and the process of converting them into extensive sheep-farms is being carried on. A political economist has no hesitation concerning the fitness of the land in view, and little scruple as to the means. Leave the bleak regions, he says, for the cattle to breed in, and let men remove to situations where they can exert themselves and thrive. The traveller who looks only at the outside of things, might easily assent to this reasoning. I have never–not even in Galicia–seen any human habitations so bad as the Highland *black-houses*; by that name the people of the country call them, in distinction from such as are built with stone and lime. The worst of the black houses are the *bothies*–made of very large turfs, from 4 to 6 feet long, fastened with wooden pins to a rude wooden frame. The Irish cabin, I suppose, must be such a heap of peat with or without stones, according to the facility of collecting them, or the humour of the maker. But these men-sties are not inhabited, as in Ireland, by a race of ignorant and ferocious barbarians, who can never be civilized till they are regenerated–till their very nature is changed. Here you have a quiet, thoughtful, contented, religious people, susceptible of improvement, and willing to be improved. To transplant these people from their native mountain glens to the sea coast, and require them to become some cultivators, others fishermen, occupations to which they have never been accustomed–to expect a sudden and total change of habits in the existing generation, instead of gradually producing it in their children; to expel them by process of law from their black houses, and if they demur in obeying the ejectment, to oust them by setting fire to these combustible tenements–this surely is as little defensible on the score of policy as of morals."

[1] *The Sutherland family also had large estates in Staffordshire, and their English title would be more familiar to Southey than their Scottish style.*

The sight of the early miseries caused by the Clearances made Southey reflect:

"Turgot used to wish that he could possess absolute power for one year. I would not be entrusted with it for all the world could give me, seeing in every instance the fatal effects which it produces in those who exercise it.

"Even when pursuing good and generous intentions, they act tyrannically, they become proud and impatient of contradiction, reckless of the feelings and sufferings of others–and the course of conduct which began in benevolence ends sometimes in injustice and cruelty."

Southey thought that "great good arises where a large estate in Scotland is transferred by marriage to an English owner, English capital and ingenuity being employed to improve it." He could not have foreseen that grouse would in due course oust the sheep as the sheep had previously ousted the Highlanders; that vast tracts of the Highlands would become game preserves kept for the pleasure of absentee English landlords during a few weeks in the autumn; and that "English ingenuity and capital" were never to be seriously deployed for the good of the Highlands and those who belonged there.

But naturally, Southey had strong English prejudices. He thought it proof of "increasing decency and civilization that the Highland philabeg, a male-petticoat, is falling into dissuse. Upon a soldier or a gentleman it looks well," he opined; "but with the common people, and especially with boys, it is a filthy, begarly, indecent garb." He claimed that it was introduced to the Highlands by an Englishman, Thomas Rawlinson, in 1728. There is, of course, no truth in this claim. The kilt, in its "modern" form as it emerged after the proscription of the Highland dress which followed the "Forty Five", is merely the lower part of the belted plaid with the pleats stitched up, the garment that had formerly covered the whole of the body.

Dining again at Kincardine, Southey had "an excellent pudding, which appears to be the legitimate cheese cake, the basis being evidently fresh curd." He discovered that bread was "brought here from Inverness by the mail-coach every day, for there is no yeast here. And the yeast in Inverness is obtained from the smugglers who make whiskey in the

Black Isle." Southey consistently spells whisky in the Irish manner.

From Dingwall, Southey and Telford set off in a chaise and gig for the West Coast, leaving the ladies of the party behind. Near Strathpeffer, on the estate of the Icelandic traveller Sir George Mackenzie, Southey noted that there was some destruction of the woods, "for since the herring fishery has increased, the scarcity of oaken staves for barrels led men to try whether birch would answer the purpose as well, and great quantities have been felled and are felling in conseq-uence–to the profit of the landholders, but to the sad deterioration of many a beautiful scene."

At the inn at Auchanault, "a miserable place", they tasted whisky, "which was pronounced to be of the very best and purest, 'unexcised by Kings'."

At the tiny hamlet of Luip, Southey was amused to find a room containing "three beds like ships' cabins, each shut in with folding doors." He also noted the other furnishings at the little inn.

"There was an air of cleanliness about the house, as far as could consist with a tinge of smoke upon the rafters and walls. The wooden chairs and tables were cleaner than they would usually be found in an English cottage; and there was one better bed, upon an open bedstead . . . . with a quilt of patchwork, ornamentally disposed, in stars, upon a white ground. There were also two plated candlesticks, a hand bell, a wire bell, and a good likeness of the Landlord, well drawn in water colours. We dined here on good mutton chops, excellent potatoes, and fresh soft curds and cream . . . . The charge was a shilling per head. And we tasted again right Highland whiskey."

One of the strangest aspects of Southey's *Journal,* for all its interest, is the almost total absence of enthusiastic comment on Highland scenery; indeed, of any kind of comment at all. The best that Southey could find to say of Loch Dougall, in the country of Mackenzie of Applecross, was:

"Loch Dougall, a fine lake on the left; a steep green mountain on the south side, so steep that such a mountain in my country would have been covered with screes; here it is green, tho' scored and ribbed with numerous deep ravines. The glen then widens into a great expanse, which seems to have been formerly under water, and with little care might become a most valuable carse."

And of Loch Carron:

"The evening set in with rain–which was to be expected in this rainy region. We saw seals swimming in the salt water, and finally on the shore of this long inlet in the sea, we took up our night's abode at Jeantown . . . We had . . . a good meal at tea, excellent butter, barley cake and biscuit (no wheaten bread) and herrings . . ."

The plan was to cross Strome Ferry, and return to Inverness via Kintail, Glenshiel, and Glenmoriston.

Shiel House, an inn built by the Government for the purpose of lodging such travellers as Telford and Southey, had, however, fallen into the hands of a new Laird (an Englishman called Dick), who had shut it up, and this posed a problem for their party. However, on arrival at Strome Ferry it was found that Mackenzie of Applecross had failed to provide a promised boat large enough to take the chaise and horses, so the projected round trip had to be abandoned. Southey casually notes: "Ours was the first carriage which had ever reached the ferry, and the road on the southern shore, up which we walked, had never yet been travelled by one."

At least he was able to enjoy the view, if not exactly to wax lyrical about it, before turning about:

"Loch Carron is a beautiful inlet. A tongue of land runs out on the north side and forms a natural pier, protecting the bay where Jeantown stands. The pier at Strome is sheltered by a smaller neck of land. The Loch is inclosed by mountains on three sides, and on the fourth the mountains in the Isle of Skye are seen even at a great distance."

Southey crossed the ferry on foot to get "a view into the wilds leading to Loch Alsh", and found that the weather had roughened for his return crossing.

On the way back to Inverness, Southey called at Brahan Castle, the seat of the head of the Mackenzies, and not only discovered that his hostess, Lady Mackenzie, knew Sir Walter Scott, of whom she talked much, but that a fellow guest was a young man who was to become one of the most celebrated of journalising Victorian travellers, described by Southey as "a visitor, by name Augustus Hare."

Crossing the Black Isle to reach Inverness over Kessock

Ferry, Southey recalled that the "anomalus shire" of Cromarty, not yet united with its neighbouring county, had on it one estate exempt from the Excise laws[1], on which enormous quantities of whisky were made, but that the Government had recently bought out the owner's privilege with "a sum of money for an exemption which could no longer be allowed."

Telford's main achievement in the Highlands was undoubtedly the construction of the Caledonian Canal, work upon which was in progress when Southey travelled down its length on the return journey from Inverness.

The party made a halt at the Fall of Foyers. The ladies looked at the Fall from above the glen, but Southey and Telford went some way down.

"The water was much less than it usually is in this wet country," Southey observed "and far too little for the chasm, still it exceeded our waterfalls when they are in full force . . . The accompaniments cannot be finer anywhere: everything is beautiful and everything–woods, rocks, water, the glen, the mountains, and the lake below, in proportion."

Passing an inn which General Wade had used as his headquarters while his troops were building the road from Fort George to Fort Augustus, they found that at the latter place the inn was "most inconveniently built." Wade's Fort itself seemed to Southey to be "very pretty–a quiet collegiate sort of place, just fit for a University", the guns from which had recently been removed. This proved to be a prophetic utterance, for when the garrison was finally removed from the Fort in 1867, the Government sold it to Lord Lovat for five thousand pounds. He presented it to the Catholic Benedictine Order, who built an abbey and school on this site, but preserved part of the old Hanoverian fort in the North West corner.

On the morning of Thursday, September 16th, before breakfast, Southey went to inspect the construction work on the locks. It inspired him to write a brisk description of what must have been a scene of amazing activity.

"Such an extent of masonry, upon such a scale, I had never before beheld, each of the Locks" –there were five–"being 180 feet in length. It was a most impressive and

[1] *The estate of Forbes of Culloden.*

memorable scene. Men, horses, and machines at work; digging, walling and puddling going on, men wheeling barrows, horses drawing stones along the railways. The great steam engine was at rest, having done its work. It threw out 160 hogsheads per minute; and two smaller engines (large ones they would have been considered anywhere else) were also needed while the excavation of the lower docks was going on; for they dug 24 feet below the surface of the water in the river, and the water filtered thro' open gravel. The dredging machine was in action, revolving round and round, and bringing up at every turn matter which had never before been brought to the air and light. Its chimney poured forth volumes of black smoke, which there was no annoyance in beholding, because there was room enough for it in this wide clear atmosphere. The iron for a pair of Lockgates was lying on the ground, having just arrived from Derbyshire: the same vessel in which it was shipt at Gainsborough, landed it here at Fort Augustus. To one like myself not practically conversant with machinery, it seemed curious to hear Mr. Telford talk of the propriety of weighing these enormous pieces (several of which were four tons weight) and to hear Cargill reply that it was easily done."

Southey was even more overawed by the work in progress when, later in the day, they walked along the works between Lochs Oich and Lochy where another lock was under construction.

"The earth is removed by horses walking along the trench of the Canal, and drawing the laden cartlets up one inclined plane, while the emptied ones, which are connected with them by a chain passing over pullies, are let down another. This was going on in numberless places, and such a mass of earth had been thrown up on both sides along the whole line, that the men appeared in the proportion of emmets to an ant-hill, amid their own work. The hour of rest for men and horses is announced by blowing a horn; and so well have the horses learnt to measure time by their own exertions and sense of fatigue, that if the signal be delayed five minutes, they stop of their own accord, without it."

On the way to Fort William, Southey was much taken by the Well of the Seven Heads. Alisdair MacDonell, the 12th of Keppoch, was murdered by seven ruffians in 1663. The clan poet, Iain Lom MacDonell, appealed in vain to the Glengarry chief, Lord MacDonell and Aros, but Sir James MacDonald of Sleat provided an effective revenge force. The poet washed the severed heads of the murderers, and presented them to Glengarry. Alistair MacDonell, 15th of Glengarry, had the monument erected over the spring in which the heads were washed, inscribed in Latin, French, Gaelic and English, seven years before Southey was his guest.

The western end of the Canal, at Corpach, attracted Southey's interest. Although the middle section had yet to be made, this end was already completed, except for the bridges.

Though the Laureate's admiration for Telford's handiwork was unstinted, he took a different view of the Highland Lairds. The chief of the Clan Cameron, Locheil, "a poor creature" according to Southey, inspired the reflection that:

"The restoration of the forfeited estates has produced no good in the Highlands. As an act of grace it carried with it not the appearance only, but the reality of great injustice, in restoring those families who were implicated in the rebellion of 1745, and not the sufferers of 1715, who had surely more claim to indulgency. Far better would it have been for the country in general, and especially for the poor Highlander, if the estates had been retained as Crown lands, and leased accordingly, or even sold to strangers."

The Highland Laird seemed to Southey to use his power badly upon a "sober, moral, well-disposed people" who, if properly treated, would still "be ready to lay down their lives in his service." A few of the fifty or so "land-Leviathans" who owned the Highlands, Southey reckoned, were "desirous of improving their own estates by bettering the condition of their tenants." But the greater number were "fools at heart, with neither undertaking nor virtue, nor good nature to form such a wish. Their object is to increase their revenue, and they care not by what means this is accomplished."

At Roy Bridge, they made a detour on Highland ponies to see what Southey called "the Parallel Roads" of Glen Roy, but which later geological knowledge has established as being old beaches, a discovery made and generally accepted not long afterwards by Lyell and other geologists. Southey, however, with Telford's support, dismissed any notion of these even-surfaced parallel terraces being made by the "action of water", and assumed that they were "intended for a display of barbarous magnificence in hunting", adding that "a genuine Ossian" would probably have informed him.

Southey found Fort William "one long, mean filthy street; the inn abominably dirty." At the inn, the spoons were of iron and pewter, as they had been also at Inverness.

Next day, the party moved down Loch Linnhe, to Ballachulish Ferry, through "country of a more cultivated and warmer appearance than any we had lately seen, well wooded with hazel, ash and alder, and thorns of every kind, and having cultivated fields close to the sea beach."

Southey and Telford walked up Loch Leven "to enjoy the glorious mountain scenery" of Glencoe. "The evening was glorious," Southey recorded. "To the west the Linnhe Loch lay before us, bounded by the mountains of Morven. Between those two huge mountains, which are of the finest outline, there is a dip somewhat resembling a pointed arch inverted; and just behind that dip the sun, which had not been visible during the day, sunk in serene beauty, without a cloud; first with a saffron, then with a rosey light, which embued the mountains, and was reflected upon the still water up to the very shore beneath the window at which we stood, delighted in beholding it . . . The effect was such that I could almost have wished I were a believer in Ossian."

Southey, however, was no believer in the cult of the sublime and the picturesque, but a poet able to accept delight for its own sake, and, as we have seen, a man with an enquiring and reasonably fair mind.

His party had to divide between the hotels on both sides of the narrow passage. Southey crossed this "perilous ferry" the next day at six in the morning, when a strong tide was running, carrying their rowing boat "far about the landing place", though, in the manner of the modern car-ferry, they then "easily made way along the shore by favour of the eddy."

"The vestibule of Glencoe" reminded Southey of Borrowdale, the glen itself of the pass from Buttermere to Borrowdale, although, as he admitted, "on a longer and greater scale." A stay was made at Kings House, which had run out of bread, but was able to supply "turkey as well as hens' eggs, a shoulder of lamb, and cream for the tea", drunk out of "handsome English china."

The journey to Tyndrum, "a wretched assembly of Hovels", was more or less uneventful, except for the jolting caused by the bad roads on that part of the route which passes through Perthshire, where the county seemed "black and dreary, with high mountains on all sides" and "no cultivation except immediately above the hovels." By Bridge of Orchy and Dalmally in whose kirkyard Southey reflected "It seems strange to engrave sculls, and other such hideous emblems of mortality upon the tomb stones" and Loch Awe, they reached Inveraray, designed by the previous Duke of Argyll. Its planned main street, "terminated by a Kirk", reminded Southey of "those little German towns which, in like manner have been created by small potentates, in the plenitude of their power. They are building a town-house, which is in good style, and will be a handsome edifice; and they have built on a line with the Inn a huge prison . . . At a little distance the appearance of the large buildings upon the shore, and the whole surrounding scenery, bore no faint resemblance to a scene upon the Italian lakes (Como more particularly) both in the character of the buildings, and the situation." This glowing account of Inveraray's charms was inspired by a day "not favourable—a grey, Scotch, sunless sky; and the water of course grey also; but not lifeless, for there was just enough wind to keep up a sea-like murmur upon the stoney beach."

Southey thought that Inveraray lost "much of its beauty at low water, the beach which is then uncovered being extensive and unsightly", and considered that the Castle "would be much improved by taking away the battlements, and substituting balustrades", since "battlements look as if intended for defence, and are therefore inappropriate for a dwelling house", a criterion which makes one wonder what impression the Gothic Castles of the ensuing Victorian "Balmorality" period would have made upon his sensibility.

The Loch Fyne herring industry was in full production in Southey's day, and he admired the place's reputation for producing "the best on the Western Coast", though he adds that "every Loch claims the superiority for its own".

As "a true lover and faithful eater of this incomparable

fish", however, he felt "bound to deliver a decided opinion in favour of the herrings of Cullen above all others whatsoever."

The development of the paddle-steamer–Henry Bell's "Comet" had made its first noisy and dangerous voyage down the Clyde in 1812–was already beginning to open up the lochs of the Clyde estuary to tourism. And so, on Saturday, September 25th, 1819, Southey wrote: "The steam boat which has lately been started to ply between Glasgow and Fort William, and touch at the interjacent places, brings a great number of visitors to Inveraray. As many as an hundred have sometimes landed there, to idle away more or less time, according to their means and leisure; many of them landing in the morning and returning in the evening."

The crossing from Glenkinlas to Glencoe was not the easy ascent and descent it is today, but a twisting, steep mountain path, so testing the traveller that a stone at the top carried the injunction put there by one of Wade's lieutenants, "Rest, and be Thankful", which Southey thought a "beautiful inscription". Although he made the crossing in the rain, he thought the scene "more impressive" than Glencoe, although on a smaller scale.

Everything . . . is wild, great, simple and severe; but there is nothing terrible or savage. The mountains are green; the stones are in fine masses; and the steep sides are cut into green channels by the rain, not into stoney ravines, nor sheeted with lines of screes." In fact, it owed its superiority to Glencoe because it was a prospect "upon which you can dwell with pleasure."

Arrochar seemed to Southey to have an inn "more beautifully placed than any Inn which I have seen either in Scotland or elsewhere", and this in spite of it having "the high summit of the grotesque mountain abominably called the Cobler, opposite and in full view."

After a night here between "coarse cotton sheets–of Glasgow fashion *sans* doubt", Southey and his friends crossed to Tarbet, and made their way down Loch Lomond over the "very beautiful, but in great part . . . very bad road" to Luss.

The outline of Ben Lomond reminded him of Skiddaw, though the rise was "rather steeper, and the summit more rounded." The best view of Loch Lomond he held to be "from a hill above the seat of the Smollet family". He inspected the column, with its Latin inscription, in memory of the picaresque Scottish novelist Tobias Smollet, who died a little too soon to inherit the Loch Lomondside seat which consequently went to his sister, Mrs. Telford, whose descendants, the Telford-Smollets, own it to this day.

On the way to Dumbarton, Southey noticed "a woman walking barefoot, and with her bare legs exposed half way up, tho' she was expensively dressed and wore a silk spencer", a custom which continued among country folk longer than those who lived in towns, although barefoot children were still a common sight in the poorer districts of Glasgow and Edinburgh up until the Second World War.

As Southey approached Dumbarton, "the prominent objects were some glass-houses pouring out volumes of smoke; and the remarkable rock upon which the Castle stands". It is amusing to find Southey bandying about the stock terms of a previous generation in which he did not really believe, when he added: "It is picturesque and singular, but has nothing of sublimity, and little magnitude, if those words may be coupled together."

He stayed at the Elephant and Castle, and there took leave of Mitchell. Southey recorded that he was "a remarkable man" and that "no fear or favour in the course of fifteen years has ever made him swerve from the fair performance of his duty, tho' the Lairds with whom he has to deal have omitted no means to make him enter into their views, and do things, or leave them undone, as might suit their humour, or interest."

When Southey left Dumbarton, "several steamboats were plying on the Clyde—yesterday morning when we rose, there was one smoking before the window at Arrocher (*sic*), on Loch Long", for the development of the Clyde had already begun.

"A City like Glasgow," Southey wrote, "is a hateful place for a stranger, unless he is reconciled to it by the comforts of hospitality and society. In every case the best way is to reconnoitre it, so as to know the outline and outside, and to be contented with such other information as books can supply." This was the method Southey chose, finding Argyle Street "a mixture of old and new buildings, but long enough and lofty enough to be one of the best streets in G. Britain",

Jakob Ludwig Felix Mendelssohn-Bartholdy (Felix Mendelssohn),
1809–1847

Above, the coach in which Mendelssohn and Klingemann travelled north; *below*, ships on the Clyde (*these and subsequent illustrations are all from Mendelssohn's sketch book*)

a character it was to retain for a few more decades before the Irish overspill from the potato famine crowded its mediaeval closes into slumdom, and the City Fathers, in an excess of understandable zeal, deprived Glasgow of its ancient heritage, including its mediaeval University.

Southey admired the Cathedral, which he wrongly thought "the only edifice of its kind in Scotland which received no exterior injury at the Reformation[1] "

Inside, he thought the seats "so closely packed that any person who could remain there during the time of service, must have an invincible nose."

Passing over Bothwell Bridge, "famous in history and in modern Scotch romance", Southey reached Hamilton, then "a dirty old town, with a good many thatched houses in the street–implying either poverty, or a great disregard of danger from fire." He thought the fifteen miles between Hamilton and Lanark "beautiful country . . . No part of England, the Lake-Land alone excepted, is more beautiful than this."

At New Lanark, the pioneering industrialist Robert Owen took them through his mills. Owen, with his father-in-law David Dale, was responsible for the development of a model village and cotton mill run on humane lines for the implementation of practical measures of factory reform, education, and the application of the principle of cooperative shopping. Southey thought the village, which today is in process of being conserved, like "a Moravian settlement", but wrote more extensively about this part of his Scottish tour than any other. His impressions are worth quoting at length:

"Owen led us thro' the works with great courtesy, and made as full an exhibition as the time allowed. It is needless to say anything more of the Mills than that they are perfect in their kind, according to the present state of mechanical science, and that they appeared to be under admirable management; they are thoroughly clean, and so carefully ventilated that there was no unpleasant smell in any of the apartments. Everything required for the machinery is made upon the spot, and the expence of wear and tear is estimated at 8,000£ annually. There are stores also from which the people are supplied with all the necessaries of life. They have

[1] *St. Magnus Cathedral, in Orkney, survived the Reformation. Victorian improvers removed two of Glasgow Cathedral's towers.*

a credit there to the amount of sixteen shillings a week each, but may deal elsewhere if they chuse. The expences of what he calls the moral part of the establishment, he stated at 700£ a year. But a large building is just compleated, with ball and concert and lecture rooms, all for 'the formation of character'; and this must surely be set down to Owen's private account, rather than to the cost of the concern.

"In the course of going thro' these buildings, he took us into an apartment where one of his plans, upon a scale larger than any of the Swiss models, was spread upon the floor. And with a long wand in his hand he explained the plan, while Willy and Francis stood by, with wondering and longing eyes, regarding it as a plaything, and hoping they might be allowed to amuse themselves with it. Meantime the word had been given: we were conducted into one of the dancing rooms; half a dozen fine boys, about nine or ten years old, led the way, playing on fifes, and some 200 children, from four years of age till ten, entered the room and arranged themselves on three sides of it. A man whose official situation I did not comprehend gave the word, which either because of the tone of the dialect I did not understand; and they turned to the right or left, faced about, fell forwards and backwards, and stamped at command, performing manoeuvres the object of which was not very clear, with perfect regularity. I remembered what T. Vardon had told me of the cows in Holland. When the cattle are housed, the Dutch in their spirit of cleanliness, prevent them from dirting their tails by tying them up (to the no small discomfort of the cows) at a certain elevation, to a cross string which extends the whole length of the stalls: and the consequence is that when any one cow wags her tail, all the others must wag theirs also. So I could not but think that these puppet-like motions might, with a little ingenuity, have been produced by the great water-wheel, which is the *primum mobile* of the whole Cotton-Mills. A certain number of the children were then drawn out, and sung to the pipe of a music master. They afterwards danced to the piping of the six little pipers. There was too much of all this, but the children seemed to like it. When the exhibition was over, they filed off into the adjoining school room.

"I was far better pleased with a large room in which all the children of the establishment who are old enough not to require the constant care of their mothers, and too young for instruction of any kind, were brought together while their parents were at work, and left to amuse themselves, with no more superintendence than is necessary for preventing them from hurting themselves. They made a glorious noise, worth all the concerts of New Lanark, and of London to boot. It was really wonderful to see how the little creatures crowded about Owen to make their bows and their curtsies, looking up and smiling in his face; and the genuine benignity and pleasure with which he noticed them, laying his hand on the head of one, shaking hands with another, and bestowing kind looks and kind words upon all."

Southey, the former idealist and dreamer of a "Pantisocracy" turned Poet Laureate and hard-working, respectable *pater familias* to his own and Coleridge's children, was moved to criticise, but on solidly practical grounds:

"Owen in reality deceives himself. He is a part-owner and sole Director of a large establishment, differing more in accidents than in essence from a plantation: the persons under him happen to be white, and are at liberty by law to quit his service, but while they remain in it they are as much under his absolute management as so many negro-slaves. His humour, his vanity, his kindliness of nature (all these have their share) lead him to make these *human machines* as he calls them (and too literally believes them to be) as happy as he can, and to make a display of their happiness. And he jumps at once to the conclusion that because he can do this with 2210 persons, who are totally dependent upon him—all mankind might be governed with the same facility.

In mid-flight, Southey suddenly remembered his past:

"*Et in Utopia ego*. But I never regarded man as a machine; I never believed him to be merely a material being; I never for a moment could listen to the nonsense of Helvetius, nor suppose, as Owen does, that men may be cast in a mould (like the other parts of his mill) and take the impression with perfect certainty. Nor did I ever disguise from myself the difficulties of a system which took for its foundation the principle of a community of goods. On the contrary I met them fairly, acknowledged them, and rested satisfied with the belief (whether erroneous or not) that the evils incident in such a system would be infinitely less than those which stare us in the face under the existing order. But Owen reasons from his Cotton Mills to the whole empire. He keeps out of sight from others, and perhaps from himself, that his system, instead of aiming at perfect freedom, can only be kept in play by absolute power. Indeed, he never looks beyond one of his own ideal square villages, to the rules and proportions of which he would square the whole human race. *The* formation of character! Why the end of his institutions would be, as far as possible, the destruction of all character. They tend directly to destroy individuality of character and domesticity—in the one of which the strength of man consists, and in the other his happiness. The power of human society, and the grace, would both be annihilated."

His verdict on Owen, who eventually lost faith in his New Lanark enterprise and crossed to America, was: "I admire the man, and like him too."

Up the valley of the Clyde and down the valley of the Annan the travellers went on to Moffat, where they discharged the coach and proceeded in two post-chaises to Lockerbie. Because it turned out to be "the last day of the races at Carlisle", they spent the night in the inn at Longtown. In Carlisle next morning, Friday, October 1st, Telford and Southey parted, Telford to take the mail coach back to Edinburgh, and Southey to return to his family by Keswick, which he reached in time for dinner, and found "all well, thus happily concluding a journey of more than six weeks", during which he "laid up a great store of pleasurable recollections."

He had one regret: the reflection that his path and Telford's lay in different directions.

"This parting company, after the thorough intimacy which a long journey produces between fellow travellers who like each other, is a melancholy thing. A man more heartily to be liked, more worthy to be esteemed and admired, I have never fallen in with: and therefore it is painful to think how little likely it is that I shall ever see much of him again."

Telford's career moved from success to success, his most difficult triumph being the construction of the Menai Suspension Bridge to carry the mail road from London to

Holyhead.[1] Southey, who took his Laureate duties seriously, brought down disaster on his head when his Funeral Ode for the sovereign who had appointed him incurred the ridicule of Byron, and, in the "*Vision of Judgment*–Byron's retort to a gibe by Southey in a poem of the same name–the famous couplet accusing Southey of being responsible for

> *. . . much blank verse and blanker prose,*
> *And more of both than anybody knows . . .*

a witty but unfair verdict upon the author of the lives of Wesley and Nelson, the fairy-tale "The Three Bears" and several ballads that have held their place in anthologies.

Southey's second marriage to his friend Caroline Bowles took place in 1839, but soon after, his mental powers began to fail him. When he died in 1843, he was buried in Crosthwaite churchyard. A monument carrying an inscription by his friend Wordsworth was put up inside the church.

By then, the age of steam, whose first portents Southey had seen outside the window of his hotel at Arrochar and on the Clyde near Dumbarton, had ushered in the beginnings of rail travel, and had begun to change not only much of the face of Scotland, but the habits and expectations of those who came to visit the country.

[1] *When the iron chains had to be replaced with steel ones in 1946, to give greater carrying weight, the work was undertaken by Sir Alexander Gibb, a descendant of Telford's assistant.*

7

Mendelssohn and Klingemann:
Two Merry Wanderers

The tradition of the carefree, youthful wanderer, celebrated in so many German folk-songs, in the lieder of Schubert and others, and given such an unpleasant twist by the organised "strength through joy" cruises of the Nazis in our own century, can rarely have been more happily exemplified than in the tour of the Scottish Highlands which Felix Mendelssohn made in the summer of 1829, in company with his closest friend, Karl Klingemann. Both men were young, good-looking and full of high spirits, and had been friends since childhood.

Karl Klingemann, born in 1798, was the son of August Klingemann, a dramatist and Director of Brunswick Theatre, who provided the romantic composer Marschner with the libretto for his opera *Das Schloss am Aetna.* Karl was an amateur musician and a graceful dilettante rhymer, who was secretary to the Hanovarian Legation in London, and spent his life as a diplomat.

Jakob Ludwig Felix Mendelssohn-Bartholdy, to give him his full name, born in 1809, was the second child and elder son of Abraham Mendelssohn, banker, and his gifted wife, Leah Salomon, and grandson of Moses Mendelssohn, whose philosophical work *Phaedon or the Immortality of the Soul* had been translated into all the languages of Europe, earning him the title of "the German Socrates". When Abraham Mendelssohn married, he and his wife, also the daughter of a rich banker, became Protestants, and added the name "Bartholdy" to their own, to distinguish them from the Mendelssohns who remained within the orthodox Jewish faith. Because the French occupation of Hamburg made life there intolerable, the Mendelssohns moved to Berlin in 1812.

Felix Mendelssohn began to receive piano lessons when he

was four years old. Like Mozart before him, he was a prodigy, his creative activity beginning to manifest itself energetically when he was ten years old. He became the favourite pupil of his teacher, Zelter, who took the boy to Weimar to play to the aged Goethe. The great poet sat in the shadows "like a Jupiter Tonans, with his old eyes flashing fire" while Mendelssohn played the music of Haydn, Mozart, Bach and Beethoven to him.

Like Schubert, Mendelssohn was brought up in a home—though a vastly wealthier one—in which family music-making was a regular occurrence, an activity in which Klingemann sometimes participated.

In March, 1829, a month before Mendelssohn left for England on a three-year tour intended by his father to be the culmination of a carefully planned education (which had included three years at the University of Berlin) the young composer conducted a performance of Bach's *St. Matthew Passion* at the Berlin Singakademie. Bach's music had been largely forgotten since his death and Mendelssohn's successful revival of one of his greatest works—the performance had to be twice repeated—laid the foundations for the gradual restoration of Bach's reputation as one of the greatest of all composers.

Mendelssohn arrived in London in the middle of April, to a room in the house of a German ironmonger in Portland Street found for him by Ignaz Moscheles, who had been Mendelssohn's most brilliant piano teacher.

A newspaper columnist reported the arrival of this ". . . son of the rich banker of Berlin and I believe, a grandson of the celebrated Jewish philosopher and elegant writer. He is one of the finest pianoforte players in Europe, and though a very young man is supposed to be better acquainted with music than most professors of the art". Naturally, the young composer wanted to present some of his music to a London audience, including his overture *A Midsummer Night's Dream,* written three years before, and his recently completed *Symphony No. 1 in C minor.* The Philharmonic Society's orchestra was then the best in London, Sir George Smart one of its regular conductors. Sir George had read his newspapers and was evidently jealous of the newcomer. (Since the English worship of Handel, English musicians had cause to fear their German rivals!) No programme-space could be found for his music, Mendelssohn eventually grew impatient as delay followed delay. Then, by chance, he met two of the Philharmonic Society's directors in a store, and, it transpired, as Mendelssohn later explained to his parents, that "Neither Sir George nor the secretary had said a word to the directors about the fact that I had brought music here and wanted to have it played. On the contrary, Sir George had told them that I really made music *only for fun,* and that 'I did not really need to do it at all', and that I was here only as a gentleman, not at all as a professor."

On 25th May, the symphony was performed, the composer seated at the piano after the manner of the time, and well received, that same journal the *Harmonicum,* whose report of his arrival had unwittingly delayed the event on which its critic now pronounced, declaring: "It is not venturing too far to assert that his latest labour, the symphony of which we now speak, shews a genius for great writing, and it is a fair presumption, that, if he perseveres in his pursuit, he will in a few years be considered as the fourth of that line which has done such immortal honour to the most musical nation in Europe."

Five days later, Mendelssohn appeared as a pianist in the Argyll Rooms, creating a sensation by playing Weber's *Konzertstück* in F minor by heart. Other concerts followed, including one on 24th June, when *A Midsummer Night's Dream* was at last performed, though to an audience of only two hundred. Even so, it had to be repeated.

The most successful appearance of all took place at a charity concert given on 13th July, in aid of the Silesians, who had suffered from serious flooding, a concert arranged in spite of some further machinations by Sir George, whom Mendelssohn called an "intriguing, deceitful and untruthful man". The concert lasted four hours, and included a further performance of the overture *A Midsummer Night's Dream,* as well as the *Double Concerto in E Major,* which the composer himself played with Moscheles. The concert brought in three hundred guineas for the Silesians, and for Mendelssohn firmly cemented the foundations of that enthusiastic admiration and affection with which his music continued to be specially regarded in England long after his death.

His reputation established, Mendelssohn sought, and got, the permission of his strict father to make a tour of the Scottish Highlands and the Lake District of England, in company with Klingemann.

They left London on July 28th, and travelled through York and Durham to Edinburgh, arriving on the post coach a week later. The two young men recorded their impressions of Scotland in letters to Berlin. Klingemann, in spite of his sometimes arch playfulness a keen observer, wrote rather more fully than Mendelssohn, who spent much of his time sketching, a common pastime among tourists in that pre-photographic age.

Mendelssohn began the story:

"It is Sunday when we arrive in Edinburgh; then we cross the meadows, going towards two desperately steep rocks, which are called Arthur's Seat, and climb up. Below on the green are walking the most variegated people, women, children and cows. The city stretches far and wide. In the midst is the castle, like a bird's nest on a cliff; beyond the castle come meadows, then hills, then a broad river; beyond the river again hills; then a mountain rather more stern, on which towers Stirling Castle; then blue distance begins. Further on, you perceive a faint shadow, which they call Ben Lomond."

This, Mendelssohn explained, was only half the view from Arthur's Seat.

"The other is simple enough; it is the great blue sea, immeasurably wide, studded with white sails, black funnels, little insects of skiffs, boats, rocky islands, and such like."

He breaks off to ask himself: "Why need I describe it? "When God Himself takes to panorama-painting, it turns out strangely beautiful," a pious sentiment which would no doubt reassure father Abraham that the sensuous delights of a foreign land were not dazzling his son's powers of moral perceptiveness.

A kind of gentle clarity illuminates the soft clash of the composer's descriptive images, in feeling characteristic both of the early spring of the romantic movement and of Mendelssohn's own music which this journey was to inspire.

"Everything here looks so stern and robust, half enveloped in haze or smoke or fog. Moreover, there is to be a bagpipe competition tomorrow. Many Highlanders came in costume from church, victoriously leading their sweethearts in their Sunday attire, and casting magnificent and important looks over the world. With long red beards, tartan plaids, bonnets and feathers, naked knees and their bagpipes in their hands, they passed quietly along by the half-ruined grey castle on the meadow, where Mary Stewart lived in splendour and saw Rizzio murdered. I feel as if time went at a very rapid pace when I have before me so much that was, and so much that is."

The "half-ruined gray castle on the meadow" was, of course, Holyrood House. Schiller's fine verse-tragedy *Maria Stuart,* which had appeared in Weimar in 1800, had brought home to cultured Germans those aspects of Scottish history which accorded with the precepts of romanticism, the part-spurious "translations" from Ossian of James Macpherson and the poems and novels of Scott quickening this interest.

"It is beautiful here!" Mendelssohn went on. "In the evening a cool breeze is wafted from the sea, and then all objects appear clearly and sharply defined against the grey sky. The lights from the windows glitter brilliantly."

The previous day, he tells his parents, he had collected a letter from them at the Post Office and read it "with a particular zest in Princes Street, Edinburgh. In Edinburgh, a letter from under the yew tree in the Leipziger Strasse. My swim in the sea was pleasant to-day, and afloat on the waves, I thought of you all, how very closely we are linked together; and yet I was in the deep Scotch ocean, that tastes very briny."

He told his mother that although he had a letter of introduction to Sir Walter Scott from one of his intimate friends in London, he was still uncertain whether or not he would be able to see him, but he hoped so, "chiefly to escape a scolding from you, dear mother, if I return without having seen the *lion* . . . What further shall I tell you? Time and space are coming to an end, and everything must terminate, in the refrain: 'How kind the people are in Edinburgh, and how generous is the good God'. The Scotch ladies also deserve notice; and if Mahmad follows father's advice and turns Christian, I shall in his place become a Turk and settle in this neighbourhood."

Later next day, Mendelssohn's interest in Mary, Queen of Scots was further gratified:

"In the evening twilight we went today to the palace where Queen Mary lived and loved; a little room is shown there with a winding staircase leading up to the door. Up this way, they came and found Rizzio in that little room, pulled him out, and three rooms off there is a dark corner, where they murdered him. The chapel close to it is now roofless; grass and ivy grow there; and at the broken altar Mary was crowned Queen of Scotland. Everything around is broken and mouldering, and the bright sky shines in. I believe I found today in that old chapel the beginning of my Scotch Symphony."

Few more widely enjoyed ideas than the gently melancholy of that opening theme of Mendelssohn's *Symphony No. 3 in A minor* can have been inspired by the roofless chapel.

Next day, July 31st, they set out for Abbotsford. According to the fanciful account of Klingemann, he remained at Melrose "as a person without a letter of invitation", while Mendelssohn drove to Abbotsford. Wrote Klingemann:

"Melrose Abbey is a ruin full of preservation and conversation: King David (of Scotland) and the magician Scott (Michael, not Walter) are there cut in stone, and the whole neighbourhood is interwoven with legends and ancient fairy dances.

"Thomas the Rhymer and the Fairy Queen held their revels a little higher up in the dark glen, and something of that still animates the castellan when he scrambles like a chamois up to the highest point of the ruins. One gets so hungry in such ruins (which by way of contrast throw the present in one's very hungry face) that I retired into the inn for bread and cheese and ale and a newspaper. So I lay in quiet enjoyment on the sofa, when the coach came back and someone rushed into our room. Thinking only of Felix, I made some scurrilous remark. That moment I discerned an elderly man: 'Oh, Sir Walter!' cried I, jumping up; and with apologising blushes I added 'familiar likenesses can alone excuse like familiarity!' Never mind!' was his brief reply—he who is so famed for prolixity! 'My dear future Parnassus brother and historical novelist, I have much pleasure in meeting you. Your friend has already beautifully told me what and how much you will yet write and may have written'. Meanwhile hands were shaken out of joint and shaken in again, and we all proceeded in happy ecstasy to Abbotsford."

That is how they would no doubt have liked it to have been. Next day, however, Mendelssohn added a postscript to his friend's letter.

"This is all Klingemann's invention, We found Sir Walter in the act of leaving Abbotsford, stared at him like fools, drove eighty miles and lost a day for the sake of at best one half-hour of superficial conversation. Melrose compensated us but little. We were out of humour with great men, with ourselves, with the world, with everything. It was a bad day."

Scott's total indifference to music may have left him unaware of the genius of the young composer who was so anxious to make his acquaintance.

Next day, from an unspecified halt on the way north, Mendelssohn wrote that "Today, however, was glorious! We have forgotten the ills of yesterday, and can laugh over them."

The intended route was to be "via Stirling, Perth, Dunkeld, and the waterfalls to Blair Atholl." The next letter, dated August 3rd, is from Blair Atholl, and Mendelssohn's pen.

"This is a most dismal, melancholy rainy day. But we make shift as best we can, which indeed is not saying much. Earth and sky are wet through, and whole regiments of clouds are still marching up. Yesterday was a lovely day. We passed from rock to rock, among waterfalls, beautiful valleys with rivers, dark woods and heath with the red heather in bloom. In the morning, we drove in an open carriage, and then walked twenty-one (English) miles."

Later on that wet evening of August 3rd, in an inn, Mendelssohn continued his impressions.

"A wild affair! The storm howls, rushes and whistles, doors are banging and window-shutters are bursting open. Whether the watery noise is from the driving rain or the foaming stream there's no telling, as both rage together. We are sitting here quietly by the fire, which I poke from time to time to make it flare up. The room is large and empty. From one of the walls the wet trickles down. The floor is so thin that the conversation from the servants' room below penetrates up to us. They are singing drunken songs and laughing. Dogs are barking.

"We have two beds with crimson curtains. On our feet instead of English slippers, are Scotch wooden shoes. Tea, with honey and potato-cakes. There is a wooden winding staircase, in which the servant-girl came to meet us with whisky. A desperate cloud-procession in the sky, and in spite of servants and door-banging, there is repose.

"It is quiet and very lonely here! I might say that the stillness rings through the noise. Just now the door opens of itself.

"This is a Highland inn. The little boys with their kilts and bare knees and gay-coloured bonnets, the waiter in his tartan, old people with pigtails, talk helter-skelter in their unintelligible Gaelic.

"The country, far and wide, is thickly overgrown with foliage. From all sides ample water is rushing from under the bridges. There is little corn, much heather (brown and red), precipices, passes, crossways, beautiful green everywhere, deep-blue water—but all stern, dark, very lonely."

According to Mendelssohn's outlined plan, the intention was to proceed "from Blair Atholl on foot over the hills to Inverarary, to Glencoe, the Isle of Staffa and the Isle of Islay", where they intended to stay for several days with "Sir Walter Campbell, the lord, owner and tyrant of the island", as Mendelssohn called him. However, Islay is clearly a slip of the pen for Iona.

Klingemann described the journey across to the West Coast in a letter dated 7th August:

"Yesterday we moved up-hill and down-hill, our cart generally rolling on the side and we ourselves stalking through heather and moss and all kinds of passes (nature here is so amply provided with them that Government does not ask for any[1]), under clouds, and in a thick drizzling rain, through the Highlands. Smoky huts were stuck on cliffs; ugly women looked through the window-holes: cattle-herds with Rob-Roys now and then blocked up the way; mighty mountains were sticking up to their knees (the latter in Highland costume) in the clouds, and looked out again from the top; but we often saw little.

"Late last night we unexpectedly stumbled upon a bit of culture again, viz: the one street of which Fort William consists. This morning we embraced the very-newest piece of culture, steam, and were again among many people, greedily enjoying sunshine and sea-green, the wide outlines of the sea, the rocks

[1] A pun, the German word for passport being *pass*.

at modest distance, good cheer and society of all kinds. A new friend told us at once that yonder young couple were on their honeymoon excursion, and that he had seen them on Ben Lomond, shortly after the wedding, dance a Scotch reel, the bride with parting tears in her eyes."

This haven of civilization was Oban, where they rested on Sunday, August 7th, setting out for Tobermory next day. Klingeman recorded:

"The youngsters of Tobermory, the capital of the Isle of Mull, are merrily bustling by the harbour. The Atlantic Ocean, which appears to contain abundance of water, is quietly riding at anchor, the same as our steamer. We have found quarters in a respectable private house, and would willingly leave a memorial of our day's work in always issuing, like Napoleon, our army-bulletins from places of note."

Early next morning, in rough weather, they set out on a paddle-steamer, for Staffa. Klingemann's account of the experiences which followed is so vivid and so amusing that it is worth setting out in full.

"On the said early morning, the agreeable steam-persons, who at first came flying towards us with nothing but olive-leaves, became lower and lower the more the barometer sank and the sea rose. For that the Atlantic did. It stretched its thousand feelers more and more roughly, twirling us about like anything. The ship household kept its breakfast almost for itself, few people aboard being able to manage their cups and saucers. Ladies, as a rule, fell down like flies, and one of the other gentlemen followed their example.

"I only wish my travelling fellow-sufferer had not been among them, but he is on better terms with the sea as a musician than as an individual or a stomach.

"Two beautiful cold daughters of a Hebrides aristocrat, at whom Felix may storm, quietly continued sitting on deck, and did not even care much for the sea-sickness of their own mother Also, there sat placidly by the steam engine, warming herself in the cold wind, a woman of two-and-eighty. That woman has six times touched me, and seven times irritated me. She wanted to see Staffa before her end. Staffa, with its strange basalt pillars and caverns, is in all picture-books.

"We were put in boats and lifted by the hissing sea up the pillar stumps to the celebrated Fingal's Cave. A greener roar of waves surely never rushed into a stranger cavern–its many pillars making it look like the inside of an immense organ, black and resounding, absolutely without purpose, and quite alone, the wide grey sea within and without. There the old woman scrambled about laboriously, close to the water. She wanted to see the cave of Staffa before her end; and she saw it.

"We returned in the little boat to our steamer, to that unpleasant steam smell. When the second boat arrived, I could see with what truth at the theatre they represent the rising and falling of a boat, when the hero saves the heroine out of some trouble. There was a certain comfort in seeing that the two aristocratic faces had, after all, turned pale as I looked at them through my black eye-glass. The two-and-eighty-years old woman was also in the boat, trembling. The boat went up and down. With difficulty she was lifted out–but she had seen Staffa before her end."

The "yellow, mulatto cook whose shining Caliban countenance" they had joyfully watched the previous day at Tobermory, "amongst saucepans, herrings and vegetables, was now frying some stale ham, the smell of which drove some suffering navigators to despair, if not to worse."

However, there was Iona to come. It inspired Klingemann to break into an almost lyrical rapture:

"Iona, one of the Hebrides sisters–there is truly a very Ossianic and sweetly sad sound about that name–when in some future time I shall sit in a madly crowded assembly, with music and dancing round me, and the wish arises to retire into the loneliest loneliness, I shall think of Iona, with its ruins of a convent, the graves of ancient Scotch kings and still more ancient pirate princes, with their ships rudely carved on many a monumental stone.

"If I had my home on Iona, and lived there upon melancholy as other people do on their rents, my darkest moment would be when, in that wide space which deals in nothing but cliffs and seagulls, suddenly a curl of steam should appear, followed by a ship, and finally by a gay party in veils and frock-coats, who would look for an hour at the ruins and graves, and the three little huts for the living, and then move off again. This highly unjustifiable joke, occurring twice a week, and being almost the only thing in the world, would be as if the inhabitants of those old graves haunted the place in a ludicrous disguise. Opposite Iona, stands a rocky island which, to complete the effect, looks like a ruined city."

The return trip, though much delayed by the rough outward voyage, was more placid.

"Gradually the sea-sick people recovered, and a sail was spread by way of tent on deck, less for keeping off the sun than the wet (which is a constant matter of dispute between Felix and me, since he calls it rain and I call it mist). We kept open table in the face of all the sea-monsters of the Atlantic. Even Felix fell to, and stood out like his old self . . .

"At seven o'clock in the evening we ought to have been back at Oban, our continent, but we only reached Tobermory. Some of the party went on shore . . .

"Night came on, the captain coolly cast anchor in some corner or other, and we lay down in the cabin. Beds there were none, and herrings are lodged in spacious halls compared to us. At times, when half asleep, I tried to drive away flies from my face, and then found they were the grizzly locks of an old Scotchman. If the Pope had been amongst us, some Protestant might unawares have kissed his slipper, for we often chanced to make unknown boots act as pillows. It was a wild night's revel without the merry cup, and with rain and wind for the boisterous songsters.

"At half past six on the Sunday morning we landed at Oban, in the rain. Not wishing to hear a Gaelic sermon, we mounted one of those eligible open vehicles that are called carts, 'sheltered' by the rain. At last, however, the sun came out, warming our hearts and drying our cloaks."

Mendelssohn's contribution to this narration, written on the same day, was brief and to the point:

"In order to make you understand how extraordinarily the Hebrides affected me, the following came into my mind there:

Thus the germ theme out of which Mendelssohn's exquisite *Fingal's Cave* Overture was to emerge—a score remarkable for its charm and clarity—apparently occurred to him in the middle of what seems to have been a highly uncomfortable voyage.

Klingemann again takes up the story:

"In Inveraray, we found an excellent inn and good quarters. Our host's beautiful daughter in her black curls looked out, like a sign over the signboard, into the harbour, in which the newest herrings are swimming about all alive at nine o'clock in the morning, and at a quarter past nine are served up fried, with the coffee. Sympathising fellow-travellers eased our minds of our past sufferings, and our feet of our torn boots.

"The Duke of Argyll's castle proudly looked forth from between the lofty trees, and from the tops of the surrounding hills the green trees held a colloquy with their relations below, who were already appointed to the navy and swam about in the water."

They came back to Glasgow over the return leg of what the Highland firm who first organised it used to call "the far-famed Loch Eck tour".

"Out of a steamboat on which we embarked, whilst our host's black-curled daughter thumped the piano, we were to have been transferred into a steam-coach; but our locomotion was effected by horses, and the former vehicle stood idly by the roadside, having already been used but not found quite practicable yet, and looking very ridiculous with a high funnel and rudder."

Coming to Loch Eck ("Hech", Klingemann called it) they "once more got on board a steamer, which finally delivered us to a final one in the mouth of the Clyde, and we sailed up the Clyde to Glasgow: a splendid sail, scarcely any waves, watering-places on the river with large vessels, seagulls, steamers fast gliding past, villas, a rock with Dumbarton Castle and a view of the clear wide distance, and the blue towering Ben Lomond.

"We saw him for the first time. The country became more flat, and soft corn-fields gave us a familiar greeting, like old acquaintances after our long roaming among the proud silent mountains.

"Everything was still and peaceful. Three kinds of stillnesses are here. Between the mountains the water rushes, but it is sternly still. In the sea, between the islands the waves roll, but it is dismally still. In the smooth water the steamboats fly, but it is mildly and recreatively still."

On August 10th, the travellers were back in Glasgow relaxing in a comfortable hotel. Klingemann wrote: "Sitting, as we are now, in the best hotel of a commercial town of 160,000 inhabitants, which has a university and common manufacturers, and coffee and sugar at first hand, we look back with equanimity on past disasters. The Highlands, however, and the sea brew nothing but whisky and bad weather. Here, it is different and smooth, but comfortable. With a blue sky overhead and a good sofa underneath, palatable victuals before and ministering spirits around us, we brave all dangers, particularly the past ones . . . In Glasgow there are seventy steam-boats, forty of which start every day, and many long chimneys are smoking. An excellent inn refreshes us. The waiters minister to us with two hands and as many feet, as steam-service in hotels has not yet been invented."

Later, he added: "We have seen and admired Glasgow. This morning we were in a stupendous cotton mill, as full of maddening noise as the divine waterfall of Monass. What is the difference to the ear?

"One old wash-woman wore a wreath of cotton, another had tied up her aching tooth with it. Hundreds of little girls toil there from their earliest days, and look yellow. But there will ever exist poetry about it. Systematic order becomes sublime, and the whole swallows itself up in succession, like seasons and vegetation."

Poetry of a less dubious order awaited them at Loch Lomond next day, August 11th. Mendelssohn continued the narrative:

"We had weather to make the trees and rocks crash. The day before yesterday, on Loch Lomond, we were sitting in deep twilight in a small rowing boat and were going to cross to the opposite shore, invited by a gleaming light, when there came a sudden tremendous gust of wind from the mountains. The boat began to see-saw so fearfully that I caught up my cloak and got ready to swim. All our things were thrown topsy-turvy, and Klingemann anxiously called to me, 'Look sharp, look sharp!' But with our usual good luck we got safely through.

"When on shore, we had to sit in a room with a cursing young Englishman, who was something between a sportsman, a peasant and a gentleman, perfectly insufferable, and with three other individuals of a similar kind. We were obliged to sleep in the next house close under the roof, so that from sitting-room to bedroom we walked with umbrellas, cloak and cap."

Back in Glasgow once more, both the travellers reflected on the scenery they had enjoyed and the social conditions they had experienced.

Mendelssohn decided that "To describe the wretchedness and the comfortless, inhospitable solitude of the country, time and space do not allow. We wandered ten days without meeting a single traveller. What are marked on the map as towns, or at least villages, are a few sheds, huddled together, with one hole for door, window and chimney for the entrance and exit of men, beasts, light and smoke; in which you get a dry 'No'; in which brandy is the only beverage known; without church, without street, without gardens; the rooms pitch dark in broad daylight; children and fowls lying in the same straw, many huts without roof; many unfurnished, with crumbling walls; and many ruins of burnt houses; and even the inhabited spots are but sparingly scattered over the country.

"Long before you arrive at a place, you hear it talked of. The rest is heath, with red or brown heather, withered fir stumps, and white stones; or black moors where they shoot grouse.

"Now and then you find beautiful parks, but deserted, and broad lakes, but without boats, the roads a solitude. Fancy in all that the rich glowing sunshine, which paints the heath in a thousand divinely warm colours, and then the clouds chasing hither and thither!"

Klingemann, on the whole took a more kindly view:

"Ever memorable country! . . . The Highland smell will be remembered by us, a certain smoky atmosphere which every Highlander has about him. I once, while going along, closed my eyes and then correctly stated that five Highlanders had passed—my nose had seen them. It is easy to determine the number of houses in the same way.

"As for the rest, the country is not as bad as certain people in great capitals would make out. It is almost exclusively a mountainous country, and as such it is remarkable. At night, when the storm rises, you find an inn with beds which you are not exactly obliged to share with cattle drovers, but with sporting John Bulls. If a fowl chances to run about the room, or a pig squeaks under you, it is a proof that you may look forward to a new-laid egg and some pork next morning at breakfast. If the cart on which you travel jolts rather murderously, that is only the more temptation to get out and walk . . . If nothing is to be had but fresh herrings and beautiful rich cream, that indicates the patriarchal primitiveness which the modern world has so often on its lips. If the people make clumsy effort at something better, with diluted wine and diluted bills, that shows a pleasing disposition for culture."

Looking back at the Highlands from the foot of Loch Lomond, Klingemann added:

"The sun did really shine out here from the blue sky, only over the Highlands black clouds were hanging. But the longer and oftener we looked back, the bluer and more misty grew the mountains, at the feet of which we had been lying, all deep shades of colour mingled; and we might have become Highland-sick and wished ourselves back, had we not known that the reality within that mountain land was grey, cold and majestic. It was a sweet farewell to the heights which we at once abuse and love."

Just before they "flew away from Glasgow on the top of the mail, ten miles an hour, past steaming meadows and smoking chimneys, to the Cumberland lakes, to Keswick, Kendal, and the prettiest villages", where the whole county was "like a drawing-room", Mendelssohn gave his verdict on their Scottish tour:

"It is no wonder that the Highlands have been called melancholy. But two fellows have wandered merrily about them, laughed at every opportunity, rhymed and sketched together, growled at one another and at the world when they happened to be vexed or did not find anything to eat, devoured everything eatable when they did find it, and slept twelve hours every night. These two were we, who will not forget it as long as we live."

Mendelssohn never again came to Scotland, but paid several visits to England, on one occasion dining with Charles Dickens, and on another playing before Queen Victoria, who shared her music-loving subjects' admiration of him. Indeed, just before the end of his last visit when he was physically worn-out, he called on the Queen and Prince Albert to say farewell. The shock of his beloved sister Fanny's death from a stroke hastened his own end. Aged 38, he died at Leipzig in November, 1847, after himself suffering two strokes, a fate which befell several members of the Mendelssohn family comparatively early in life.

In 1845, Karl Klingemann married Sophie Rosen of Detmold, described by Mendelssohn as having "smooth fair hair parted in the middle, and a thorough German face, round, with blue eyes". The Klingemanns settled in London, where Mendelssohn stayed with them the following year.

Klingemann remained in the diplomatic service for the rest of his life as Secretary to the Hanoverian Legation in London, where he died in 1862. He provided the text for Mendelssohn's opera *Die Heimkehr aus der Fremde (Son and Stranger).* His son, also Karl, who was born in 1859 in London, survived until 1946, dying at Bonn, having reached a position of considerable eminence in the German Lutheran Church. In 1909, Karl Klingemann the younger published the delightful letters forming the correspondence between his father and Mendelssohn.

When Mendelssohn left Scotland and the Lake District, he visited Wales, staying with the family of John Taylor, a musical mining engineer, at Coed-Du (where, incidentally, the composer was extremely rude about Haydn and Beethoven's arrangements of Welsh national airs, then being widely performed). One of Taylor's three daughters analysed and noted down the impression Mendelssohn made on her:

"I suppose some of the charm of his speech might be in the unusual choice of words which he, as a German, made in speaking English. He lisped a little. He used an action of nodding his head quickly till the long locks of hair would fall over his forehead with the vehemence of his assent to anything he liked."

His charm of speech finds some reflections in his share of the joint account of the Hebridean journey of 1829. The quality of his mind and the distinctiveness of his imagination —for too long under-valued during the inevitable reaction against Victorianism, but now beginning to be recognised again for its true worth—reflects in musical terms through the Overture *Fingal's Cave* and the "Scottish" Symphony a kind of music which Scotland might have produced herself if the Reformation and its aftermath had not so crudely severed her musical arteries.

8

Hans Christian Andersen:
The Innocent Eye

To his readers on this side of the English Channel, Hans Christian Andersen is remembered as a writer for children, the teller of some of the finest fairy-tales ever set down on paper. To his European contemporaries, he was a writer of travel books, a novelist, a poet, the author of several plays and opera libretti, and a character whose loveable gentleness endeared him to everyone he met. To his fellow countrymen, along with Søren Kierkegaard, he is one of the two greatest Danes their nineteenth century produced.

He was born at Odense, in the island of Fünen, on 2nd April, 1805, the son of a 23-year-old shoemaker and his 38-year-old washerwoman wife. The whole family lived and slept in a single room. As a child, Hans Andersen already showed signs of an emotional and imaginative temperament: so much so that when in 1816 his father died, having urged his mother to let the boy have his head whatever he wanted to do in life, the widow, who could not understand this wise direction, nevertheless obeyed it.

He was allowed to give up going to school, spending his time at home making a little toy theatre and clothes for his puppets, as well as digesting the plays of Holberg and Shakespeare.

Attempts to get him apprenticed to a tailor proved disastrous, and in 1819, bearing in mind her late husband's injunction but with many misgivings, his mother allowed him to set out for Copenhagen. His tall, lean figure and eccentric manner led some people to think him a lunatic, but he was taken on at the Royal Court Theatre as a singer until his voice broke, and befriended by the composer Christoph Weyse, and among others the poet Frederik Högh-Guldberg. When Guldberg lost interest in him, Jonas Collin, the director of the Royal Theatre, took his place and became Andersen's life-long friend. King Frederick VI then took an interest in him, and sent him to the grammar school at Slagelse. He learned much from the tyrannical teacher Simon Sørensen Meisling, whose realisation of his pupil's superior talents induced behaviour not far removed from mental cruelty. Nevertheless, Andersen followed Meisling when he moved to a school at Elsinore.

Considered educated at last by Collin, but full of self-doubts, Andersen returned to Copenhagen. His first success came in 1829, with his travel-book *A Journey on Foot from Holman's Canal to the East Point of Amager*, followed quickly by a play and a book of poems. Danish monarchs in these days showed more enlightenment in their patronage of promising artists than the rulers of most other European states. The King gave Hans Andersen a small travelling stipend, and he set out on the first of what were then long European journeys, culminating in his arrival at Rome. His play *Agnate and the Merman* written at Le Loc, in the Jura, won him some recognition at home, while his novel set in Italy, *The Improvisatore*, published in 1835, attracted international recognition. In the same year, the first of his fairy-tales was published in Copenhagen. A novel, *O.T.*, and another travel book, *In Sweden*, followed, and at first won more fame for their author than the fairy tales, on which he himself set small value, though he continued to write them. Another romance, considered by Danish critics today to be his best, *Only a Fiddler*, followed, together with several plays which scored purely ephemeral success. Meanwhile, the fairy tales, more of which had appeared, were finding their way into other European languages.

Andersen was by now famous throughout Europe, and on his travels was received as an equal by writers like the Grimm brothers, Heine, Dumas père et fils and Victor Hugo, and by the composers Spohr, Mendelssohn and Liszt. The great families of Europe opened their palaces to him, and over tea he read his fairy-tales to the last Habsburg Emperor, Franz Joseph.

Although he knew Italy, Germany and Switzerland well, the success in 1846 not only of his badly-translated fairy-tales but of his miscellany *A Poet's Bazaar*, published in

London and New York, together with his admiration for the work of Dickens and Scott, made him want to visit England and Scotland. In June 1847, therefore, he set sail from Rotterdam on a Dutch steamer, "a true snail of a ship", its decks crowded with emigrants *en route* for America, and baskets of cherries.

The Thames, crowded with ships of all sorts and surrounded by smoky chimneys and at ebb-tide revealing its slimy bed, seemed to Andersen truly Dickensian.

Leaving the Customs House, a cab drove him into a sunset "red-gold as if it was shining through the glass of a beer-bottle", and the smell of Dickensian London exerted itself to the full:

"The throngs in the street became denser and denser, there was carriage after carriage in two directions; there were omnibuses filled both inside and on top, great carts which were only huge packing-cases with posters of the latest news stuck on them; there were men with large signboards on a stick which they lifted high above the crowds and on which one could read of something or other that was to be seen or bought. Everyone was in motion, as though half London were streaming to one side of the town and the other half to the other side. Where the streets cross each other there are raised stone sections in the middle of them; thither folk departed from one pavement, in and out of the nearest stream of traffic and on to the footpath on the other side. London, the city of cities. Yes, that is what I immediately felt. . .".

Count Reventlow, the Danish Ambassador, introduced him to London society. Some years before, Andersen had fallen in love with Jenny Lind, "the Swedish nightingale", but she could regard him only as a dear brother. (All his previous love-affairs had settled into a similar pattern, possibly because his romantic idealisation of women implied some lack of male assertiveness.) Her presence in London at this time greatly enriched his visit, for she let both the aristocrats and the public understand quite clearly that for her, Andersen was someone special. He was taken up by the redoubtable Lady Blessington, of Gore House, Kensington, and found some difficulty in understanding why there was a silence in company when he mentioned her name, her reputation being "bad" because her son-in-law was said to prefer her company to that of his young wife. His gratitude to Lady Blessington, however, was immense, for she introduced him to Dickens, then thirty-five years old. To Andersen, Dickens looked "handsome with an intelligent and kind expression and a mass of beautiful hair which fell to both sides. We shook hands with each other, looked deep into the other's eyes, talked to each other and understood each other. We went out on the veranda and I was so moved and delighted to see and speak to the one living English author I loved more than any other, that tears came to my eyes."

The Irish poet William Allingham entered in his diary for 9th July:

"I met Andersen the other day at dinner and we were mutually unintelligible. I had the pleasure of feeling his arm, in mine, on the way to dinner: It was the thinnest arm I ever felt. He looks like a man in the last stage of consumption . . . a large child, a sort of half-angel. There were many people of rank present, yet no one in the room looked more *distingué* than Andersen, the shoemaker's son."

Andersen also met Disraeli and Leigh Hunt, and, among the Scots in London, John Wilson ("Christopher North"), Lord Jeffrey, and Scott's son-in-law and biographer, John Gibson. Lockhart who, with his wife, suggested that Hans Andersen should visit Abbotsford.

It was, however, the son of Baron C. J. Hambro, the founder of the international banking firm which still bears his name, who persuaded his father to bring Andersen to Scotland with him. Joseph Hambro had rented a house outside Edinburgh for the summer. Having felt too unwell to accept Queen Victoria's invitation to visit her on the Isle of Wight, and with a further invitation to visit her in the Highlands, Andersen agreed to accompany the Baron, mistakenly believing that he would find Scotland restful, after the hectic delights of London.

They travelled by train, a daring adventure, as Andersen's best English biographer, Monica Stirling, points out, fatal railway accidents at the time being fifteen times as frequent as in Germany. They divided the journey into two days, travelling in an express train, which "dashed along without rest or pause."

At York railway station, Andersen met the Duke of Wellington. Andersen and the Baron stayed at the Black Swan hotel. "Swallows were flying in flocks above the streets," the poet recorded, "and above my head I saw my own bird, the stork."

Next day they travelled on to Newcastle, "enveloped in dense smoke and steam." As the viaduct was then still under construction, they had to take "an omnibus through the town to the station on the other side".

Apparently it was not altogether a comfortable journey from Newcastle to Scotland:

"In England one does not receive a ticket for one's luggage as is the case in other countries; it is a case of looking after it oneself, and it was a terrible bother in the places where it was necessary to change. This particular day the crowds were especially bad; there were so many travellers, and early in the morning an express train had left which had been put on for gentlemen for going hunting in Scotland with their dogs. All the first-class carriages were occupied, and so we had one and all to travel in the second class which is as bad as it can possibly be, with wooden seats and wooden shutters, just as other countries have in the fourth class."

At last they reached "the river which forms the border between England and Scotland; the land of Walter Scott and Burns lay before us. The countryside began to be mountainous and we could see the sea; the railway runs along the coast; there were lots of boats out there."

They reached Edinburgh through "a narrow, deep valley, which was like a dried-up moat on a large scale."

Young Hambro met them with a carriage and they went off "at a gallop" to Mount Trinity, where "a happy and gay reception" awaited Andersen.

By next day, he was "already like one of the family among charming and clever people", who, however, practised the family evening prayers in the manner of Burns's *The Cotter's Saturday Night*. A prayer was said and a bit of the Bible was read aloud in the same way as I later saw it in all the families I visited. It made a good and beautiful impression on me."

Although Andersen felt he "needed physical rest and quiet," there was too much to explore to allow for these things. Approaching Edinburgh in the train, it "stopped outside a tunnel under the rock, up which several of the streets in new Edinburgh lead; most people got out. 'Have we arrived already?' 'No' said my companion, 'but there are not many who go further; people are afraid the tunnel is not strong enough and that it might collapse with all the streets, and so most people prefer to get out here; but I do not expect it will collapse when we are in it.' And we rushed into the long, black vault; and it did not collapse on that occasion, but it was not pleasant."

Safely out on the street again, Andersen found that "The view from the new part of the city to the old is magnificent and impressive, and it offers a sight which, with its picturesque grouping, puts Edinburgh on a level with Constantinople, or Stockholm. There is a long road there, which can almost be called a quay if the chasm along which the railway runs, is regarded as a river-bed; thence one can see a panorama of the whole of the old part of the city, with its Castle and Heriot's Hospital; where the old town slopes down towards the sea, there is the hill called 'Arthur's Seat', famous from Walter Scott's novel *The Heart of Midlothian*; the whole of the old town is like a mighty commentary on these great works which are read in all lands".

So wrote the Romanticist, stimulated, perhaps by the proximity of his viewpoint to the Scott Monument, which George Kemp had completed only a few months before "in the shape of a great Gothic tower, and under this . . . a statue of the poet seated on a chair; his dog, Maida, is lying at his feet, and in the topmost arches of the tower, figures from his works, figures who are now known the world over are to be seen, Meg Merrilees, the Last Minstrel and so on."

His enthusiasm entirely lay in the direction of the Old Town. Beyond the seated statue of Sir Walter, it seemed to Andersen as if "The new part of Edinburgh has straight roads and uninteresting modern buildings; one line cuts another or runs parallel to it. There is nothing more Scots about it than the fact that it has regular squares just like the Scots plaids."

Very different in his eyes was the fairy tale appearance of the Old Town: "so picturesque and magnificent, so old, so murky, so characteristic. The houses, which in the main street have two or three storeys, back on to the valley which divides the old and the new part of the city, and there they have between nine and eleven storeys; and in the evenings when the lights have been lit by the various people living there, storey upon storey, and they, together with the bright gas-lamps, stream over the roofs of the other houses in the street, high up as it is, it presents a characteristic, almost festive appearance with lights high up in the air."

But Andersen was realist enough to appreciate that what lay beneath the lights was not always so romantic. The discoverer of chloroform, Sir James Simpson, was Hans Andersen's guide when they walked down the High Street.

"The many side streets off it," the poet wrote, "are narrow, filthy, and with six-storeyed houses; the oldest of them seem to be built of heavy stone; one has to think of the great buildings in the dirty towns of Italy; poverty and misery seem to peep out of the open hatches, which normally serve as windows, and rags and tatters are hanging out to dry. In one of these streets, I was shown a dirty, gloomy building, with a courtyard, which looked like a stable; it had once been an important hotel in Edinburgh, the only one there had been, where kings had stayed, and where Samuel Johnson had lived for a long time."

This building, like so much else in the old Town entered upon its Victorian decline, was the White Horse Inn.

Hans Andersen looked at the house where Burke, the partner of Hare in an enterprising undertaking to supply cadavers to the anatomist Dr. Knox, had once lived, and "where the unfortunate victims had been lured in and strangled in order to be sold as corpses". The poet also saw through "almost tumbling down, Knox's little house . . . still standing in the main street and a statue of him talking from a pulpit", this of course being the supposed Edinburgh home of that other Knox, John, the Reformer.

The Old Tolbooth seemed to Andersen to attract attention "not because of its exterior, but because of Walter Scott's novel", *The Heart of Midlothian.* Holyrood, the Dane thought, contained "a number of uninteresting rooms to go through, with, in the great hall, a lot of bad portraits", a fair enough comment on the hundred and ten Scottish kings, mythical and real, from Fergus I to Charles II, painted by a Dutch hack artist James De Witt at two pounds a time in 1684.

"It was only when I entered Mary Stuart's bedroom," Andersen went on, "that it became Holyrood House for me. The tapestry there represented 'The Fall of Phaeton;' so that is what she always had in front of her eyes; it was almost like a forewarning of her own fall. In the little room at the side, the unfortunate Rizzio had been dragged to be murdered; spots of blood are still to be seen on the floor." Rich, indeed, would have been the Italian musician's blood had it retained its colour unaided by paint over the passing of more than three centuries!

Hans Andersen admired the Chapel, "now a lovely ruin; ivy, which in England and Scotland spreads with a fullness, the likes of which I have only seen in Italy, covers the walls of the church here; it looks like a rich carpet.The eternally green plant winds its way up round the windows and columns; grass and flowers grow around the gravestones."

With Baron Hambro, Andersen visited George Heriot's Hospital, "a magnificent castle-like building, the founder of which was a goldsmith whom we all know from Walter Scott's novel *The Fortunes of Nigel*.

"Visitors must come provided with written permission and in addition they must personally write their names in the porter's lodge; I wrote mine in full, Hans Christian Andersen, as it is as such I am always known in England and Scotland. The old porter read it and then, with striking readiness, he followed Mr. Hambro who had a kind, jovial face and silvery hair, and he asked him if he were not the Danish writer. 'That is just as I imagined him to be with such a gentle face and such distinguished hair!' 'No,' came the reply, and then I was pointed out. 'So young!' exclaimed the old man; 'I have read him, and the boys here read him. It is strange to see such a man; they are usually all old or dead before one hears of them.'

"I was told of what he had said, and I went across to the old man and shook hands with him. He and a few of the boys, who came and were asked, knew all about 'the ugly duck and the red shoes'. It surprised and moved me to think that I was known up here and had friends among the poor boys and those about them. I had to step aside to hide my tears; God knows the thoughts of my heart."

The editor of *The Literary Gazette*, Charles Jerdon, had

given the poet a letter of introduction to Francis, Lord Jeffrey, described by the young wife of John Wilson as "a horrid little man", but the much-feared editor of the *Edinburgh Review,* to whom Dickens had dedicated his novel *The Cricket on the Hearth,* and who was then living at Craigcrook; "a real old romantic castle, the walls of which were almost hidden by evergreen. A huge fire was roaring in the hearth in the great hall, where the family soon congregated, and where young and old alike surrounded me, and, showed their affection for me. Children and grand-children came along, and I had to write my name in the front of the different books of mine they possessed. We wandered about in the large park until we came to a point from which there was a view of Edinburgh, which from there, is not unlike Athens. . . ."

A few days later, Jeffrey and his family repaid the visit, coming out to Mount Trinity. As they parted, Jeffrey said to the poet: "Come to Scotland again soon, so that we can meet again: 'I have not many years to live.' " Indeed, he had not. He died in January, 1850, without having ever again met Hans Andersen.

At the home of Sir James Simpson, the poet met "the jovial critic, Mr. Wilson", Professor of Moral Philosophy at the University of Edinburgh, and the "Christopher North" of *the Noctes Ambrosianae*. Wilson, a hearty man of leonine appearance, much given to vigorous joking, seemed to the delicate Hans Andersen, "full of life and humour . . . . he called me brother in fun." Others in the company, which included such long-forgotten writers as Mrs. Crowe, the authoress of the novel *Susan Hopley,* dubbed him "The Danish Walter Scott . . . unworthy though I was."

Though he enjoyed the company at Sir James's home, he was less happy at being involved, with "the large circle which was gathered there" in "several experiments . . . made with breathing in ether; I thought it distasteful, especially to see ladies in this dreamy intoxication; they laughed with open, lifeless eyes; there was something unpleasant about it, and I said so, recognising at the same time that it was a wonderful and blessed invention to use in painful operations, but not to play with; it was almost like tempting God." An elderly gentleman, who had sided with Hans Andersen, chanced to meet the poet in the street a few days later, just after he had bought "the Holy

Bible in a cheap, but beautiful edition, and now he became even more friendly towards me, patted my cheek, and made some warm remarks, which I by no means deserved, about my pious mind. Chance had put me in a light which he found beautiful."

A week later, Hans Andersen set off to see part of the Highlands, particularly, "the places which Walter Scott depicted in *The Lady of the Lake* and *Rob Roy*".

Over at Kirkcaldy he visited Ravenscraig Castle, founded by James II in 1460, and reputedly the first Castle to be built for defence against firearms. Andersen, however, believed it to be the Ravenswood Castle of *The Bride of Lammermoor*. Even although "an old man from the town", told him that this was merely "something people had invented to tell strangers"; that "the name was an invention on the part of the author"; and that the real setting of the story was further north, the prototype of the Ashtons being the Stair family, Hans Andersen found the castle fascinating.

"The ruin itself, with its murky, vaulted dungeons, and luxuriant evergreens, which covered the remains of the walls like a firm carpet and hung fast to the cliff jutting out over the sea, was so picturesque and so characteristic; the sea had receded because of the ebb-tide, and the view from here to Edinburgh was magnificent and unforgettable."

Hans Andersen enjoyed a sail on the Forth in a paddle-steamer, a pleasure which finally became impossible only in 1939.

"We sailed up the Firth of Stirling by steamer; a modern minstrel, sang Scottish ballads and accompanied himself on a violin; it sounded so melancholy, and to the sound of these notes we approached the Highlands where the cliffs lay like outposts. Mist descended over them and then lifted again; it was like a hasty arrangement to show us Ossian's land in the proper light. The mighty Stirling Castle, high up on a rock, which is like a gigantic figure of stone rising from the flat plains, dominates the town, the oldest streets of which are dirty, badly cobbled and just as they were in olden days."

However, Andersen thought the view from the castle "absolutely wonderful". The stone where "King Edward planted his standard before Bannockburn" interested the poet, as did the fact that so many people had chipped bits of it away that iron railings had to be put round it to preserve what

Above, '. . . a rock with Dumbarton Castle and a view of the clean wide distance'; *below*, Edinburgh Castle, 'like a bird's nest on a cliff'

Above, Oban . . . 'sunshine, the wide outlines of the sea, good cheer and society of all kinds', recorded Mendelssohn; *below*, Loch Tay, with Ben More and Ben Lawers in background

Hans Christian Andersen, 1805–1875

Above, a view of the old city of Edinburgh from the New Town in 1847. Andersen found it 'magnificent and impressive'; *below*, Loch Katrine . . . 'long and narrow with deep, dark water and lying between brownish-green slopes'

remained. He also saw the "poor smithy" where, after the battle of Sauchieburn, James III—Andersen erroneously calls him James IV, who, of course, was killed at Flodden—"sought shelter, sent for a priest, and confessed, and when the priest heard it was the King, he plunged a knife into his heart." The smith's wife showed Andersen "the corner where her bed now stood, where the murder had been done." Near Darnley's house, he met a cobbler full of stories of Scottish history. He even thought that "The whole region looked rather Danish but it was poorer, and it looked as though the season were colder than it really was. The limes were in bloom there, while at home they were still in bud." He also observed: "Travel is dear in England and Scotland, but one receives value for one's money. Everything is excellent: guests are looked after, and even the smallest village inn is comfortable;" a view so much running counter to the generally expressed opinions of travellers that one can only assume the Hambros shielded Andersen from the filthier establishments.

In Callander, then "not much more than a hamlet", Andersen felt "almost as though I were staying at a Count's residence; there was soft carpet on the stairs, and in the passages; the fire was blazing merrily and we were glad of that, although the sun was shining outside and all the Scots were going about with bare knees; and that is indeed also their winter dress. They wrapped themselves in their colourful plaids; even the poor boys had one, although it might only have been a rag."

Next morning, Andersen set out early to catch the steamer on Loch Katrine.

"The road became wilder and wilder; heather was to be seen and it was in bloom; we passed a few lonely houses which were built of stone. Loch Katrine, long and narrow with deep and dark water, lay between brownish green mountain slopes; heather and scrub covered the shores and as far as I could see. I had the impression that if the Jutlandic heath is a sea in motionless calm, then this region is the heath in a tempest! The waves of mountains are dead, but they are all green, covered with grass and scrub."

To his left, as he sailed up the loch, Andersen looked with European interest on "Ellen's Isle" from which "the Lady of the Lake" had steered her boat, "the island which Walter Scott has made known to us and interesting for us through his poem."

By the northerly pier, Andersen inspected, "the poor inn" in which fifty beds were ranged alongside each other, "the place where travellers from Loch Lomond could find shelter until the following morning when the steamer sailed over Loch Katrine."

His fellow passengers set out on foot, a few on horseback, over the neck of land down to Loch Lomond. But "Hambro had procured a little carriage for his wife and myself, since we were both too weak to manage the tiring journey across the heath on foot. There was no proper road here, only a path; we drove where the carriage could best progress, over hills and through valleys, over clods and stones which were marked in a way indicative of a future road"—a road which had been laid when, a few years later, Queen Victoria crossed from the one loch to the other.

Andersen, sensitive as always to place atmosphere, captured the feeling of this mountain pass with his usual economy of words:

"The coachman walked alongside the horse; one moment we reeled and jolted down hill at a wild speed, the next, we were slowly being tugged up hill; it was a journey the likes of which I have never seen elsewhere. There was not a house to be seen, and we did not meet a soul; all around us there were the silent, gloomy mountains shrouded in mist; monotonous and always the same. The one and only living creature we saw for miles was a lonely shepherd, who was bitterly cold, and wrapped himself in his grey plaid. Silence reigned over all the landscape. Ben Lomond, the highest mountain peak, finally broke through the mist, and soon we could see Loch Lomond below us. Although there was a sort of road leading down, the descent was so steep that it was extremely dangerous to go with a carriage; it had to be left behind, and on foot we approached the well-equipped inn where a crowd of people were waiting for the steamer to arrive."

As he walked up the gangway at Inversnaid, Andersen met a fellow Dane already aboard, the geologist C. Puggaard.

It was a not untypical Loch Lomond day. "On board we were all wrapped in our plaids; in rain and drizzle, mist and wind the steamer went right up to the most northerly point of the lake, which ends where a little river [the Falloch] flows into it. Some passengers left and others joined us. We were in the countryside where 'Red Robin' [Rob Roy MacGregor] had moved."

As the steamer sailed southwards, past Rob Roy's cave, where, "great chunks of rock had fallen into the lake", a small boat brought a whole party out to us; in it was a young lady who looked fixedly and closely at me. Soon afterwards, one of the gentlemen stepped across to me and said there was a young lady . . . . who would like to know if I were not the Danish poet Hans Christian Andersen. I said I was, and the young lady flew across to me filled with heart-felt delight, and with a show of confidence as though we were old acquaintances, she pressed my hand and said in a natural and beautiful way how glad she was to see me . . . Her father and all her family gathered round me . . . Hambro enjoyed the homage which was paid to me; soon the attention of all the passengers was turned on me, and it was surprising how large the circle of my friends became. It is a strange feeling of gladness to be given a good reception when one is so far from home, and, so to speak, to belong to so many kind and friendly people."

Andersen and the Hambros went ashore at Balloch, and drove past Smollett's monument at Bonhill, to Dumbarton, "a real Scottish town close to the Clyde. That night there was a gale with long, extremely powerful gusts of wind; it was as though we could hear the roar of the sea all the time, everything creaked, the windows rattled, and a sick cat miaowed the whole night through."

Sunday morning broke "quiet as the grave after such a night". Andersen was not impressed by the Scottish Sabbath.

"Everything rests there, even the trains are not allowed to go; only the one from London to Edinburgh does not stop, to the annoyance of the strictly religious Scots. All houses are shut, and people sit at home reading the Bible or getting themselves drunk–that is what I have generally been told.

"It was foreign to my nature to sit indoors a whole day in that way, and see nothing at all of the town," Andersen protested; "and I suggested going for a walk but I was told that it just would not do, people could be annoyed. However, towards evening, we all went for a walk out of the town, but there was silence everywhere, and folk peeped out of their windows and looked at us, so we soon turned round again."

Andersen, whose form of Danish protestantism was Lutheran, untainted by the psychological blight cast by Calvin and Knox, was not slow to diagnose the nature of the Scots disease.

"Such piety on Sundays cannot be genuine in all people; where it is genuine, I will respect it, but as a habit which has been handed down from father to son, it becomes a mask and results in hypocrisy."

Next day, he and Hambro went into a bookshop in Dumbarton, and by way of a joke Hambro asked the man if he stocked a portrait of "the Danish poet Hans Christian Andersen". The shopkeeper said he did, adding that the poet was supposed to be in Scotland. Producing the portrait, he looked at Hambro and said: "Why, it must be you", on which Andersen commented: "That shows how much the portrait resembled me."

The mistake corrected, the bookseller begged the poet to meet his wife and children.

"They came and seemed happy to meet me," Andersen recorded: "And I had to shake hands with them all. I felt and understood that I was really known up there in Scotland, or at least that my name was."

At Dumbarton, he said good bye to the Hambros and their children, who were going to a watering place on the Clyde. Andersen caught the steamer to Glasgow, "profoundly melancholy" at the thought that he would probably never again see "these charming people".

He had decided that he was too tired to travel north again to Loch Laggan, where Queen Victoria and Prince Albert were then staying, and where he had been told the royal couple "would be graciously pleased" to see him. Also, the travelling grant he had received from the Danish king, Christian VIII, was running low, and there was no prospect of receiving a speedy reply if he were to write to Denmark seeking an extension of it.

From Glasgow, he crossed to Edinburgh, abandoning his plans to go to Abbotsford for the same reason that had led him to decline with so much reluctance the royal invitation. At Edinburgh, waiting on the station platform for the London train, a curious incident occurred. Driving from Loch Katrine to Loch Lomond one of the Hambro boys had seized Andersen's walking-stick and, pointing it towards Ben Lomond, said (inaccurately, as Ben Nevis has the honour accorded Ben Lomond by Master Hambro): "Now palm-tree, can you see the highest mountain in Scotland? Can you see the great lake?" The poet promised that when he next went to Naples, where he had bought the walking-stick, it should tell its friends "all about the land where the red flowers of the thistle were held in honour since it was given a place in the coat of arms of the people and nation."

At Inversnaid, the stick was left behind. Andersen asked Puggaard who went ashore there on the downward trip, to try to find it, and take it back to Denmark for him.

A few moments before the London train pulled out of the Edinburgh platform, the guard came along to Andersen's carriage carrying the walking-stick "saying with a little smile, 'It has travelled quite well alone.' A letter had been attached to it with the inscription, 'The Danish Poet, Hans Christian Andersen', and it had been handled with such order and care that it had been passed from hand to hand, first with the steamer on Loch Lomond, then with the omnibus driver, then by the steamer again, and then by train, all with the help of its little address card. It was put into my hands just as the signal sounded to fly away from Scotland; I have still to tell of my stick's adventures; I hope I may do it one day just as well as it managed to travel all alone."

Hans Andersen never told the story of his stick, and never came back to Scotland, though he paid a second visit to England ten years later to stay with Dickens at Gad's Hill.

Jenny Lind, the love of his life, married Otto Goldschmidt, a Jewish pianist nine years younger than herself, turning gradually into a middle-aged mother devoted to religion, who bore little resemblance to the talented young artist Andersen once hoped to marry but who had never regarded him as anything other than a gentle brother. Resigned to his bachelor state, Andersen continued his travels, winning fame and friendship wherever he went, and becoming a favourite guest at the palaces of the Danish royal family.

He had one last contact with Scotland in 1869, when Anna Mary Livingstone, daughter of the famous explorer David Livingstone, wrote to him from Ulva Cottage, Hamilton:

"Dear Hans Andersen,"

I do like your fairy tales so much that I would like to go and see you, but I cannot do that, so I thought I would write to you.

When papa comes home from Africa, I will ask him to take me to see you . . . ."

Andersen replied to his "Dear Little Friend," and the correspondence was kept up until, in September, 1874, the year before Andersen's own death, Mary Livingstone told him: "I did so expect to have had Papa take me to see you in Denmark. Instead of going to different places I fully intended to with Papa, I was obliged to take the sad journey to London to see him buried in Westminster Abbey."

Andersen's later years were much eased through his friendship with Moritz Melchier, a merchant and banker, and his wife, who owned the eighteenth-century house of Rolighed, overlooking the sound between Denmark and Sweden. There Andersen died on August 4th, according to one of the Melchior's servants having "just given a sigh and stopped breathing".

Few authors have had a happier fame: for, as Monica Stirling so aptly puts it, "There is never a moment when there is not somewhere in the world a child who is reading Hans Christian Andersen for the first time." That curious blend of wisdom and wonder which gives his tales their quality of greatness spilled over into his travel books, and into his autobiography *The Fairy Tale of my Life* in which the recollections of his Scottish visit are to be found. It is pleasant to think that Scotland had a small share in stimulating the imagination of one of the world's kindest and best loved travellers.

9

Queen Victoria:
The Royal Seal

In this age of constitutional monarchy, when the sovereign engages in rapid and regular journeying, it is perhaps fairly difficult to appreciate that throughout the seventeenth and eighteenth centuries travelling monarchs were not regarded with much favour in Scotland. A royal presence was always expensive, sometimes offensive, and often dangerous.

When King James VI of Scotland and I of England made his leisurely and expensive progress South in 1603 to occupy the English throne, and so for the first time unite Scotland and England under one ruler, the Scottish nobility soon followed after the Court. London became the centre from which favours could be anticipated and preferments granted. James come back to his native land in 1618, hunting and feasting and, in the eyes of some observers, strangely renewing his youth. But he imported with him a gilded organ for use in the Anglican services held for him at Holyrood Palace, and his attempts to persuade the Scots, who had given him so hearty a homecoming welcome, to accept the Anglican system of church ritual, led to a stormy session with the Scottish Parliament.

Charles I came north, somewhat reluctantly, in 1633, and on 18th June had himself crowned at Edinburgh with full Anglican ceremony, a gesture which aroused the hostility of most of his Scottish subjects. Charles II landed in Scotland in June 1650, having accepted the Presbyterian system of Church government set out in the Covenant, and on 1st January 1651 was duly crowned King of the Scots at Scone. But this was the year of the Battle of Worcester, prelude to the ensuing years of exile. After his Restoration, he did not return to Scotland. His brother, the Duke of York, did, taking up residence in Holyrood Palace where his civilized encouragement of the drama and his persistent belief in his right publicly to practise his own religion so angered the Protestant burghers of Edinburgh that he was recalled to London. The following year he returned as High Commissioner, accompanied by his Duchess, and by his daughter Princess Anne, the future Queen. Once he had become James VII and II in 1685, his attempts to establish Catholicism, though neither more biased nor more unfair than the measures used by Protestant monarchs against the English Catholics throughout the previous hundred and fifty years, fanned into active hostility his intense unpopularity, and eventually led to his deposition and defeat at the Battle of the Boyne. To celebrate the arrival of William of Orange and James VI's daughter Mary in these islands, the mob of Edinburgh broke into Holyrood House and sacked the tainted Chapel where the Catholic rites had been practised.

The "Old Pretender", as the Hanoverians called James II's surviving son, but who called himself James VIII and III, landed at Peterhead in December 1702. Finding that there was no prospect of a rising in favour of the Stuart cause, he soon re-embarked for France. His twenty-five year old son, the "Young Pretender", Charles I's great-grandson Prince Charles Edward Stuart, landed at Loch Shiel in 1745, and at the head of a Jacobite army marched as far south as Derby. There, the momentum of the thrust wavered and broke, and Bonnie Prince Charlie could do no more than retreat to the Highlands. Through months of hardship, during which those of his men who had not been killed in skirmishes on the weary march North, butchered as they lay wounded on Culloden Moor on 16th April, 1746, or executed after English trial, had to endure rigorous repression at the hands of George II's third son, the twenty-four year old Duke of Cumberland, and the alarmed and revengeful British Government. Prince Charles himself eluded the forces scouring the Highlands to capture him, until, in September the arrival of two French ships, at Loch-na-nuagh, enabled him to escape to France. Then followed his long years of frustrated, and latterly drunken, decline as the self-styled Count D'Albany, ending with his death in Rome in 1788.

Thereafter Scotland managed to exist without benefit of royal visit until, in 1822, King George IV announced that he intended to visit Edinburgh. The Royal Company of Archers, associated with royalty in Scotland since the days of King James I of Scotland, offered to be his bodyguard, and the offer was accepted. Sir Walter Scott stage-managed the proceedings for the royal stay, which lasted two weeks. The corpulent monarch, dressed in a kilt of Stuart tartan, took part in much of the pageantry, and held a levee at Holyrood Palace. As a result of this visit, Government money was provided for the restoration of the Palace of Holyrood House (as it is now known), some of the peerages forfeited after the Jacobite risings were restored, and by publicly toasting "Health to the chieftains and clans, and God Almighty bless the Land of Cakes", the King helped to heal some of that bitterness which the inhumanity of the measures taken after Culloden had seared into the Scottish consciousness.

He thus prepared the way for the first visit of the young Queen Victoria who, in 1842, asked her Prime Minister, Sir Robert Peel, to arrange that she should spend an autumn holiday in Scotland. She was then twenty-three, happily married to Prince Albert, second son of the hereditary duke of Saxe-Coburg-Gotha, the mother of two children expecting a third, and five years Queen of Great Britain. She had already given her patronage to the recently invented railway train, which, by the end of her reign, was so dramatically to speed up the pace of life and broaden the outlook of her subjects.

Peel was at first reluctant to allow her to go to Scotland, because of his fear of possible Chartist riots. But the determined young Queen, backed by Lord Melbourne, won her way, and set sail aboard the yacht *Royal George* from Woolwich on Monday 29th August, having made the journey from Windsor to London by "railroad", and driven by carriage from the station to the docks. Off the Yorkshire coast, the Queen recorded that she "remained on deck all day lying on sofas: the sea was very rough towards evening, and I was very ill."

Next day, the weather improved. Bonfires had been lit at Dunbar, at Tyninghame, the home of Lord and Lady Haddington, and at other points along the Scottish coast. There was also a certain amount of diversion aboard the royal yacht.

"We let off four rockets, and burned two blue lights. It is surprising to see the sailors climb on the bowsprit and up to the top of the masthead—this, too, at all times of the day and night. The man who carried the lantern to the main-top ran up with it in his mouth to the top. They are so handy and so well-conducted."

Next morning, 1st September, the ship anchored off Leith, and the Queen stepped ashore at Granton Pier, to be met by the Duke of Buccleuch, Sir Robert Peel and others. The "crowd and crush" of the Edinburgh people kept the Queen "continually in fear of accident". But the impression Edinburgh made on her and her husband was "very great: it is quite beautiful, totally unlike anything else I have seen; and what is more, Albert, who has seen so much, says it is unlike anything *he* ever saw . . . The country and people have quite a different character from England and the English. The old women wear close caps, and all the children and girls are barefooted."

They stayed at Dalkeith Palace, seat of the Earl of Dalkeith. At the beginning of the eighteenth century, this Palace, once the home of James Douglas, Earl of Morton, who held the council which plotted the trial and execution of Mary, Queen of Scots, was rebuilt for the Duchess of Monmouth, a Buccleuch before her marriage to the unfortunate leader of the Monmouth Rebellion. She chose Sir John Vanbrugh to be its architect, and the resulting heavy red-faced pile with recessed centre and projecting wings standing on a knoll above the North Esk was modelled on Lee Palace, in Holland.

Next morning, the Queen made her first acquaintance with a Scots breakfast, tasting "the oatmeal porridge, which I think very good, and also some of the 'Finnan haddies'." She thought Dalkeith itself "full of people, all running and cheery", while Prince Albert thought both people and town very "German-looking".

Driving into Edinburgh in a barouche, the Queen and the Prince saw Holyrood Palace, but because of a recent case of scarlet fever at the farm of Lord Strathearn, who had apartments in the Palace, did not go into it. They inspected John Knox's house, that "curious old building" which certainly once housed a Mr. Knox who may, or may not, have been the famous Reformer, the Tron Kirk, the Castle, and Heriot's Hospital, which, as the Queen noted, was "founded, in the time of James, by a goldsmith and jeweller whom Sir Walter Scott made famous in *The Fortunes of Nigel*."

Lord and Lady Roseberry entertained the royal couple to lunch at their "quite modern" Dalmeny House, by the banks of the Forth. They were "all civility and attention". After lunch, the Queen and the Prince Consort drove through Leith, which the Queen thought "not a pretty town".

Once again the crowds were enthusiastic: "The Porters all mounted, with curious Scotch caps, and their horses decorated with flowers . . . But the fisherwomen are the most striking-looking people, and are generally young and pretty women—very clean and very Dutch-looking, with their white caps and bright-coloured petticoats. They never marry out of their class."

And so, back to Edinburgh. "There was that beautiful large town, all of stone (no mingled colours of brick to mar it), with the bold Castle on one side, and the Calton Hill on the other, with those high sharp hills of Arthur's Seat and Salisbury Crags towering above all, and making the finest, boldest background imaginable. Albert said he felt sure the Acropolis could not be finer."

After a visit to Dalhousie, "a real old Scotch castle, of reddish stone", though much altered a few years before by the ninth Earl of Dalhousie, raised to the peerage for service in the Peninsular War, and a day spent in holding "a Drawing room at Dalkeith" attended by the Ministers and Scotch Officers of State, the Lord Provost, and representatives from the Scotch Church, and from the Universities of St. Andrews, Glasgow and Edinburgh, all of whom delivered addresses, the royal pair set out for the North, visiting Hopetoun House on the way to South Queensferry.

The distant sight of Dunfermline reminded the Queen that Robert the Bruce was buried there. She was further reminded of her Scots ancestors as the carriages rolled past Loch Leven, and she caught a glimpse of the castle on the island from which "poor Queen Mary escaped" in 1568.

There was a lunch party at Lord Kinnoull's seat, Dupplin, a new-Tudor replacement mansion completed in 1832, after which the royal couple drove into Perth, which put Albert "in mind of the situation of Basle". From Perth it was only a short drive to Lord Mansfield's Palace of Scone, two miles North of the town. This castellated mansion had been put up between 1803 and 1808 to replace the beautiful seventeenth century Palace once visited by both the Chevalier St. George and Prince Charles Edward Stuart, but which the Stormonts, who succeeded to the Mansfield title, apparently thought lacking in becoming grandeur.

Outside Dunkeld, "before a triumphal arch, Lord Glenlyon's Highlanders with halberds, met us, and formed our guard—a piper playing before us". This, however, was as nothing compared to the reception which awaited the Queen at Taymouth Castle, the seat of Lord Breadalbane.

"At the gate, a guard of Highlanders, Lord Breadalbane's men, met us . . . There were a number of Lord Breadalbane's Highlanders, all in the Campbell tartan, drawn up in front of the house, with Lord Breadalbane"—the 2nd Marquis and fifth Earl—"himself in a Highland dress at their head, a few of Sir Neil Menzies' men (in the Menzies red and white tartan), a number of pipers playing, and a company of the 92nd Highlanders, also in kilts. The firing of the guns, the cheering of the great crowd, the picturesqueness of the dresses, the beauty of the surrounding country, with its rich background of wooded hills, altogether formed one of the finest scenes imaginable. It seemed as if a great chieftain in olden feudal times was receiving his sovereign. It was princely and romantic."

The building of Taymouth Castle, set in a circuit of thirteen miles of what were described as "pleasure-grounds", was begun in 1801 and only completed shortly before the Queen's visit. The new building, which replaced a sixteenth-century castle, was adorned by Italian craftsmen in a princely style.

For six days, its "great chieftain" took Prince Albert shooting, while the chieftain's lady took the Queen to see Loch Tay, the River Tay, and Glen Dochart. The Queen was constantly reminded of *The Lady of the Lake.*

On Saturday, September 10th, Drummond Castle was reached on the return journey. This, the home of Lord Drummond, was an ancient seat which had been visited by

James IV and Queen Mary, before being badly damaged by Cromwell's troops and falling into neglect after the Revolution of 1688. Royalist troops used it in 1715, and to prevent a recurrence of this disagreeable experience, the Jacobite Duchess of Perth levelled it almost to its foundations in 1745. It was partly rebuilt about 1822, and much improved in 1842 to make it fit for royal visitors. A temporary wooden pavilion was used as a banqueting hall, and Prince Albert occupied a bedroom where Prince Charles had previously slept.

The Sabbath being wet, the Queen read to Albert the first three cantos of *The Lay of the Last Minstrel,* which delighted them both. This early enthusiasm of Victoria for Scott's poems and novels suggests that her own almost immediate love for the Scottish Highlands was at least in part a product of that kindly romanticism with which "the Wizard of the North" fired the European imagination.

Leaving Drummond Castle, the royal party returned by Dunblane to Stirling, where "the crowd was quite fearful, and the streets so narrow that it was most alarming; and order was not very well kept." She thought the situation of Stirling Castle "extremely grand; but I prefer that of Edinburgh Castle". The road up to the castle was "dreadfully steep; we had a foot procession the whole way, and the heat was intense". Their progress continued, through Falkirk to Linlithgow, and through Edinburgh back to Dalkeith. After a day spent visiting Rosslyn and Hawthornden, the home of the sixteenth century Scottish poet William Drummond, whom the Queen does not mention though she thought his house "beautifully situated at a great height above the river", the Queen, the Prince and their party boarded "the Trident, a large steamboat belonging the General Steam Navigation Company". Soon "the fair shores of Scotland receded more and more", and the Queen felt quite sad that this very pleasant and interesting tour was over"; adding, "but we shall never forget it".

Indeed, she did not. Two years later, in September 1844, she returned, this time sailing to Dundee. A great crowd turned out to greet her, but "everything was very well managed, and there would have been no crowding at all, had not, as usual, about twenty people begun to run along with the carriage, and thus forced a number of others to follow". She thought "the situation of the town is very fine, but the town itself not so".

Coupar Angus and Dunkeld were briefly visited on the way North. At Moulin, she tasted Athole Brose, the hot mixture of honey, whisky and milk, and at Killiecrankie, recorded: "The road winds along it and you look down a great height, all wooded on both sides. I cannot describe how beautiful it is. Albert was in perfect ecstasies."

Her destination on this occasion was Blair Castle, Blair Atholl, where she and her husband were to be the guests of Lord and Lady Glenlyon for just over two weeks. During this time, Albert went deer-stalking with his host, the Queen and her hostess visiting the chosen scene of action by pony or carriage. Together they visited the Falls of Bruar, planted by the Duke of Atholl in accordance with Burns's *Petition*, the Pass of Killiecrankie, which the Queen wanted to inspect more closely, the Falls of Tummell, which she thought inferior to those of Bruar. At this period the enjoyment Victoria mirrors in her journal is not so much the interest of a sovereign in her subjects as the contentment and satisfaction of a young wife still very much in love.

"Oh! what can equal the beauties of nature!" she exclaimed. "What enjoyment there is in them! Albert enjoys it so much; he is in ecstasies here".

It was thus not surprising that when, on 1st October, the time for departure came, and the return journey to re-embark was begun, they were "very sorry to leave Blair and the dear Highlands!" Two days later to the royal eyes: "The English coast appeared terribly flat."

At the end of this second visit, the Queen systematically enumerated the considerations which were eventually to lead her to acquire a Scottish home of her own.

"There is a great peculiarity about the Highlands and Highlanders; and they are such a chivalrous, fine, active people. Our stay among them was so delightful. Independently of the beautiful scenery, there was a quiet, a retirement, a wildness, a liberty, and a solitude that had such a charm for us."

Three years later, on 11th August, the Queen and the Prince Consort left Osborne pier, in the Isle of Wight, aboard the royal yacht, the paddle-steamer *Victoria and Albert,* attended by a flotilla of warships, one of which, the *Fairy,* acted as a tender. They visited the Scilly Isles and Wales, where Stevenson's Britannia tubular railway bridge was being constructed across the Menai Straits near Telford's earlier road suspension bridge, and where Albert went ashore to see the then new but still fantastic Penrhyn Castle. The Queen's first sight of Scotland on this occasion was the Mull of Galloway as the royal yacht approached Loch Ryan. Next day, 17th August, the ship sailed up the Clyde, past Ailsa Craig the formation of which the Queen thought "very curious", and Arran, reaching Greenock at half-past twelve on the morning. "The shore and the ships were crowded with people, there being no less . . . than thirty-nine steamers, over-filled with people, which almost all followed us. Such a thing never was seen. Add to these steamers boats and ships of all descriptions, moving in all directions; but not getting out of the way!" In spite of this congestion, aboard the *Fairy* the Queen sailed safely up-river to land at Dumbarton Castle, from which the view was spoiled by mist. The *Fairy* then cruised up Loch Long: "splendid, fifteen miles in length surrounded by grand hills, with such beautiful outlines, and very green–all so different from the east part of Scotland–the loch winding along most beautifully, so as to seem closed at times." The royal tourists then sailed to Rothesay, "a pretty little town built round a fine bay", where the *Victoria and Albert* was waiting for them, and where at night the whole town was "brilliantly illuminated, with every window lit up, which had a very pretty effect".

Next day, the *Fairy* took the Queen through the Kyles of Bute, "which, as you advance become very fine, the hills lying so curiously one behind the other, sometimes apparently closing up all outlet".

Rounding Loch Fyne, the ship sailed to Inveraray, past "a fine range of mountains splendidly lit up–green, pink and lilac".

At Inveraray, the Queen was treated to one of those tartan receptions which nineteenth-century Highland noblemen enjoyed laying on for her benefit. The landing-stage was decorated with heather, pipers walked in front of the royal carriage, which was flanked by a bodyguard of kilted Highlanders, and at Inveraray Castle, the Duke of Argyll's two-year old heir, the Marquis of Lorne, was waiting in "a black velvet dress and jacket, with a 'sporran', scarf, and Highland bonnet!" During lunch, there were "Highland gentlemen standing with halberds in the room".

From Inveraray, the *Fairy* took the Queen and her children to Lochgilphead, where they were driven to the Crinan Canal. There, "a most magnificently decorated barge, drawn by three horses, ridden by postillions in scarlet" awaited. Although at first the barge "glided along very smoothly", the eleven locks which had to be negotiated were tedious and instead of the passage lasting one hour and a half, it lasted upwards of two hours and a half; therefore it was nearly eight o'clock before the royal party reached Loch Crinan and went aboard the *Victoria and Albert.*

This, however, was the voyage which encouraged Messrs. David MacBrayne to dub their tourist and passenger service from Greenock to Islay, via Tarbert and the Crinan Canal, *The Royal Route,* a nomenclature which has no doubt added relish to the enjoyment of travellers making the journey in such famous pleasure steamers as the *Columba, Saint Columba* and *Lochfyne* during the ensuing century.

Sailing south next day, the Queen viewed Oban from the sea, and thought it "one of the finest spots we have seen", noting that "the famous stone which supports the Coronation Chair, in which the sovereigns are crowned at Westminster Abbey", came from Dunstaffnage Castle, from which it is said to have been removed to Scone by Kenneth MacAlpin.

At three in the afternoon, having passed Rum, Eigg, Muck and the Treshnish Isles—the Queen made a little sketch of The Dutchman's Cap—the royal yacht reached Staffa. Aboard a barge, she and the Prince sailed into Fingal's Cave, where "the effect was splendid, like a great entrance into a vaulted hall . . . The sea is immensely deep in the cave. The rocks, under water, were all colours—pink, blue and green—which had a most beautiful, and varied effect. It was the first time the British standard, with a Queen of Great Britain, and her husband and children, had ever entered Fingal's Cave, and the men gave three cheers, which sounded very impressive there."

At Iona, Prince Albert landed to see the ruins, and the

Above, Queen Victoria with her family, a painting executed in 1848; *below*, Queen Victoria passing the Royal Triumphal Arch, Glasgow, in August 1849 (*from the 'Illustrated London News'*)

Above, Stirling Castle, the road up to which Queen Victoria found 'dreadfully steep'; *below*, the Palace of Holyrood House, where Queen Victoria stayed on her visits to Scotland

"fine old caves and tombs of ancient kings" while the Queen remained aboard, sketching. By nine o'clock, they reached Tobermory, to find that "the place was all illuminated".

Then a cold rain came on. It accompanied them as they sailed up Loch Linnhe to Fort William, and persisted during their stay at Lord Abercorn's house "Ardverikie" on Loch Laggan, the walls of which were decorated by Sir Edwin Landseer with the *Monarch of the Glen,* and other appropriate symbols of Highland wild-life, but which was to be destroyed by fire in 1873.

Albert went up the Caledonian Canal, which had been opened in 1822, to attend a ball at Inverness. It was still raining as the Queen and the Prince came back down the Crinan Canal by barge. The warship *Black Eagle* took them to Campbeltown, which the Queen thought "a small and not pretty place". Aboard the *Victoria and Albert* again, a squall blew up as she made her way to anchor in Loch Ryan. Next day, when she set out for the South, the sea became so rough that the paddle-steamer turned back from the open sea and put into Loch Ryan for shelter. When the ship was eventually able to sail, the sea was still rough, and the Queen recalled "I was very ill." Not ill enough, however, to forget to add, as the ship passed "the Mull of Galloway, a great rock with a lighthouse on it", that this was "our last glimpse of dear Scotland".

Back in Windsor, the Queen and the Prince decided that they must definitely establish a Highland home of their own. The Queen had already begun to be troubled by occasional twinges of rheumatism, and in view of the weather experienced on the West Coast holiday, she sought advice as to a suitably dry location from her physician, Sir James Clark. Clark's own son had recently convalesced at Balmoral, on Deeside, enjoying sunshine while the royal yacht had been pitching her way through storms of rain. So Deeside was the district he recommended.

Balmoral–whose name seems to derive from "bal" meaning "dwelling-house", and "mhoral" meaning "majestic"–the Deeside home of Sir Robert Gordon, who had been Her Majesty's ambassador in Vienna, became vacant because of the sudden death of its owner. The lease was therefore taken by Prince Albert, and early in September, 1848, the royal pair arrived at Aberdeen—several hours earlier than expected because of the speed which the *Victoria and Albert* had made on the voyage from the south—to a welcome through cheering crowds and triumphal floral arches.

The people into whose lives their sovereign thus came were crofters, whose holdings rarely exceeded twelve acres, living on a simple diet based on oatmeal and milk, supplemented by the annual killing of an ox and the occasional salmon poached from the river. They were simple in their dress, and narrowly intense in their religious observance.

The house which received the Queen had been the home of the Farquharsons for generations; but when Sir Robert Gordon acquired it, he brought down an Aberdeen Architect, John Smith, to transform it according to the tastes of a more expansive age. Not much more of the original than a seventeenth-century tower was left by 1839, when "Tudor Johnnie", as Smith was nicknamed, had finished with it. To Queen Victoria, as she arrived before lunch on September 8th, it seemed "a pretty little castle in the old Scottish style". After lunch, she and Albert "went up to the top of the wooded hill" opposite their windows, where "there is a cairn, and up which there is a pretty winding path. The view from here, looking down upon the house, is charming. To the left you look towards the beautiful hills surrounding Loch-na-Gar, and to the right, towards Ballater, to the glen (or valley) along which the Dee winds, with beautiful wooded hills, which reminded us very much of the Turingwald. It was so calm, and so solitary, it did one good as one gazed around and the pure mountain air was most refreshing. All seemed to breathe freedom and peace, and to make one forget the world and its sad turmoils."

For more than fifty years, Victoria was to come to her Highland home, to "breathe freedom and peace", much of the time as a widow who never forgave the world the "sad turmoil" into which the death of her beloved husband plunged her.

But for the moment, and for some years to come, there was to be the shared joy of their joint explorations, on foot or riding on ponies.

The Queen's days at Balmoral fell into three phases: the period between 1848 and 1853, when the old house still did duty; the all too short years from 1853 to 1861, ending with the death of the Prince Consort; and the long years of widowhood, when, because Balmoral had been so much Albert's creation, the Queen finally took to coming north in the spring as well as in the autumn.

In the earlier of her two volumes, *Leaves from the Journal of our Life in the Highlands,* there are happy accounts of new discoveries during the first phase. There was, for instance, the ascent of Loch-na-Gar on ponies, the summit being "cold, and wet and cheerless" and "the wind blowing a hurricane", although lower down, "the fog disappeared like magic and all was sunshine below, about one thousand feet from the top".

In that same year, 1848, the Queen and Albert set off on a stag-hunt in the forest of Ballochbuie, in the glen below Craig Gowan. "We scrambled up an almost perpendicular place to where there was a box, made of hurdles and interwoven with branches of fir and heather, about five feet in height. There we seated ourselves, . . . Macdonald (one of the ghillies) lying in the heather near us, watching and quite concealed; some had gone round to beat, and others again were at a little distance. We sat quite still, and sketched a little: I drawing the landscape, and some trees, Albert drawing Macdonald as he lay there. This lasted for nearly an hour, when Albert fancied he heard a distant sound, and in a few minutes Macdonald whispered that he saw stags, and that Albert should wait and take a steady aim. We then heard them coming past. Albert did not look over the box, but through it, and fired through the branches, and then again over the box. The deer retreated; but Albert felt certain he had hit a stag. He ran up to the keepers, and at that moment they called from below that 'they had got him', and Albert ran on to see. I waited for a bit; but soon scrambled on with Bertie (the Prince of Wales and future King Edward VII) and Macdonald's help; and Albert joined me directly, and we all went down and saw a magnificent stag, a 'royal' (a stag with twelve points to its antlers) which had dropped, soon after Albert had hit him, at one of the men's feet. The sport was successful, and everyone was delighted–Macdonald and the keepers in particular–the former saying: 'that it was her Majesty's coming out that had brought the good luck'. I was supposed to have 'a lucky foot', of which the Highlanders 'think a great deal'."

In August, 1849, on the way up north, the *Victoria and Albert* took the Queen and her party to Dublin, and then across to the Clyde. Loch Long, Loch Goil and the Gareloch were all visited, though only Albert and some of the male members of the party braved the weather–"it poured with rain most hopelessly"–to visit Loch Lomond, where the Prince saw Rob Roy's Cave.

On Sunday 14th August, the *Fairy* steamed up the river, both banks lined with loyal subjects, to Glasgow, where several addresses were presented, and the Cathedral, "a very fine one", was visited. The Queen noted that it was in its crypt that "the famous scene in Rob Roy is laid, where Rob Roy gives Frank Osbaldistone warning that he is in danger."

Of Glasgow, she wrote: "The town is a handsome one with fine streets built in stone, and many fine buildings and churches. We passed over a bridge commanding an extensive view down two quays, which Albert said was very like Paris. There are many large shops and warehouses, and the shipping is immense."

That afternoon, they travelled by train to Perth, where they stayed at the George Inn, next day making the journey by carriage to Balmoral over the "sharp turn" of the Devil's Elbow. On her arrival, Victoria recorded: "It seems like a dream to be here in our own Highland home again; it certainly does not seem like a year since we were here."

That year, they made their first stay in their two huts enclosing "a charming little dining-room, sitting room, bed-room and dressing-room, all *en suite*" at Alt-na-Giuthasach by the head of Loch Muick. Here they could relax without formality, and until Albert's death it became a favourite retreat of the Queen's.

The following year, they climbed on ponies to the summit of Ben-na-Bhourd [Benabourd, 'flat or table mountain'], 3,940 ft. high, from which they saw Ben-y-ghlo [Ben-y-Gloe, 'the hazy mountain'], very clear, Cairngorm and Ben Muick Dhui [Ben Macdhui, 'mountain of the black sow'] quite close but in another direction, the Moray Firth, and, through the glass, ships could be seen; and on the other side rose Loch-na-Gar, still the jewel of all the mountains here." Coming down, the Queen's pony made "great haste, though he had half a mind to kick", and "Albert found some beautiful little rock crystals in the Sluggan."

Six days later, on 12th September, they attended the Braemar Gathering, a festivity which went back about a thousand years, although originally it was a gathering of clansmen summoned so that King Malcolm Canmore could select, by competition, his hardiest soldiers and his fleetest messengers. Later, John Erskine, sixth Earl of Mar, raised his standard for the Jacobite cause on the Braes of Mar in 1715. Early in the nineteenth century, the gathering was held to raise subscriptions for the poor and needy. In 1826, the Braemar Highland Society took it over to foster interest in Highland customs, language and sport. The Queen first attended it in 1848. The 1850 visit was notable for the race up Craig Cheunnich (Craig Choinnich, "Kenneth's rock") won by one of the royal ghillies, Duncan, whose health suffered so severely by what the Queen called this "fearful exertion" that the race was thereafter discontinued.

Next day, the menfolk went leistering (spearing) salmon in the Dee (a sport of which Sir Walter Scott was fond, but which has long since been made illegal) while the Queen looked on from "above the bridge, where all our tenants were assembled with poles and spears, or rather leisters, for catching salmon. They all went into the river, walking up it, and then back again, poking about under all the stones to bring fish up to where the men stand with the net. It had a very pretty effect, about one hundred men were wading through the river, some in kilts with poles and spears, all very much excited."

Eventually, seven salmon were caught, "some in the net, and some speared. Though Albert stood in the water some time, he caught nothing: but the scene at this beautiful spot was exciting and picturesque in the extreme. I wished for Landseer's pencil."

There was a sad moment during the holiday of 1852, when, on 16th September, a dispatch reached the Queen informing her of the death of the eighty-three year old Duke of Wellington. At first the Queen was reluctant to believe the news, and went off on an expedition to the top of Glassalt ("grey stream"). But on her return, confirmation from the Duke's son, Lord Charles Wellesley, was awaiting her.

"The Crown never possessed—and I fear never *will*—", the Queen entered in her *Journal*, "so devoted, loyal, faithful a subject, so staunch a supporter! To *us* (who alas! have lost, now, so many of our valued and experienced friends), his loss is *irreparable,* for his readiness to aid and advise if it could be of use to us, and to overcome any and every difficulty, was unequalled. To Albert he showed the greatest kindness, and the utmost confidence . . . He was a link which connected us with bygone times, with the last century. Not an eye will be dry in the whole country." But there was good news as well as bad. This year the legal negotiations with the Fife Trustees, which had dragged on since 1848, were successfully concluded, and William Smith, the son of "Tudor Johnny", was commissioned to build a new Balmoral. The site chosen was a hundred yards north-west of the old house, and Prince Albert interested himself closely in every detail. Work began in the spring of 1853 and the plans came to fruition when the Queen arrived at her new home in September.

"Strange, very strange, it seemed to me to drive past, indeed *through* the old house," she mused; but sentiment for the old soon gave place to enthusiasm for the new.

"The house is charming; the rooms delightful; the furniture, papers, everything perfection."

Indeed, she came almost to forget William Smith's share in the creation of her Scots baronial style *schloss* made of granite from the Glen Gelder quarries on the estate, when she rhapsodized: "Every year my heart becomes more fixed in this dear Paradise, and so much more so now, that *all* has become my dear Albert's *own* creation; own building, own laying out, as at *Osborne:* and his great taste and the impress of his dear hand, have been stamped everywhere."

There were only to be six summers left for the Queen and her Prince to enjoy together the pleasures of the Highlands she loved so much from the splendid castellated home he had caused to be built for her. Some of the expeditions which they undertook together during these six years would have taxed the energies of younger and hardier people. On Friday, October 7th, 1859, for instance, they set out to climb Ben Muick Dhui, 4,227ft., driving by carriage to the foot of Glen Derry, and thereafter mounting ponies, the Queen noting "my pony being led by Brown most of the time both going up and down". As they reached the top of the mountain, the cold mist surrounding them was so thick that they "hardly knew whether we were on level ground or the top of the mountain." They lunched at the very top", at a cairn of stones, "in a piercing cold wind. Just as we sat down, a gust of wind came and dispersed the mist, which had a most wonderful effect, like a dissolving view and exhibited the grandest, wildest scenery imaginable! . . . The wind was fearfully high, but the view was well worth seeing . . . Ben-y-Ghlo and the adjacent mountains, *Ben Vrachie* [the speckled mountain] then *Ben-na-Bhourd Ben A'an* [mountain of the river] etc–and such magnificent wild rocks, precipices. It had a sublime and solemn effect; so wild, so solitary–no one but ourselves and our little party there."

They were "not at all tired" by the time they got back to Balmoral "at a quarter past eight, precisely," although the expedition had lasted almost twelve hours. "*Never* shall I forget this day," wrote the Queen, "or the impression this very grand scene made upon me; truly sublime and impressive; such solitude!"

It was perhaps the enjoyment of "such solitude" which led them to undertake what the Queen called their "great expeditions", the first of which, to Glen Feshie and Grantown, took place in the early days of September, 1860. The idea was that, as far as possible, they should travel incognito, and stay at inns and hotels. On this occasion, they had with them General Grey, the Prince Consort's private Secretary, and Lady Churchill, the Queen's Lady-in-waiting.

After a diversion on ponies to see Loch Inch, they crossed the Spey on a ferry to rejoin their carriages. The Queen's own words admirably capture the sense of adventure which animated the expeditions:

"The ferry was a very rude affair; it was like a boat or cobble, but we could only stand on it, and it was moved at one end by two long oars, plied by the ferryman and Brown, and at the other end by a long sort of beam, which Grant took in hand." (Grant was a keeper). "A few seconds brought us over to the road, where there were two shabby vehicles, one a kind of barouche into which Albert and I got, Lady Churchill and General Grey into the other–a break; each with a pair of small and rather miserable horses, driven by a man from the box. Grant was on our carriage, and Brown on the other. We had gone so far forty miles, at least, twenty on horseback. We had decided to call ourselves *Lord and Lady Churchill and party,* Lady Churchill posing as Miss Spencer and General Grey as Dr. Grey! Brown once forgot this, and called me 'Your Majesty' as I was getting into the carriage, and Grant in the box once called Albert 'Your Royal Highness', which set us off laughing, but no one observed."

Having already driven twenty miles and ridden a further twenty on their ponies, they now drove for a further three hours. Setting out at six o'clock in the evening, they passed "close to Kinrara but unfortunately not through it . . . It was very beautiful–fine wooded hills–the high Cairngorm range, and Ben Muick Dhui, unfortunately much obscured by the mist on the top–and the broad Spey flowing in the valley, with cultivated fields and fine trees below. Most striking, however, on our whole long journey was the utter, and to me very refreshing, solitude . . . It gradually grew dark . . . The mountains gradually disappeared. On and on we went, till at length we saw lights and drove through a long and straggling 'town', and turned down a small court to the door of the inn. Here we got out quickly . . . We went up a small staircase, and were shown to our bedrooms at the top of it–very small but clean."

Next day, they rode to "Castle Grant, Lord Seafield's place–a fine (not Highland looking) park, with a very plain-looking house, like a factory", which had be n modernised in 1836. From there, they drove through drizzle to Tomintoul, the highest village in Scotland, but to the Queen merely "a long street with three inns, miserable dirty-looking houses and people, and a sad look of wretchedness about it."

After lunch just outside the village, alleged by her host to be at that time "the poorest village in the whole of the Highlands", they mounted their ponies, and rode 'towards Inchory, "seeing as we approached, two eagles towering splendidly above, and alighting on the top of the hills." At Loch Bulig, "beautifully lit up by a setting sun", their carriage was waiting and they reached Balmoral at half past seven in the evening.

This "never to be forgotten expedition" led them to make no fewer than three further expeditions in what proved to be the final summer of the Prince Consort's life, 1861.

The first to be carried through, called by Victoria the

Second Great Expedition, was to Invermark and Fettercairn, and they left Balmoral on Friday 20th September. The night was spent at the Ramsay Arms Inn, Fettercairn, which provided them with "a very nice, clean, good dinner". Next day, in driving morning rain, they made their way back by Spittal Bridge, the Bridge of Aboyne, up Glen Tanar, and back to Balmoral, a distance of eighty-two miles having been covered in the two days by carriage—the "fine large" sociable, left by the Queen's mother, the Duchess of Kent, who had died in March, to Albert—on ponies, in a double dog-cart, and in the carriage again. Once more, despite the variable weather, they were "much pleased" with their expedition.

The Third Great Expedition, begun on 8th October, took them to Glen Feshie, Dalwhinnie and Blair Atholl. They drove by carriage through Castleton to the Geldie Water, where they mounted their ponies.

"The ground was wet, but not worse than last year. We had gone on very well for about an hour, when the mist thickened all round, and down came heavy, or at least beating, rain with wind. With the help of an umbrella, and waterproofs and a plaid, I kept quite dry. Dearest Albert, who walked from the time the ground became boggy, got very wet, but was none the worse for it, and we got through it much better than before; we ladies never having to get off our ponies." Fording the Feshie, they rejoined their carriages, and set off for Dalwhinnie at five o'clock in the evening, reaching it at a quarter to nine, having travelled almost thirty miles since they left their ponies, latterly driving through the cold and rainy darkness. Here, alas! "there was only tea, and two miserable Highland chickens, without any potatoes . . . It was not a nice supper, and the evening was wet" commented the Queen. Next day, they drove through the Pass of Drumochter, past Loch Garry, to Dalnacardoch Inn, passing, on the way "many drovers, with their herds and flock," returning from the great annual autumn Tryst at Falkirk. From Dalnacardoch, they rode towards Blair Atholl, being met a few miles down the road by the kilted Duke of Atholl "on a pretty little chestnut pony". After coffee, they rode to the foot of Glen Tilt, and crossed the hills, fording Poll Tarff, "which is very deep—and after rain almost impassable". The Duke offered to lead the Queen's pony, but "I asked for

Brown, whom I have far the most confidence in". As they climbed the hillside, the road "became almost precipitous, and indeed made riding very unpleasant; but being wet, and difficult to walk, we ladies rode, Albert walking the greater part of the time. Only once, for a very few steps, I had to get off, as the pony could hardly keep its footing. As it was, Brown constantly could not walk next to the pony, but had to scramble below, or pull it after him . . . The Tilt becomes narrower and narrower, till its first source is almost invisible. The Tarff flows into the Tilt, about two miles or more beyond the falls. We emerged from the pass upon an open valley–with less high hills and with the hills of Braemar before us." Here, the Duke of Atholl produced some whisky out of a silver flask, and made a speech proposing the Queen's health. The Duke set out to return to Blair Atholl. Then the royal party rode on to Bainoch "which we reached," the Queen noted, "at ten minutes to six: when it was already dark. As we approached the 'shiel', the pipes struck up and played. The ponies went so well with the pipes, and altogether it was very pleasant to walk and ride with them."

Home safely at a quarter-past eight, they had completed one hundred and twenty-nine miles in two days. And the Queen felt "This was the pleasantest and most enjoyable expedition I *ever* made; and the recollections of it will always be most agreeable to me, and increase my wish to make more!"

The Last Expedition was a one-day affair, and took place on 16th October, "a most beautiful morning. Not a cloud was on the bright blue sky, and it was perfectly calm:" They drove to Castleton again, then proceeded up Glen Clunie to Glen Callater, to Loch Callater. They climbed Little Cairn Turc on the north side of Loch Callater, and found the summit "quite flat–with moss and grass–so that you could drive upon it." Half-an-hour's ride brought then to "the edge of the valley of Cairn Lochan", from which it was possible to see Glen Isla, "the Lomond Hills behind Kinross, at the foot of which is Loch Leven . . . We sat on a very precipitous place, which made our dread any one's moving backwards; and here at a little before two o'clock, we lunched. The lights were charmingly soft . . . like the bloom on a plum. The luncheon was very acceptable for the air was extremely keen, and we found ice thicker than a shilling on the top of Cairn Turc, which did not melt away when Brown took it and kept it in his hand.

After lunch, they came round by Cairn Glaishie, Glas Meall [Glas Maol] Shean, Spittal Bridge and back to Balmoral. From Castleton "we went back on our side of the river; and if we had been a little earlier, Albert might have got a stag—but it was too late. The moon rose and shone most beautifully, and we returned at twenty minutes to seven o'clock, much pleased and interested with this delightful expedition."

The Queen ended her account of this expedition, and the first volume of her *Highland Journal* with the prophetic words: "Alas! I fear our last *great* one."

Prince Albert, whose constitution had never been robust, died of typhoid at Windsor Castle on 14th December, leaving Balmoral to his widow. The Queen was inconsolable, and, as she declared in a letter to her uncle, the King of the Belgians, a few days after Albert's death:" . . . *his* wishes, *his* plans about everything, his views about *everything* are to be *my* law." This applied particularly to Balmoral, and to the memory of the happiest days of her life which she had passed in and around it. It was therefore not surprising that, in due course, she had the idea of having extracts from her *Journal* published for private circulation among her friends and those of her late husband.

Conscious, perhaps, of the literary deficiencies of her writing, she showed the chosen portions of her manuscript to Arthur Helps, a distinguished civil servant, who, in 1862, had written an introduction to *The Speeches and Addresses of the Prince Consort.* Helps took the view that however limited the edition, extracts would leak to the press. The only way to avoid this, in his view, was for the Queen to allow the book to be made available to the general public. To persuade her conclusively, he argued that the book showed clearly how much the support and companionship of her late husband had meant to her. The Queen accepted his advice, but proved stubborn over some of his attempts to correct her grammar. But in 1867, a private edition of *Leaves From The Journal of our Life in the Highlands* appeared, being followed by the first general addition a few months later. It became an instant best-seller, the considerable profits from which the Queen used to benefit charities of her choice.

The youthful enthusiasm and ardour which the Queen experienced, and captured unconsciously in her writing, reminds one of the gently sentimental but limpid melodiousness of the Scotland Mendelssohn reflected in his "Scottish" Symphony. Disraeli wrote of the Queen's book:

"Its vein is so innocent and vivid, happy in picture and touched with what I ever think is the characteristic of our Royal mistress. There is a freshness and fragrance about the book like the heather amid which it was written". It is still easily possible to agree with his sensitive appreciation, in spite of the changes the century which has passed since the book's first publication has wrought on the castles, towns and villages of the Highlands, on the fabric of Highland life, and on the taste of the reading public.

By the time her book appeared, the Queen had already written some of the material which was to go to make up her second volume, *More Leaves.* Here, the tone was no longer Mendelssohnian. Sentiment thickened into sentimentality. Wars or rumours of wars and the weight of an Empire's glory present rather the complicated mingling vulgarity and nobility of Elgar, the laureate of the Queen's son's short reign.

On 26th August, 1862, she and the Princesses Helena and Louise went up Craig Gowan with Grant, the keeper, to the cairn which had been put up to commemorate the ascent she and Albert had made in 1852. "I thought you would like to be here today, on His Birthday," Grant said to her, adding that this, like the day of the Prince Consort's death, "must not be looked upon as a day of mourning." No wonder her heart went out to Grant, John Brown and her other Highland servants, so that she added: "There is so much true and strong faith in these good simple people."

Until she grew older, the Queen liked to maintain her late husband's determination never to let the Highland weather deter her from a decision to go on an excursion. There was the visit to Dunkeld, on Monday October 9th, 1865, when it turned out to be "a thick, misty, very threatening morning! There was no help for it, but it was sadly provoking. It was the same once or twice in former happy days, and my dear Albert always said we could not alter it, but must leave it as it was, and make the best of it."

So the Queen and her party set out by carriage to Spittal of Glenshee, and, on to Strathardle, where at the farm of Pitcarmich, they mounted their ponies—the Queen her favourite pony, Fyvie—and plodded across the hills, past Loch Oishne and Loch Ordie. "Here, dripping wet, we arrived at about a quarter-past six, having left Pitcarmich at twenty minutes to four. It was dark already from the very bad weather. We went into a lodge here, and had tea and whisky . . . About seven we drove off from Loch Ordie . . . in a phaeton which had a hood—Brown and Grant behind. It was pitch-dark, and we had to go through a wood, and I must own I was somewhat nervous.

"We had not gone far when we perceived that we were on a very rough road, and I became much alarmed, though I would say nothing. A branch took off Grant's cap, and we had to stop for Brown to go back and look for it with one of the carriage lamps. This stoppage was most fortunate, for he then discovered we were on a completely wrong road."

After some discussion, and a forward reconnaisance, they discovered that the track wound its way back to a more serviceable road. "Grant took a lamp out of the carriage and walked before the horses, while Brown led them, and this reassured me . . . At length at a quarter to nine, we arrived quite safely at Dunkeld," sitting down to dinner at half-past nine, at the end of a travelling day that had lasted almost twelve rainy hours.

They spent three nights at a house on the Atholl estate. On the second day the Queen was "much distressed at breakfast to find that poor Brown's legs had been dreadfully cut by the edge of his wet kilt on Monday, just at the break of the knee, and he said nothing about it; but today one became so inflamed, and swelled so much, that he could hardly move. The doctor said he must keep it up as far as possible, and walk very little . . ." But Brown was not forbidden to go out with the carriage, and there were trips to the three Lochs of the Lowes, to the village of Inver, and to Dunkeld Cathedral, before the royal party returned to Balmoral by the route they had come, when the Queen found it "really most distressing to see how poor Brown suffered, especially in going up and down hill."

In 1867, before going to Deeside, the Queen paid a visit to the Border country, arriving at Kelso to stay with the Duchess of Roxburghe at Floors Castle, built by Sir John Vanburgh in 1718, though added to in early Victorian days. The Duchess showed the Queen and her children to their rooms; for the Queen, a single bed: "the feeling of loneliness when I saw no room for my darling, and felt I was indeed alone and a widow, overcame me very sadly! It was the first time I had gone in this way on a visit (like as in former times), and I thought so much of all dearest Albert would have done and said and how he would have wandered about everywhere, admired everything, looked at everything–and now! Oh! must it ever, ever be so?"

A good dinner, bonfires and illuminations seen from the window, and in the ensuing days' drives to see the Eildons, Melrose Abbey, which the Queen thought looked "very ghostlike", reminding her a little of Holyrood Chapel, and Abbotsford, cheered her up. At Abbotsford she was received by Hope Scott, whose first wife had been John Gibson Lockhart's daughter, Sir Walter Scott's last surviving grandchild, and whose daughter, then a girl of eleven, carried forward Sir Walter's line. Hope Scott's second wife, Lady Victoria, sister to the Duke of Norfolk, was a god-daughter of the Queen. The Queen, a warm admirer of Sir Walter's poems and novels, was warmly received by the Hope Scotts.

"They showed us the part of the house in which Sir Walter lived, and all his rooms"–Hope Scott, a Catholic convert, added the "modern" wing to Abbotsford, together with the Chapel–"his drawing room with the same furniture and carpet, the library where we saw his MS. of *Ivanhoe,* and several others of his novels and poems in a beautiful handwriting with hardly any erasures, and other relics which Sir Walter had himself collected. Then his study, a small dark room, with a little turret in which is a bust of bronze, done from a cast taken after death, of Sir Walter. In the study, we saw his journal, in which Mr Hope Scott asked me to write my name (which I felt it to be a presumption in me to do), as also the others.

"We went through some passages into two or three rooms where there were collected fine specimens of old armour, etc., and where in a glass case are Sir Walter's last clothes. We ended by going into the drawing room, in which Sir Walter Scott died, where we took tea . . ."

Thirty-five years after Sir Walter's death, the pattern of preservation which so strongly re-creates the surroundings of his personality had already been set in a manner which still exercises the same fascination on visitors as it did on Queen Victoria more than a century later.

Next day, the Queen visited the town of Jedburgh, which she thought "very prettily situated . . . the same size as Kelso, only without its large shops." She recalled the historical events which had occurred there: the death of Malcolm IV; the residence there of both William the Lyon and Alexander II; the marriage of Alexander III to his second wife, Jolleta; and the visits of Queen Mary, the last sovereign before herself to set foot in the town. She also admired the "four pretty triumphal arches" specially erected, "one with two very well chosen inscriptions, viz. on one side 'Freedom makes all men to have lyking', and on the other side 'The love of all thy people comfort thee'," apparently seeing nothing incongruous in this association of the noble and the banal (John Barbour did not, however, go so far as to assume that the pleasures of freedom were enjoyed by all men).

After a week which she clearly enjoyed, the Queen "took leave of the dear Duchess and the Duke", and entrained for Ballater.

On 15th October of that year, "at a quarter-past eleven in distressing rain, which twice had given hopes of easing", the Queen and her family went to an assemblage of all the servants and tenants and the detachment of the 93rd Highlanders, for the ceremony of the unveiling of a statue of the Prince Consort.

"A verse of the 100th Psalm was sung, and Mr. Taylor then stepped forward and offered up a beautiful prayer (in pelting rain at that moment), after which the order was given to uncover the Statue; but (as happened at Aberdeen) the covering caught, and it was a little while before it could be loosened from the shoulder.

"The soldiers presented arms, and the pipes played, as we gazed on the dear noble figure of my beloved one, who used to be with us here in the prime of beauty, goodness and strength."

The following year, on Wednesday 1st September, the Queen with her daughters Louise and Beatrice left Balmoral by train at half-past eight in the morning. They arrived at Callander at a quarter past three. This pretty little town, famous a century after this royal visit as the setting for Tannochbrae, the place of practice of the television folk-hero Dr. Finlay, seemed to Queen Victoria "one long street with very few shops, and fewer good houses, but many poor ones."

The Queen and her daughters drove to the house of Invertrossachs, the home of Mr. and Lady Emily Macnaghten, overlooking Loch Vennacher. Next day, the Queen and her party drove over the Duke's Road, from which they saw "Ben Ledi, a splendid hill; to the north Ben Vorlich, and to the east the heights of Uam Var, a pink heathery ridge of no great elevation, and in the distance, rising up from the horizon, Dun Myat, and the Wallace Monument and the Abbey Craig, near Stirling."

The Lake of Menteith and the Clachan of Aberfoyle interested her, the one because Queen Mary had lived there as a child before setting out for France to be educated, and the other because of its place in Scott's *Rob Roy*. When she came upon Loch Ard, she thought that "a lovelier picture could not be seen. Ben Lomond, blue and yellow, rose above the lower hills, which were pink and purple with heather, and an isthmus of green trees in front dividing it from the rest of the loch. We got out and sketched."

Driving on to Loch Katrine, she "went on board a very clean little steamer, *Rob Roy*—the very same we had been on under such different circumstances in 1859 on the 14th of October, in dreadful weather, thick mist and heavy rain, when my beloved husband and I opened the Glasgow Waterworks."

Sailing on the loch, this time in warm sunshine, the Queen took out her copy of *The Lady of the Lake*, so that later, driving through the Trossachs, she was able to remember:

The Western waves of ebbing day
Rolled o'er the glen the level way.
Each purple peak, each flinty spire
Was bathed in floods of living fire.

Adding: "The drive back was lovely, for long after the sun had set the sky remained beautifully pink behind the dark blue hills."

Next day, she drove back to Loch Katrine, and boarded the *Rob Roy* to sail to Stronachlacher, driving over the short hill road past Loch Arklet to descend on Loch Lomond at Inversnaid, with its "high mountains, looking shadowy in the mist (dry mist), rising abruptly from the loch. We went at once on board the fine steamer *Prince Consort* (a pleasant idea that that dear name should have carried his poor little wife, alas! a widow, and children on their first sail on the beautiful lake which he went to see in 1847). She is a fine large vessel . . . with a fine large dining-cabin below, and a galley underneath, on which people can stand and smoke without incommoding the others above.

"We steamed southward, and for the first half nothing could be finer or more truly Alpine . . ."

They sailed to Rowardennan pier, "a lovely spot from whence you can ascend Ben Lomond," past, "all the beautifully wooded islands, to the number of twenty-four," and past the island of Inch Murrin on which the Duke of Montrose had his deer preserve. "The sun had come out soon after we went on board, and it was blowing quite fresh as we went against the wind. At two o'clock we stopped off at Portnellan for luncheon, which we had brought with us, and took below in the large handsome cabin . . . This over, we went to the end of the lake to Balloch, and here turned . . . It became pretty warm. To the left we passed some very pretty villas (castles they resembled) and places, amongst others Cameron (Mr. Smollett's) Arden (Sir J. Lumsden's, Lord Provost of Glasgow) Ross-Dhu (Sir J. Colquhoun), the road to Glen Fruin, and several more islands," before coming to Luss "a very prettily situated village," the "ferry of Inveruglas opposite Rowardennan," and "Tarbet, a small town, where dearest Albert landed in 1847, and here began the highest, and finest mountains, with splendid passes, richly wooded, and the highest mountains rising behind . . . The head of the lake with the very fine glen (Glen Falloch along which you can drive to Oban) is magnificent."

The Queen and the Princesses then returned to Inversnaid and Stronachlachar where, aboard the *Rob Roy* again, they had "a splendid sail over this most lovely loch. How dearest Albert would have enjoyed it!"

As the years passed, the Queen's comments became briefer and more perfunctory. The old sadness, which would not leave her, cast itself on much that she saw and did. A visit to Edinburgh, in August, 1872, began with her arrival on "a dull gloomy, heavy morning;" but "a great many people were out, and all most enthusiastic, reminding me forcibly and sadly of former days. We had an escort of the Scots Greys. We drove up to the door of the old, gloomy, but historical Palace of Holyrood, where a band of the 93rd Highlanders were stationed in the quadrangle of the Court. We got out, walked up the usual stairs, and passed through two of the large gloomy rooms we used to occupy, and then went past some passages up another and very steep stair-case to the so-called 'Argyll rooms', which had been arranged for me, with very pretty light paper, chintz and carpets . . ."

The Queen drove round Edinburgh, and was especially interested in "Charlotte Square, where my dear one's monument is to be placed, and where I was to have stopped and looked at the site. But the crowd, which was very great everywhere, and would run with us (facilitated by the great steepness and slipperiness of the streets), as well as the great number of cabs and vehicles of all sorts which would drive along after us everywhere, made this impossible."

There was a return visit to Dalhousie Castle, and trips to Granton and Newhaven, "where we saw many fishwives who were very enthusiastic; but not in their smartest dress"; and Leith, with its "new and very splendid large docks, with the ships all decked out", named after Albert.

September brought a visit to Dunrobin Castle, the seat of the Sutherlands, travelling by rail via Keith and Elgin, where the Provost presented an address.

"The ruins of the Cathedral are said to be the finest in Scotland, and the town is full of ancient recollections," the Queen noted, adding: "No British sovereign has ever been so far north."

Passing Culloden, the Queen noted: "the moor where that bloody battle, the recollection of which I cannot bear, was fought." The train stopped for ten minutes, outside Inverness, and then proceeded past "the Beauly Firth like an enormous lake with hills rising above it which were reflected on the perfectly still water," Dingwall, which reminded Victoria of "a village in Switzerland," Tain, and Bonar Bridge, where the third Duke of Sutherland "came up to the door. He had been driving the engine (!) all the way from Inverness but only appeared now on account of this being the boundary of his territory, and the commencement of the Sutherland railroad." Under the hand of a professional driver, the train "entered the glen of Shin. The railway is at a very high level here, and you see the Shin winding below with heathery hills on either side and many fine rocks, wild, solitary and picturesque."

At Golspie station, the Duchess and a detachment of the Sutherland Volunteers were invited to welcome the Queen. They drove through three welcoming floral arches that were a feature of Victoria's royal processions, and reached Dunrobin "with its very high roof and turrets, a mixture of an old Scottish castle and French chateau."

During the five days spent at Dunrobin, the Queen laid the foundation stone for "the memorial to be raised by the clansmen and servants of my dear Duchess of Sutherland, who was adored in Sutherland." This Duchess had been a friend of the Queen's, and daughter-in-law of the first Duke of Sutherland, believed at the time to be the wealthiest man in Britain and whose institution of that practice of forcibly removing crofters from the interior of the country, later to develop into the Clearances, had hardly endeared his family to the inhabitants in the manner Queen Victoria supposed. Indeed while there is abundant evidence of personal concern for those of her "dour highlanders" who lived on or around her estate, there is no evidence whatever that the Queen even appreciated, let alone condemned, the cruel roof-burnings and enforced transportations which were being used as an instrument of economic policy to increase still further the Sutherland wealth.

The year 1873 was notable for a visit to Inverlochy, on the way to which the Queen saw Ardverikie from the other side of Loch Laggan, recalling the happy though wet month's stay she had enjoyed there in 1847. She called at Moy Lodge, where she met Richard Ansdell, the painter in 1846 of the famous *Stag at Bay* picture, as well as of other popular animal and sporting pictures reflecting the fashionable interest in the Highlands which the Sovereign's own enthusiasm had inspired.

She was not impressed with the town of Fort William, built first as Maryburgh by General Monk in 1655 to keep down the Cameron men, and enlarged and renamed in 1690, by General Hugh Mackay. she thought the place "small, and excepting where the good shops are, very dirty, with a very poor population, but all very friendly and enthusiastic". By the year of the Queen's visit, the fort, which had defied the Jacobites both in 1715 and 1745, had been dismantled, though it was not demolished to make way for the railway until 1890.

She visited Achnacarry, the seat of Cameron of Lochiel, and sailed on Loch Askaig "on board a very small but nice screw steamer which belongs to Cameron of Lochiel". One of her aides, General Ponsonby, remarked to the Queen that she, whose great-great-grandfather Charles Edward Stuart had striven to de-throne, was being shown the scenes made historical through Prince Charlie's wanderings by the very man "whose great-grand-uncle had been the real moving cause of the rising of 1745".

"Yes," the Queen reflected, "and *I* feel a sort of reverence in going over these scenes in this most beautiful country, which I am proud to call my own, where there was such devoted loyalty to the family of my ancestors—for Stewart blood is in my veins, and I am *now* their representative, and the people are as devoted and loyal to me as they were to that unhappy race."

There was also a visit to Glencoe, on another splendid morning. The Queen was surprised at the kind of homes in which her subjects by Loch Eil lived.

"The cottages along the roadside here and there hardly deserve the name and are indeed mere hovels—so low, so small, so dark with thatches, and overgrown with moss and heather, that if you did not see smoke issuing from them, and some very rugged dirty old people, and very scantily clothed, dishevelled children, you could not believe they were meant for human habitation. They are very picturesque and embedded in trees, with the heathery and grassy hills rising above them. There were poor little fields, fuller of weeds than of corn, much laid by the wet, and frequently a 'calve' or 'coo' of the true shaggy Highland character was actually feeding in them."

At Ballachulish, where the slate quarries were then fully in operation, "the poor people, who all looked very clean, had decorated every house with flowers and branches or wreaths of heather and red cloth."

The Queen also visited Glencoe and was moved by the setting of the massacre: "Stern, rugged, precipitous mountains with beautiful peaks and rocks piled high one above the other, two and three thousand feet high, tower and rise up to heaven on either side, without any signs of habitation, except here, halfway up the pass, there are some trees, and near them heaps of stones on either side of the road, remains of what once were homes, which tell the bloody fearful tale of woe. The place itself is one which adds to the horror of the thought that such a thing could have been conceived and committed on innocent sleeping people. How and whither could they fly? Let me hope that William III knew nothing of it."

She also saw "Ossian's Cave . . . more than a thousand feet above the glen, and one cannot imagine how anyone could live there, as they pretend that Ossian did."

Though a century after its origination the Ossianic legend had thus worn decidedly thin, the Queen here experienced the beginnings of the fairy-tale legend of royalty which is still with us.

"In this complete solitude, we were spied upon by impudently inquisitive reporters, who followed us everywhere; but one in particular (who writes for some of the Scotch papers) lay down and watched with a telescope, and dodged me and Beatrice and Jane Churchill who were walking about, and was most impertinent when Brown went to tell him to move . . . However, he did go away at last, and Brown came back saying he thought there would have been a fight; for when Brown said quite civily that the Queen wished him to move away, he said he had quite as good a right to remain there as the Queen," a radical sentiment of which Brown managed to disabuse him peacefully. "Such conduct ought to be known," the Queen reflected.

Two days later, at the head of Loch Shiel, the Queen stood

beside the "very ugly monument to Prince Charles Edward, looking like a sort of lighthouse surmounted by his statue, and surrounded by a wall, reflecting the expectations of his landing in 1745. "What a scene it must have been in 1745! And here was I, the descendant of the Stewarts and of the very king whom Prince Charles sought to overthrow, sitting and walking about quite privately and peaceably. Macdonald of Glenaladale fanned her romantic ardour by showing her "an old-fashioned, strange silver snuff 'mill' which had been given to the Prince by Macdonald's ancestor, when he slept for the last time in Scotland at Borrodale." A watch which had belonged to him, and a ring into which some of his fair hair had been put, were also shown.

Next day, the Queen sailed on the Caledonian Canal aboard MacBrayne's paddle-steamer the *Gondolier* (which survived to become a block ship in the 1939 war). Although Ben Nevis was "hid in the mist", the Queen thought "the Caledonian Canal . . . a very wonderful piece of engineering, but travelling by it . . . very tedious."

Early that evening, she arrived at Inverness, "where no Sovereign has been since my poor ancestress Queen Mary," and where, as usual, "the streets were full of decorations and arches, and lined with volunteers." By ten o'clock, the train had deposited the Queen at Ballater, and at twenty minutes to ten she arrived back at Balmoral in an open Landau "preceded by the outrider with the lamp . . . very thankful that all had gone off so well."

There was a visit to Inveraray in 1875, by which time her daughter, Louise, was the wife of the Marquis of Lorne. The Queen, with her daughter Beatrice, and her lady-in-waiting, Jane Churchill, set off from Balmoral on 21st September, 1875. Next morning, she had breakfast on the train "Brown having had the coffee heated which we had brought with us" at Tyndrum, "a wild picturesque, and desolate place in a sort of wide glen with green hills rising around."

At Tyndrum, they got into a carriage, and drove through Dalmally, where "four horses were put on to drag us up the first hill, which was long and high, and brought us in sight of Loch Awe." They drove round the head of Loch Awe. As they drew near to their destination, they encountered a show-piece reception.

"On we went along Glen Aray, the road as we approached Inveraray Castle being bordered on either side by trees. When we reached the gate there were two halberdiers whilst others were posted at intervals along the approach, dressed in Campbell tartan kilts with brown coats turned back with red, and bonnets with a black cock's tail and bog-myrtle (the Campbell badge). With them were also the pipers of the volunteers. In front of the house the volunteers in blue and silver, of whom Lorne is the Colonel, were assembled. The Duke and Duchess of Argyll and their six girls were at the door."

A busy week was spent in touring the surrounding district, and there was a ball in the Castle in honour of the Queen's visit. They left on September 29th, and, pulled by extra horses, climbed over Rest-and-be-Thankful, passing through Arrochar and Tarbet on the way to join their train at Balloch.

"The drive along Loch Lomond, which we came upon almost immediately after Tarbet, was perfectly beautiful. We wound along under trees on both sides with the most lovely glimpses of the head of the loch, and around Loch Lomond itself below the road . . . Such fine trees, numbers of hollies growing down almost into the water, and such beautiful capes and little bays and promontories. The loch was extremely rough, and so fierce was the wind, that the foam was blown like smoke along the deep blue of the water."

The following year, the Queen came to Edinburgh to unveil Steell's monument to Prince Albert in Charlotte Square, a visit which painfully reminded her that "The last time . . . my dearest Albert ever appeared in public was in Edinburgh on October 23rd, 1861, only six weeks before the end of all, when he laid the foundation stone of the new Post Office."

In 1877, there was a trip to Loch Maree, "beautiful in the extreme," and now and again making the Queen fancy it "some Italian view", passing on the way Upper Loch Torridon and Kinlochewe. At Gareloch, she found "the midges dreadful . . . you cannot stand for a moment without being stung."

Yet another part of Scotland was explored on a visit to Dunbar and and Broxmouth in 1878, and on the Prince Consort's birthday, that "dear and blessed anniversary," she gave her "faithful Brown an oxidized silver biscuit-box, and some onyx studs. He was greatly pleased with the former, and the tears came to his eyes, and he said 'It is too much'. God knows, it is not, for one so devoted and so faithful."

The second volume of Queen Victoria's Highland memories ended with an account of the celebrations at Balmoral when news of the victory of Tel-el Kebir came in. On the edge of the Egyptian desert, the British forces under Sir Garnet Wolseley defeated the Egyptian army of Arabi Pasha. The Queen's son, Major-General the Duke of Connaught, commanded the Brigade of Guards in the action.

When the Queen was ready to prepare her second volume for the press, she could no longer have the assistance of Sir Arthur Helps, who had died in 1875. She had to rely on such advice as she could get from a Miss Macgregor, who had the good sense to counsel repeating Helps' recipe for success.

Between her compilation of the two volumes, John Brown, the Highland ghillie, had been her constant servant and companion, a fact which produced a campaign of scandal against both Queen and servant. That Queen, who more than twenty years before, had told her uncle Leopold, King of the Belgians, "my spirit rises when I think . . . I am to be *made to do* anything," insisted that her loyal servant would stand behind her whenever she appeared in public. Believing that she would die before he did, she built him a house for his retirement at Craig Gowan. But on a day in March, 1883, the Queen fell, hurting her leg. John Brown helped her to her feet. A few days later, he caught a chill, and on March 27th, succumbed to erysipelas.

As the first volume ended with the death of her husband, so the second ended with a note added to the final manuscript prepared for the press, commemorating a man whose loyalty and devotion, through a different kind of relationship, had touched the widowed Queen's deepest affections.

"The faithful attendant who is so often mentioned through these Leaves," the Queen wrote, "is no longer with her whom he served so truly, devotedly, untiringly.

"In the fulness of health and strength he was snatched away from his career of usefulness, after an illness of only three days . . . respected and beloved by all who recognised his rare worth and kindness of heart, and truly regretted by all who knew him.

"His loss to me . . . is irreparable, for he deservedly possessed my entire confidence; and to say that he is daily, nay, hourly, missed by me, whose lifelong gratitude he won by his constant care, attention, and devotion, is but a feeble expression of the truth."

A statue by Boehm was put up to Brown, on the Queen's orders, at Balmoral. She planned a third volume of *Leaves,* to be centred upon John Brown, but Sir Henry Ponsonby and others among her admirers persuaded her that it would be misunderstood, and so the project was abandoned. The second volume, however, was almost as successful as the first had been.

The closing years of the Queen's life brought celebrations to Balmoral again: there were the events connected with her growing number of grand-children, and with her own Jubilees of 1887 and 1897.

In May, 1900, she went to Balmoral to be there on the 24th, when she wrote, "Again my old birthday returns, my eighty-first." Before she returned to Windsor in the Autumn, she drove round the cottages on the estate saying good-bye. Few of those who wiped their hands on their aprons as her carriage drove up to their doors for them to drop their curtsies to her, could have expected to see her again, for she had suddenly grown small and shrunken. She died on January 22nd, 1901, having had by three days the longest Royal life and by four years the longest reign in British history.

During that reign, the countries that constituted her United Kingdom had been opened up by the development of the steamship, and the spreading fingers of the railway lines to even the remotest corners. Her special fondness for Scotland particularly encouraged her English subjects to visit it, and in some cases to set up northern residences or shooting lodges there. The first motor cars had even begun to stir up the dust of Scotland's unmetalled roads by the turn of what was, for Scotland, Victoria's century.

A decade later, the consequences of the world at war were to uncement not only the social structure over which she presided at home, but the "far-flung" Empire over which she ruled. With the redistribution of wealth and the increasing ease and availability of private travel, the new men and women rarely stayed long enough in any place for them to take time to note down their reactions to it. In any case, journeys to every part of Scotland become easily and cheaply repeatable.

Queen Victoria was thus the last of those romantic travellers whose journals reflect the arduousness, the freshness and pleasures of personal discovery. After Sir Walter Scott, she probably did more than any other single writer to encourage what was to develop into the Scottish tourist industry. Her love of Scotland was as intense as it was sincere. Because of this, her spontaneous and simply-expressed sharing of that love makes a fitting conclusion to our survey of the writings of some of those travellers who came to Scotland to feed the romantic hunger of their imaginations, and who recorded a satisfaction still of interest to us long after their several departures.

Index